Goethe

Goethe

by

Joseph-François Angelloz

Translated from the French by R. H. Blackley

With 16 illustrations

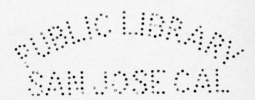

The Orion Press   **New York**

Distributed by Crown Publishers, Inc.

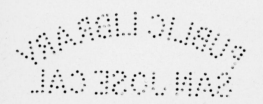
© 1958, by The Orion Press, Inc., New York
First published in France, 1949, by Mercure de France
All rights reserved
Library of Congress Catalog Card Number: 58-7922
Manufactured in Italy
by Officine Grafiche Stianti, Sancasciano Val di Pesa (Florence)

Contents

Contents

List of illustrations

Goethe

Introduction

The case for Goethe

England has Shakespeare, Italy has Dante, Spain has Cervantes, France has a continuity and wealth of literature which in its totality manifests a unique and living personality [1]: Germany has Goethe.

On emerging from the prolonged stagnation into which she had been plunged in the middle of the seventeenth century by the Thirty Years War, Germany suddenly produced the man who was to become the keystone of her literature. At first Goethe tended toward " Anacreontism," then threw himself into the first wave of German idealism, and soon became the standard-bearer of the " Sturm-und-Drang." [2]

[1] Curtius, *Die französische Kultur*, p. 91, quoted by Charles Du Bos in *Approximations V* (Editions Correa, 1932, p. 115, note 1).

[2] For all literary movements we refer the reader to our *Littérature Allemande* (Presses Universitaires de France, Collection " Que sais-je? " 3rd edition 1948, 128 pages). We will limit ourselves here to pointing out that at its birth, modern German literature was influenced by French rationalism. This was the period of " enlightenment " (*Aufklärung*), which lasted from 1700 to 1770, though it did not then die out, for its last and most famous representative was Kant. About 1770 a literary revolution broke out, which has been labelled with the

Together with Schiller he created classicism which he
rapidly brought to perfection. He flirted with romanticism,
then rejected it in favor of a mystic symbolism. And finally,
he knew the dawning realism of " Young Germany." Before Goethe, German literature was seeking its own course
by imitating or rebelling against French classicism. After
him, its best forces seemed exhausted. Thanks to him,
around him, sometimes even in opposition to him, that
" Cathedral of Literature " was erected which constitutes
the " Spiritual Space " [1] of the German people. One may
justly speak of a " Goethe Era."

History offers few men who can be compared to Goethe
for universality of genius. As a poet, he created modern
German lyricism; as a novelist, he overwhelmed the pre-
Romantics with *Werther*, then bestowed on his contemporaries and on posterity the consummate beauty of
Wahlverwantschaften, and *Wilhelm Meister*. In the epic
field he became the Homer of the bourgeosie with *Hermann
und Dorothea* and of the animal kingdom with *Reineke
Fuchs*. Finally, as a dramatist, he gave his country both
Shakespearean plays and " dramas of the soul." Above
all he created *Faust*. The writer was an artist as well.
As a theorist, he maintained a life-long interest in problems
of aesthetics; as a practising artist he worked with pencil
and brush. In fact, he long hesitated between poetry and
the plastic arts.

untranslatable title of a play of Klinger's *Sturm-und-Drang*, which
we may call " Storm and Stress." Born of a reaction against reason
and rule, it was the projection of the subjectivism of the pietists, exalt-
ing feeling and individualizing religion. One may consider " Sturm-
und-Drang " as the literary expression of a secularized Christianity.
Its two essential dogmas were: the divine character of genius, and
the divinity of nature. The poets of this school are called " Stürmer-
und-Dranger " or " Stürmer." The most representative work is undoubtedly *Werther*.

[1] The expression is borrowed from the remarkable lecture on *Das
Schrifttum als geisteger Raum der Nation* delivered by Hofmannsthal
at Munich on January 10, 1927.

As a scientist, he was not a mere dilettante, but a researcher who sought to discover fundamental laws and types. Though he created no system of philosophy, though he always refused to " think about thought," he was none the less a thinker [1] whose dicta, maxims and aphorisms [2] constitute a substantial breviary of wisdom. We must also mention his accounts of travel and of war and particularly his autobiographical writings in which, as a brilliant observer, he appears as the chronicler of nature, of history, of men, and of himself. No realm of the human spirit escaped his passionate interest except pure mathematics, a subject undoubtedly too abstract to attract a man devoted to his senses.

Although he created works of literature, which Herder aptly referred to as " emanations of his ego," he was in no sense a " man of letters." He remained a vital being who made his own life his greatest work. No doubt he could be condemned on moral grounds, and his example can only justify imitation by exceptional beings endowed with equal genius. Yet neither would it be difficult to show him as a middle-class conformist, respectful of established powers, as jealous of his time as Cézanne who would not spare a few hours from his painting to attend the burial of his mother. But is not egocentricity one of the essential characteristics of genius? There exists a unique harmony between Goethe's work and his life for he never ceased to work at the development of his personality, his *Bildung*. We must assign an almost religious sense to this word which is very imperfectly translated by the English " formation."

[1] On this point Simmel's important work *Goethe* (1913) or the third part of K. Vietor's *Goethe* (Francke Verlag, Berne, 1949) should be consulted.

[2] Among the many editions, we recommend Günther Müller's *Goethe Maximen und Reflexionen* (Kroner, Stuttgart). Read also *Welt und Geist im Goethewort*, by Th. Friedrich and Carl Diesch (Köhler and Voigtländer, 1949, p. 376).

It was his vocation to " raise even higher the pyramid of his existence." [1]

The way in which Goethe set about this process of formation reveals his originality. Convinced that he could not escape the domination of his " daimôn," Goethe achieved self-realization through a series of metamorphoses. The " dying and becoming " which he expounded in *Selige Sehnsucht* was a process which he underwent continually. He would allow his present self to die in order to become what he was to be, perhaps criticizing but never rejecting his previous self. This " pyramid of his existence " [2] was built of equally valuable strata even if for him the coping-stone was the only one that counted. In his view, what he possessed was less important than what he still lacked. One can distinguish in him three kinds of metamorphosis. The first consists of the development of what was already in him, notably through the education which he received in his family and through his years of study at Leipzig. The second is an evolution sparked by the acquisition of what was not within him, by his meeting and relationship with Herder, for example. The third and most decisive form of metamorphosis is exemplified by his experiences at Weimar, where a revolution against himself led him to desert his previous aims, both in his life and in his poetry. Thus, the outside world constantly intervened in the development of his ego, either helping him to attain an equilibrium or threatening this equilibrium. This world, alternately favorable and hostile, had to be reckoned with. When Goethe created an art of living with minute and sometimes unattractive care, when he avoided illness and the sight of suffering and death, when he selfishly deserted a mistress who had become a burden or repulsed a young romantic needing

---

[1] In a letter to Lavater on September 20, 1780, which we will look at more closely in connection with the Italian journey.

[2] *Approximations V*, p. 115.

encouragement, it was always to avoid compromising the self that he wanted to become.

No one has been the object of so much study, and yet we know that much remains to be learned about this inexhaustible genius. The scope of his work explains, in the opinion of the greatest Goethe experts, why there so far exists no great definitive monograph. This would doubt-less have to be the work of many scholars. We have not pretended to write such a work, for our ambitions are more modest. Every age recreates an image of a great man which suits the period, which reflects its state of knowledge, the degree of its abilities, and its current needs. We have set out to provide a work of medium size for the literary public wishing to deepen its knowledge of Goethe, in which it may find the essential results of the " *Goetheforschung.*" We have had recourse to the work of the poet, particularly to his correspondence; we have made use of such old books as are still of value, and also of the most modern French, German and English works; we have underlined the results achieved and have indicated the gaps, in order to point the way to future researchers. As heirs of the past, we have tried to prepare the future.

Frankfurt, April 1948-Paris, October 1949. We would like to thank very sincerely our friends P. Isler, L. Bonne-rot, S. de Sacy, P. Hartmann, A. Sauvageot, M. Averseng, P. Golliet and F. Delmas for their advice and criticism, their encouragement and their suggestions.

Part I

Liberty against the law
1749-1775

Chapter 1

Goethe's childhood (1749-1765)

> " My life, a unique adventure. Not an adventure through the effort to develop what nature had put in me, but an adventure through the effort to acquire what nature had not put in me." [1]

Chance, which is often only the veiled face of destiny, occasioned the birth of Johann Wolfgang Goethe at noon on August 28, 1749, in the free city of Frankfurt. It would be a great mistake to treat the astrological horoscope which stands at the head of the first book of *Dichtung und Wahrheit* as a humorous sally.

" On August 28, 1749, on the second stroke of twelve, I came into the world at Frankfurt-on-Main. The constellations were propitious; the sun was in the sign Virgo and at its zenith for that day; Jupiter and Venus were friendly and Mercury was not hostile; Saturn and Mars were in-

---

[1] Follows a work which Goethe had undertaken before writing *Dichtung und Wahrheit*. Quoted by E. Beutler in his introduction to the *Gedenkausgabe der Werke, Briefe und Tagebücher* in 24 volumes, begun by Artemis-Verlag, Zürich, in 1948 (X, p. 884).

different; the moon alone, just come to the full, exercised the full power of her opposition, the more so as her planetary hour had begun at the same time. She prevented my delivery until that hour was over." [1]

Goethe, who wrote that admirable orphic strophe of the " daimôn," who in his childhood placed a shelf by his bed on which he set the stars, Jupiter and Venus, in order to receive their " amicable " influence, was not ignorant of the fact that the chance of birth had placed him in surroundings of social class, city and family all favorable to the formation of a far from ordinary existence.

In the Germany of the Holy Roman Empire the nobility had played no important part for several centuries, and by the end of the middle ages literature had become more or less the property of the bourgeoisie. The Reformation enlisted humanism in the service of religion, and the Thirty Years War destroyed the country. The opening of the eighteenth century marked the beginning of a new era: around the frontiers of Germany, in the cities of Hamburg, Bremen, Frankfurt, Strassburg, Basle, Breslau, Leipzig and in Silesia, there rapidly grew up a great merchant class, capable of becoming the social support of a new literature, and in general strongly influenced by France. About 1740 a lesser middle class appeared. The life it led was simpler and more austere than that of its predecessor, but it claimed a new life for the spirit and for the heart, and was soon dreaming of a national life. It was above all an urban society of merchants, officials, university people, savants and pastors; the imprint of the latter is discernible in the new literature from 1750 and particularly from 1770 onwards.

---

[1] E. Beutler points out in his introduction (page 893), that Goethe here follows the Italian savant Girolamo Cardano (1501-1576), who set his horoscope at the head of his autobiography *De vita propria*; Goethe had read it in 1777, 1778, 1808 and 1809.

Goethe was destined to become the leader of this new literature. His great-grandfather was a shoesmith, his grandfather was a tailor who later became an innkeeper, his father was a jurist who from 1741 onwards bore the title of " Imperial Counsel." His mother was the daughter of Johann Wolfgang Textor (a Latin translation of the very common name Weber), a Doctor of Laws, burgomaster, then, from 1748 to 1770, first magistrate (Schultheiss) of Frankfurt. To Goethe was reserved the task of providing this bourgeois literature with its patent of nobility and of creating a class of writers, since, with the last edition of his works begun in 1828, he was the first writer to receive a real copyright.[1]

His urban environment was no less important, not because Frankfurt already had some literary standing, but because this town of 30,000 souls, a free city and a republic, was situated on a dividing line both in space and in time. The old quarter and the " Römer " belonged to the past, while the fairs at Easter and Michaelmas gave evidence of great commercial activity and presaged the future. Situated near the great artery of the Rhine, Frankfurt was at the intersection of the highways connecting the North and the South, the East and the West. Goethe's travels, true journeys of the spirit, seem to have been predestined, imposed by his birth at the crossways in the old house in the " Hirschgraben." full of corners and hiding-places, which his father transformed in 1775 into a fine rococo dwelling.

The atmosphere of middle-class serenity, which reigned in the town and house of his birth and which he evoked in *Dichtung und Wahrheit*, also permeated his family circle where everything, even the contrasting natures of his par-

---

[1] W. H. Bruford, *Die gesellschaftlichen Grundlagen der Goethezeit* (H. Bohlau, Weimar, 1936, p. 277). A well-documented work on political and social life in Saxe-Weimar and Germany. Goethe sometimes sold his manuscripts to publishers for considerable sums.

ents, predisposed him to become what he was. In a well-known quatrain he described his debt to each of them:

> From my father I have stature,
> And austerity of life;
> Little mother's lively spirit,
> And delight as storyteller.

His parents represented two human types so different as to be almost opposites, and their marriage was happy although not always gay. He was to realize a true synthesis of North and South, of nationalism and pietism, of the working class and the bourgeoisie.

His father, born in 1710 of Thuringian extraction, had spent his mother's heritage on law studies and then on a long trip to Vienna, Venice, Rome, Florence, Milan, Genoa and Paris. He was a cultivated man, interested in science, and an adherent of the rationalist movement introduced from France. He also had the passion of a true collector which made it possible for his son to grow up among prints and objets d'art brought back from Italy and to have the run of a very well-stocked library. While examining starfish near Fano, this gifted dilettante glimpsed the " close relation of the three kingdoms of nature." His taste for art led him to invite the painters of Frankfurt and Darmstadt to his house. He read a great deal and wrote an account of his voyage in Italian. Honest, good and serious, not without tenderness despite his iron severity, he was an impenitent pedagogue, held in awe by his wife and children, and he passed on to Johann Wolfgang his fondness for letters, his taste for the arts and his passion for science.

This austere man, son and grandson of working men, had crowned the social advance of his family by marrying, at the age of thirty-eight, the daughter of the burgomaster of Frankfurt, Elisabeth Textor, who was only seventeen. She came from a family of lawyers of Hessian and Franconian descent, in which the women had always played a predominant role. Brought up to be the mistress of a household, her education had been only rudimentary, and her husband labored methodically to perfect it. Yet she had plenty of common sense, a spicy talent for letter writing, a youthful gaiety which made a pleasing contrast to her husband's severity, and a great talent as a story teller which she transmitted to her " Hütschel-Hans." She also prepared her son for an understanding of religious experience, for she had followed the pietist movement introduced at Frankfurt by Spener, who was dean from 1665 to 1686, and led by Zinzendorf after 1736.[1] Her deep and simple faith gave her a feeling of security and the courage to bear her troubles and bereavements: she lost three children and was spared only Cornelia, for whom Johann Wolfgang had a warm affection.

Before we place this young being in relation to the world, let us try to characterize him, keeping in mind the danger of crediting him with innate dispositions which in fact only showed themselves later. There is a great deal of fantasy in *Goethes Briefwechsel mit einem Kind*, published in 1835 by Bettina, sister of Clement Brentano and wife of Achim von Arnim. Yet Gundolf [2] makes use of it to distinguish in Johann Wolfgang three fundamental characteristics; a sense of beauty, a consciousness of his own originality, and the power of creative imagination, and to document his

[1] The religious movement called by its opponents " piétisme " is associated with Jacob Böhme, but it was particularly the work of the Alsacian Spener (1635-1705), who collected into " collegia pietatis " the faithful who were discontented with the official Lutheran church, and wished to reach God by a movement of the spirit; among them were Langer and Mellin, who were to play a part in Goethe's development, and Zinzendorf (1700-1760), who founded the order of Moravian Brothers. On this question see our *Littérature allemande* (p. 26) and also A. Grosser's article *Le jeune Goethe et le piétisme* in the special number of *Études germaniques* (Nos. 14-15, 1949) devoted to Goethe.

[2] Gundolf, *Goethe*, pp. 32 et seq.

precocious aptitudes for pedagogy, religious feeling and analytical thought.

Bettina, who had talked much with " Frau Rat," Goethe's mother, relates that he would not willingly play with young children unless they were very beautiful. When he was three years old he attended a party where he met a child whose ugliness he could not bear. He began to scream that the " black child " should be removed, and did not cease to weep until he was back at home. Gundolf interprets this incident as a manifestation of the child's sense of beauty: we know that later Goethe could not bear caricature or ugliness or even a simple blot. If not the proof of an innate gift for poetic creativity, it at least promised an artistic disposition.

When his mother asked him why he courted the favorable influences of the stars when other children were not concerned about them, he answered proudly that what was good enough for others would not do for him. He was seven, and already had a sense of his uniqueness. This sense of his own originality allowed him to dominate his comrades and to play the part of arbiter. It led him later to become the " *jeune premier* " of Leipzig, the Titan of Strassburg, the Olympian of Weimar.

If these two characteristics seem to promise Goethe artistc mastery, the third seems to justify his pretensions. Not only did he outstrip his comrades in his zeal for drawing but he possessed a creative imagination which his mother described in an anecdote. Whenever she told him stories, he could not bear that the hero should have an unhappy fate, and sometimes interrupted to prevent the princess from marrying the tailor; if the narrator had to put off the conclusion of the story to the following day, he would take advantage of this respite to arrange matters, and to finish the story in his own way. Was the child to become a poet?

It is not surprising that in the century of *Emile*, in a country and family of pedagogic tastes, the young Goethe

1. *Goethe's birthplace at Frankfurt (1755, before alteration)*

should have volunteered his services as tutor to his sister Cornelia. Bettina relates a revealing tale. When his little brother Jacob died, Johann Wolfgang did not weep; he even seemed irritated by his parents' tears. His mother asked him if he had not loved his brother. He ran into his room, and brought back a quantity of lessons and stories which he had prepared for his brother's instruction. He seemed to reproach Jacob for having deprived him, by dying, of the pleasures of educating him. All his life he was to teach himself and mankind. This is, in the words of André Gide, the essential lesson of Goethe, whose work "is entirely education. His genius appears essentially didactic." [1]

We have a curious manifestation of his childhood piety at the end of the first book of *Dichtung und Wahrheit*. In order to "enter into direct communication with the great God of nature" Johann Wolfgang erected an altar in the manner of the Old Testament: it was a lectern, upon which he placed the finest specimens from his natural history collection. Then he used the rays of the rising sun falling on a lens to burn Armenian pastilles, whose perfumed vapors arose toward God like the aspirations of his child's heart. This pagan need to worship God in a tangible form already foreshadowed the adoration of deified nature which was to characterize German thought from 1770 to 1787. [2]

Finally, like all children, Goethe was observant of things around him, but he also knew how to observe and judge himself. Every Sunday the boys of his age used to meet to read their poems, each naturally feeling that his own were the best. Since he thought that some of them were terrible, he began to wonder whether he was not wrong

---

[1] Prefaces, p. 89.
[2] This story can be found in *Pages immortelles de Goethe* (pp. 44-46) or, with commentary, in Charles Du Bos' *Goethe*, pp. 180 et seq.

2.

in attributing great value to his own verses. This doubt worried him for a long time, for " it was quite impossible for me to discover any outward sign of truth."

These essential traits, which were doubtlessly innate and which were manifested very early, make up an inner portrait of the child. It reveals a being in whom, to repeat a formulation of Gundolf's, [1] vitality and creative force could attain equilibrium; we discern an individual conscious of his individuality, ready either to extend his power over the outside world, or to absorb it into himself. Thus it is particularly important to observe his reaction when he comes into contact with life, and when he discovers the world of culture.

The child's first contact was with his classmates. For three terms he was placed in Schellhaffer's school. There he received a few blows and contracted the usual illnesses of childhood, which persuaded his family to have him educated at home instead. There, under his father's guidance, professors and friends gave him encyclopedic instruction. He learned Latin, Hebrew, French, Italian, history, religion, natural science and mathematics, drawing and music. He also practised dancing, fencing and horsemanship. Avid for knowledge and extremely gifted, the young Goethe absorbed information and laid the foundations for the reading which was to nourish his future work. This reading included Homer and Virgil, Fénélon, Diderot, whose *Neveu de Rameau* he later translated as well as part of the *Essai sur la peinture*, Voltaire, for whom he retained a deep admiration, Buffon, whose *Histoire Naturelle* had an early influence on him, novels such as *Robinson Crusoe* and J. G. Schnabel's *Die Insel Felsenburg*, folktales and legends like those of *The Four Sons of Aymon*, *Eulenspiegel*, *Melusina* and *Fortunato*. In sum, he received a very

[1] Gundolf, *Goethe*, p. 22.

complete education in which his reading often provided an escape into space or time, dream or legend. We also note that French influence appears to have played a preponderant role.

To his literary education we must add the formative influence of the town and its spectacles. Here Goethe could witness fairs, ceremonies, the coronation of the Emperor in 1764 and, above all, the events of the French occupation of 1759-64. The latter led to the installation of the Comte de Turance, a lover of the arts, in the family household and to the establishment of a French theatre which made a strong impact on his orientation. There he saw the works of the seventeenth and eighteenth century authors performed in French. When his grandmother gave him a marionette theatre for Christmas in 1753, she opened the world of fantasy to him, while the French actors introduced him to a literary form which was to have an important place in *Wilhelm Meister*, and which inspired many of his works.

His religious formation did not keep pace with his intellectual and dramatic education, no doubt because his rationalist father attached less importance to it. At first, his religious education was limited to the reading of the Bible, his mother's favorite book. He regarded it—especially the Old Testament—as an epic and hymn. It gave him a taste for natural simplicity, and in later life in constituted for him a collection of poetry and symbolism. The dogmatic instruction which he next received discouraged him, for, as he later wrote in *Dichtung und Wahrheit* (I, 1.), " Protestantism, as transmitted by the official Church, is but a dry orthodoxy; it satisfies neither soul nor heart." For similar reasons, numbers of the faithful had formed dissenting sects in order to reach better God, through Christ as intermediary. Goethe as a child showed the same tendency, but chose nature as his intermediary. His confirmation in 1762 precipitated an unfortunate crisis which reached its climax at Leipzig, where the young student finally left the Church.

From this period on, Goethe's emotional life deserves mention. Let us note first his affection for his intelligent and forceful sister, Cornelia, who loved him jealously; then the amorous curiosity which Derones's sister, a little French actress, inspired in him; and finally his somewhat childish passion for the mysterious Gretchen, whose name is borne by the heroine of *Faust*.

More important were his relations with the "*Arkadische Gesellschaft zu Phylandria*." This was a hierarchical secret society which derived from the masonic lodge, [1] whose principal object was " The Cult of God and Virtue." Goethe felt drawn toward it, perhaps because the proposed ideals seemed likely to satisfy his religious feeling, or because of a taste for mystery, or through vanity—for it was a very exclusive and elegant circle—or perhaps because of a desire to meet other young people. On May 23 and June 2, 1764, he wrote very humble letters to E. K. L. Ysenburg von Buri in which he begged admission and confessed his principal faults: he was violent, impatient, loved to command, dared write to a stranger to offer his friendship, and resembled a chameleon. [2] This apparent humility did not prevent him from enumerating his good points and qualities as well. None the less, he failed to gain admission to the society. [3]

---

[1] In *Die Freimaurerei und ihr Einfluss auf die geistige Kultur in Deutschland am Ende des XVIII Jahrhunderts* (Taussig, Prag, 1919) J. F. Scheider has detailed (pp. 113-114) that L. Y. von Buri, " Archonte " of the Society, was initiated into the secret of the lodges by a French officer in a Swiss regiment. Thus we are indeed considering a para-masonic society, whose hierarchy, at the beginning of 1765, numbered not less than six degrees.

[2] In his book *A Study of Goethe* (pp. 4-5) Barker Fairley rightly points out that this comparison is dear to the young Goethe; it is found also in a Leipzig poem of before 1765, and in the first version of *Götz von Berlichingen*.

[3] F. J. Scheider adds the detail (ibid. p. 114) that the Order had

By the time that Goethe was ready to leave the town of his birth, it was evident that he was an exceptionally gifted being. He had received excellent training and had suffered some painful disappointments. If we also consider the inevitable oppression of his home atmosphere, it is understandable that he went forward into the future both confidently and joyfully. But one cannot yet discern the shape of this future. [1] There was a risk that his intellectual and rationalist education might lead to the dryness and skepticism of the philosophy of enlightenment. He had already been turned away from religion, and his sentimentality sought the nourishment it lacked. His father had recognized his talent, but had in mind for him no other study than jurisprudence, no other profession or future than a high official position to crown the social advancement of the family. Yet the young man seemed drawn toward poetry. He composed poems with astonishing facility; these he destroyed, however, with the exception of *Poetische Gedanken über die Höllenfahrt Jesu Christi* and some fragments of a play entitled *Belshazzar*. He had also a very sure artistic sense, trained by contact with the painters who worked for his father or for Comte de Thorenc. The eye, as he wrote in Book VI of *Dichtung und Wahrheit*, was the organ through which he grasped the world. On his walks he was already that " seeker after pictures " described by Jules Renard and, always working from nature, he brought back batches of drawings which his father criticized sternly but hoarded with passionate hope. Had his friend Seekatz not predicted that Johann Wolfgang had the painter's vocation? At this stage, there-

appointed Karl Schweitzer to make inquiries about Goethe; the report was not favorable, doubtless because of the Gretchen episode and what went with it (see *Dichtung und Wahrheit*).

[1] In his well-documented work on Goethe, A. Fuchs distinguishes (pp. 50-61) what he calls " the features of the personality " at the moment of departure for Leipzig as an adolescent.

fore, one might still wonder whether he would become a lawyer, a poet or an artist. Leipzig was to show him his true course.

Chapter 2

The years of apprenticeship
(1765-1771)

If one looks at the period preceding and following his twentieth year, a period of utmost importance in the formation of a poet, one can distinguish three stages in the adolescence of Goethe: two periods at universities separated by a period of rest in his father's house. For nearly three years (October, 1765-August, 1768) he was a student at Leipzig, for fifteen months (April, 1770-August, 1771) he continued and finished his studies at Strassburg; this last period was decisive, as was the interval of nineteen months during which he remained at Frankfurt. Emerging from a very sheltered, if carefully directed and supervised, childhood, particularly after his adventure with Gretchen which had led to his being placed under the care of a tutor, he found himself projected into the freedom of life in which he was to serve an apprenticeship; after the setback at Leipzig he turned inward, enriching his inner life before, wiser and riper, tackling the new experience of Strassburg.

Leipzig was no more important a city than Frankfurt, but the fact that it was a capital had led to its being called " a little Paris "; less mediaeval, less middle-class and conservative than Frankfurt, more active, more lively, looking towards the future, it went to the head of the young " provincial," who made haste to exchange his wardrobe, more sensible than elegant, for fashionable clothes, and who tried, with less zeal and less success, to rid himself of the Frankfurt dialect in favour of " High-Saxon," the language of Gottsched and Gellert. Provided by his family with letters of introduction, he launched himself into society, whose manners he tried to adopt. Frau Boehme, though a kindly mentor to him, was unable to prevent him from making himself ridiculous and disagreeable, at times, so much so that in 1766 his comrade J. A. Horn declared that " his society becomes daily more intolerable." In a movement of revolt against the austerity of his father's house he haunted the taverns, notably the Auerbach; he frequented girls who were " better than their reputation " and made himself intolerable to the bourgeois he wished to impress.

The student's life is not enough to explain so rapid a change in an adolescent of seventeen scarcely free of the strict family home. There must be added the lessons and the example of a guide and adviser, of an older friend, of whom we shall find several examples during the course of Goethe's life. This time it was E. W. Behrisch, eleven years older, tutor in the household of Comte de Lindenan. The young man attached himself to him and wrote to him on November 2, 1769: " To have found a good friend is to have found a worthy man, and there are such men, whatever the *Misanthrope* may say. " Behrisch has been variously judged, sometimes severely, [1] sometimes with a certain indulgence. [2] He was a " roué," a skeptical and sarcastic man whom the poet doubtless had in mind when he conceived the character of Mephistopheles; but he was

[1] R. D'Harcourt, *L'éducation sentimentale de Goethe* (Colin, 1934, pp. 163-178).
[2] A. Fuchs, *Goethe*, pp. 87-93.

a better man than Faust's companion. His effect was double: on the one hand, rich in the experience of life which the young Frankfurter lacked he passed this on to him, not always to his benefit; on the other hand, as a literary critic with taste he was a clear-sighted judge of his poems, selected the best and inspired the three *Odes to My Friend*, which are already rich in talent.

If the future author of *Faust* met Mephistopheles, he also discovered one of the models of Gretchen: it was Anne-Katherine Schoenkopf, the pretty daughter of an innkeeper and wine merchant. Once again the man who was to write in *Faust*,

> The girl who, on Saturday, handles the broom,
> The best will caress you on Sunday,

was captivated by a girl of rank inferior to his own; but it was no longer, as it had been at Frankfurt, mere puppy-love; Goethe could write to W. K. L. Moors on October 1, 1766, at the age of seventeen: " I love a girl of modest station and without fortune and now I am experiencing for the very first time the happiness brought by a true love." It was a total love, aware that marriage was impossible, but bringing to the young man the joy of knowing himself preferred as well as the tortures of jealousy and the grief of separation; it lasted from April, 1766, to March, 1768. [1]

This libertine existence was hardly favorable to his legal studies, and Goethe soon abandoned the university. Philosophy aroused no response in him, and logic seemed to him merely the art of artificially demonstrating the most natural and elementary workings of the human mind. In law, his disillusionment was still greater; his father had already introduced him to what he was expected to learn, and he was wasting time listening to certain professors who were actually learning while they taught. He was undoubt-

---

[1] Read the story in D'Harcourt's work (pp. 139-162) and also in Du Bos (pp. 124-147).

edly exaggerating in order to please when he wrote to his father at the beginning of his residence on October 13, 1765: " What a wonderful thing to be a professor; I am delighted to have seen some of them in this magnificence, and the only thing I really long for is the honor of a chair." His enthusiasm cooled quickly, and he was soon merely a dilettante student.

But it was not his normal program of life and study which was most important for his development as a poet: the pseudo-lawyer displayed the greatest interest in literature and art. It is certain that he owed little to Gottschel, a specialist in modern literature who was out of touch with the younger contemporaries and who preached imitation of the French; or to Gellert, a moralizing novelist already left behind by the new writers. But he discovered Wieland, who " had the finest nature of them all," and above all, Lessing, the most important and challenging, whose plays he saw and even acted in (*Minna von Barnhelm*). Here was the Lessing who crusaded relentlessly against French literature in his *Hamburgische Dramaturgie*, who made himself the herald of Shakespeare, and who bestowed the revelations of *Laokoon* (1776).

Goethe was also drawn towards art. He attended Professor Oeser's course at the School of Fine Arts, studied drawing with him and engraving with J. M. Stock. Nor did he fail to visit the famous gallery in Dresden. He already felt a vague presentiment for antiquity and followed Winkelmann's work with passionate interest; he was prepared to follow him, for Oser, whose lessons were to remain important to him all his life, was already expounding to him that the idea of beauty is simplicity and calm (*Einfalt und Stille*) and that consequently it was impossible for a young man to achieve mastery (letter of February 20, 1770, to Ph. E. Reich).

While working at graphic art, he was also writing poems and comedies. His conception of his vocation appears in a letter of October 12, 1765, to his sister, in which he jestingly used the expression " we poets," later to become " we savants." On May 11, 1767, he wrote to her more seriously: "As I am without pride, I cannot trust my inmost convictions which tell me that I possess certain qualities . necessary to a poet and that I may one day become one." In the same letter he posed the problem of genius and criticism in a way which foreshadowed the " Sturm und Drang ": if he has genius, he will become a poet, whether or not he is adversely criticized; if he has not, no favorable criticism in the world will help him. In August, 1767, he informed her, in French, that the great mentor of poetry (he undoubtedly meant Behrisch) had listened to a reading of his poems and had decided " that the whole shall be condemned to the eternal obscurity of my coffer except for twelve poems which shall be inscribed in their full magnificence, hitherto unknown to the world, on fifty small octavo sheets, and that the title shall be Annette... " In truth, the poems which make up *Annette* are still full of the rococo anacreontism of the period; they abound with dalliance and shepherds, moon and lust, zephyrs and kisses; yet one can discern the promise of true emotion and of a nature ready for self-expression. Two comedies, French in technique and versification, are worthy of attention: *Die Laune des Verliebten*, which dates from Frankfurt although he worked on it for eight months, in which the character of Annette is introduced; and *Die Michuldigen*, a satire on bourgeois society, which was only finished in Frankfurt. The former is still a pastoral, yet the characters have come alive in a subject based on real life. Already piercing through the conventions of the eighteenth century rococo we glimpse the stark simplicity of nature herself.

In Book VII of *Dichtung und Warheit*, Goethe described his development:

And thus began this sense of direction from which during my whole life I was never to stray; to express as a symbol, a poem, what delighted me or tormented me or preoccupied me in any way and thus to concentrate it in myself, partly to correct my ideas on the outside world, partly to achieve inner peace. No doubt this gift was more necessary to me than to anyone else, for my nature cast me incessantly from one extreme to the other. Consequently, all of my published work represents only fragments of a great confession.

We also know that he told Eckermann on September 18, 1823, that he had composed only " poetry of circumstance " (*gelegenheitegedichte*), and that he placed no value on " subjects in the air " (*aus der Luft gegriffen*). This is precisely what interests us in his works: the expression of his own life and therefore of life itself.

The experience of Leipzig was largely, though not entirely, positive. His legal studies hardly came into the picture, but he embarked upon his apprenticeship in a life of freedom. He made new friends in literature as represented by Wieland, Lessing, Winkelmann and Klopstock, whose *Messias* he had read as a child. He developed his taste and his knowledge of art, and above all, began to feel himself a poet. But his sojourn, initiated in drink, ended in disillusionment and illness. In June, 1765, he fell seriously ill; could it have been syphilis? One of his recent biographers, G. Muller, speaks of a dangerous glandular infection. On August 28, he left Saxony to return to his father's home.

It would be misleading merely to present Goethe, the child prodigy, as a shipwrecked soul, sick in body and spirit, who returned to his family to seek healing and comfort. His destiny demanded that, at the age of twenty, after plunging himself into life for the first time, he cure himself of disease and pietist religious sentiment in preparation for the revelations of Strassburg.

He was, in fact, seriously ill for many months, to the extent that his mother, fearing the worst, implored the doctor to use his famous universal panacea, a closely-guarded secret cure. He was so distraught that in a letter to Friederike Oeser, the daughter of his friend from Leipzig, he wrote, after paying homage to the care with which he was surrounded:

Myself alone bars happiness complete.

The lines which follow are highly revealing:

And yet I know of no one who, like you
Can quickly calm tormented suffering
And, with a look, bring soul's tranquillity.

Foreshadowing his homage to the Baroness von Stein, Goethe here appealed to the tranquillity which a woman can bestow. He appealed with confidence because Friederike, for whom he felt a loving friendship, had saved him from despair in Frankfurt by the example of her own happy and serene existence.

Goethe's sojourn in Frankfurt during his twentieth year was the equivalent of a religious retreat, in which he ceaselessly struggled for his physical well-being and for inner certainty. He felt indebted to the illness itself for teaching him things he could not have learned elsewhere, he wrote to Katherine Schoenkopf, December 30, 1768. On January 17, 1769, he wrote even more pointedly to his friend Langer, whose influence had replaced that of Behrisch: " ... I have suffered and once more I am free; this fiery ordeal was very awful to my soul." He added that, if physically cured, he would never again know " any happening (*Vorfall*) more fortunate than this, which was horrifying." On April 29, 1770, after his cure, he wrote from Strassburg, as if to underscore the idea: " That is the advantage we have, we invalids; we are more sensitive, more delicate and, up to a certain point, happier than people in perfect health."

His malady rendered him more accessible to religious sentiment; this was a victory of his mother and pietism over his rationalist father, who was, however, very tolerant. The victory was so complete that he was able to announce a " singular transformation " (*Wendung*) in a letter to Langer on January 17, 1769. His father, whose resolution weakened in the face of the illness, was willing to allow Mellin and other Moravian monks to attend him. From then on " we had a freer exercise of religion." Two days previously there had been a religious meeting in the house, with singing of sacred music, about which Goethe recorded a significant incident. Finding himself somewhat in the rear and without sufficient light, he cried out: " Why is it dark here? " and lit a lamp. Then he declared to Mellin: " See, this typifies the new Jerusalem, when the Church of the Cross shall have become the Church of the Spirit." Without immersing himself in the pietism of his mother and sister, he approached it sufficiently to visit Marienborn, where he could see the Moravians on their own territory and hear the sermons of Bishop Spangenberg.

At this moment, as was often the case throughout his life, Goethe submitted to the influence of a woman, that of Catherine von Kellenberg (1723-1774), whose conversations and letters were to appear in *Die Bekentnisse einer schöne Seele*. She was the most remarkable of his mother's pietist friends, he wrote in Book VIII of *Dichtung und Wahrheit*, and her dress recalled the habit of the Moravians; she had the greatest admiration, moreover, for Count Zinzendorf. Although frail and weak, she possessed an unshakable serenity, and considered her affliction a necessary constituent of her transitory earthly existence. She was interested almost exclusively in religious phenomena and in " moral experiments which the observant man can make on himself." In addition to this, she was, furthermore, a noblewoman, and had known the world and even the court, a fact which did not displease the future friend of Baroness von Stein. She was intrigued by this wayward but brilliant youth who was seeking his salvation where she had already found it and she attempted to reconcile him to God.

But she did not limit herself to the task of religious edification; she exercised a more durable and fruitful influence by introducing him to the realm of the occult. This was a decisive revelation, which has not yet to our knowledge been afforded adequate study, as most biographers have used only *Dichtung und Wahrheit*. Susanna von Klettenberg had secretly read Welling's *Opus mago-cabbalisticum et theosophicum* (1735), without being able to lift the veil that he drew over things while pretending to explain them. She had no difficulty in " infecting him with this malady." After plunging into the works of this Neo-Platonist, the two readers, eager to know his forerunners, delved into the works of Paracelsus, Basile Valentin, Helmont and Starcky. Goethe took particular pleasure in reading the *Aurea catena Homeri* (1723) of Anton Kirchweger, as well as Arnold's *Kirchen und Ketrerhistorie* (1698).

When Goethe came to write his memoirs, he was amused at his youthful diversion in these readings, which did not teach him to understand things but merely to express them in a particular terminology. Yet at that formative age they did help to prepare him for his work as a poet, just as his experiments in alchemy disposed him towards his intuitive scientific researches. On August 26, 1770, he wrote from Strassburg to Susanna von Klettenberg: " Chemistry is still my secret love." If one were to study his work in the light of his readings of this year, one would undoubtedly find the key to many of his poems (for example, to *Die Geheimnisse* which were dear to the Rosicrucians, and to parts of *Faust* and *Wilhelm Meister*), and one would understand the inner meaning of that " *Streben* " which was not to leave him until his death. Susanna von Klettenberg would be assigned a more important role in his development alongside of Charlotte von Stein, another noble friend, with whom he also engaged in fruitful reading. G. Müller emphasizes that Goethe's discovery of crystallization was to play a determining role in his scientific research, and observes, not without reason, that in the cosmos of Paracelsus and Plotinus a new reality was slowly emerging alongside of the world of Leipzig. He cites this passage from the *Ephemerides*, which dates from the end of his stay in Frankfurt and which expresses a conception already far removed from pietism: " To speak separately of God and of nature is as difficult and as delicate as thinking of the body and the soul as separate entities. We know the soul only through the body; we know God only through nature."

By the beginning of 1770 Goethe had almost completely regained his health and found it ever more difficult to endure the atmosphere of Frankfurt, his confining family life and the tension which existed between his father and himself. He was longing for freedom. From this moment on, we can think of this longing in terms of the phenomena of systole and diastole which were to assume so great an importance in his eyes. The period of uninhibited expansion in Leipzig was succeeded by the months of withdrawal and consolidation in Frankfurt, to be followed in turn by another phase of enrichment and absorption in the world. As before his departure for Leipzig, the young poet burned a part of his recent work; he felt a new vital energy which could only express itself in freedom, and which had to find release to provide him with new experiences. He decided to complete his study of law at Stassburg, whereas in 1765 he would have chosen Göttingen. He was therefore seeking a French atmosphere, and it has been claimed that he wanted to settle in France in order to become a French poet. In January he wrote a revealing letter to Kätchen, who was to marry Dr. Kanne in March, 1770. After having told her that she had always been a charming girl and would become an equally charming wife, he continued: "As for myself, I shall remain Goethe," expressing pride, no doubt, but also manifesting faith in his own destiny.

2. *Johann Caspar Goethe, father of the poet (Portrait by J. Schmoll)*

How did he then foresee the years to come? He envisaged a stay at Strassburg, then a journey to Paris where he hoped " to enjoy life very much, perhaps to remain for some time." In a letter of February 20 to Ph. E. Reich, he acknowledged three masters: Oeser, whose classical teaching we have already mentioned, Wieland, who was influenced by the French, and Shakespeare. Finding himself at a crossroad, he turned towards France, and we shall see that he soon turned towards Italy, that is to say, towards the Mediterranean world. The Strassburg experience was to lead him, temporarily, to Shakespeare and turn him away from French classicism. It proved as decisive for the young man as Weimar was to be at the threshold of his maturity.

The letters which Goethe wrote to his young friends during the first months of his residence at Strassburg are not paeans of joy like those from Leipzig. Instead, they reveal a surprising degree of reflection and maturity. In a letter to Hetzler of August 24, 1770, Goethe marked out a course of conduct for the young. After asserting their right to disregard their conventional milieu and to work at tasks of their own choice, he proposed a real program:

> To observe things, as well as we can and inscribe them in our memory, to be attentive and let no day pass without its harvest; then to cultivate the sciences, which give balance to the mind; to compare things, to set each in its place, to check each value, that is what we have to do now. Beyond this we should not be anything, but wish to become everything, and above all we should not stop and rest any more than is demanded by the needs of a tired mind or body.

He followed his own program, which was to bring him three benefits: self-development through the life and environment of Strassburg and Alsace, the intellectual revolution thorugh his intimacy with Herder, and finally, the experience of happy love with Friederike.

Goethe's sojourn was truly dominated by the " Munster " (cathedral), and it was not without reason that he rushed to see it as soon as he arrived. Here he was face to face with the " Colossus," which made an extraordinary impression on him. He immediately set about analyzing it, and hastened to climb the tower to view the magnificent countryside of Alsace, which seemed to him a " new Paradise." Enchanted, he blessed the destiny which had brought him there to live. The ninth book of *Dichtung und Wahrheit*, his letters and his famous essay *Von deutscher Baukunst* (1772), published by Herder in *Von Art und Kunst* are witnesses to the enthusiasm produced by this " marvelous work." Its great size would have appalled him, had it not at the same time been ordered and comprehensible, finely executed and visually agreeable. Schickete devoted a very interesting passage in *Die Grenze* (1932) to Strassburg Cathedral, in which he endeavored to distinguish the part played by Germanic influence in this Gothic realization of French genius. He demonstrated how Goethe, confronted with this astonishing but intelligible masterpiece, saw the revelation of a kind of beauty which we may call classic, and which differed from that which he defined in his letter of February 13 to Friederike Oeser: " She is not day and is not night. Twilight: daughter of truth and of lies; a between-thing " (*Ein Mittelding*). He allowed this fascinating monument to act upon him by its very presence.

The young student also frequented Strassburg society, to which he was introduced by Salzmann, a master in manners like Mme. Boehme. He even learned to play cards, and took dancing lessons from a Frenchman whose two daughters fell in love with him. We know that one of them, resentful that she was not his favorite, embraced him furiously, cursing whoever would next kiss his lips.

But the essential part of his Strassburg experience is to be found neither here nor in his law studies, which he laboriously completed with the aid of a crammer. It was rather in his constant efforts to vanquish his weak body, to overcome his vertigo by climbing to the summit of the cathedral, and to get used to the sight of blood by attending surgical operations. It was in the birth of a new poet, the disciple of Herder, the lover of Friederike Brion.

" Goethe's Meeting with Herder, or the Birth of Modern German Literature " could be the title of an essay on the literary revolution of 1770. Lessing possessed learning, a critical mind and polemical force, but although not lacking in talent, he was without spontaneous genius. Wieland had culture and taste, intelligence and the gift of pleasing, but he could not surpass his own limitations, nor could he impose his creations and those of the German language upon the world. Klopstock possessed ardent feeling and a rigorous poetic theory, but he was more a versifier than a poet. Herder had at his disposal an encyclopedic learning as well as an intuition bordering on genius which made him as apt to discover truth as error; but he was not born a poet. German literature seemed to be awaiting someone who could unite the genius of the Word and the flame of the Spirit, poetry and knowledge, creative power and critical sense. Goethe was already twenty but he was still seeking his own direction when Herder appeared. It was necessary that the citizen of Konigsberg should undertake a veritable Odyssey across Scandinavia and France, and should come to Strassburg for treatment of a lachrymal fistula, in order to meet there, on the border of the French and German worlds, the son of Frankfurt, on his way to Paris and Latinity.

They were two very different personalities. Herder was five years older than Goethe, which at that age is considerable. He had already published the *Fragments on Modern German Literature* (1757), inspired by Lessing, in which he advised his compatriots to immerse themselves in the German past, the *Silva Critica* (1769), and numerous literary, philosophical and religious essays. Goethe, we recall, had burned his first poems. Herder was a pupil of Kant, an admirer of Lessing and the heir of the "Aufklärung," but he was even more the disciple of Hamann, the " Magi of the North," enemy of the enlightenment. Goethe, son of a rationalist, heir to a classical tradition and pupil of Oeser, a man of art and of poetry, stood in contrast to the historian whose weapon was not cold logic but feeling and intuition. When Herder told him " Observation is everything for you," he was underlining the difference between himself, who thought and felt in flashes, and the poet who needed light. Goethe found a needed guide in him, and visited him frequently. He knew that the " benevolent grumbler " (*dieser gutmutige Polherer*) would have an important influence on him; the pages devoted to him in Book X of *Dichtung und Wahrheit* honor equally the writer and the man. Goethe had been treated with the greatest respect within his own circle, and had developed a feeling of superiority which flattered his pride. Here we find him face to face with a man whom he recognized as his superior, and who did not spare him criticism, sarcasm, or rebuffs, and even ventured a joke in poor taste on his name: the Gods (*Götten*) or the Goths or mud (*Kot*). He submitted to such treatment because, for the first time in his life, he found himself in the presence of an infinitely rich mind, already filled with the ideas which were to form his future work. He knew that he had need of such an example, and he absorbed his teachings.

To begin with, Herder passed on to him the teachings of Hamann. In aesthetics, for example, he learned the aphorism, " Poetry is the mother tongue of the human race " and the rule of drama, " action, not chatter." He was also exposed to Hamann's religious thought, for the " Magi of the North " professed to a cult of the Bible, and he was prolonging the influence of bourgeois pietism at the moment when the limited intelligence of the Strassburg pietists was discouraging Goethe (to Susanna von Klettenberg, August 26, 1770). And, above all, Goethe imbibed a lesson in human psychology which was to become dogma to the

" Sturmer-und-Dranger ": to avoid analysis and abstraction and to seek the complete man, permitting the senses to comprehend the world of imagery and poetry and allowing the passions, the motive force of action, to become weapons. Being more systematic, Herder went still further. By introducing him to Hebrew and folk poetry, he made him realize that " poetry is a universal and popular gift, not the prerogative of a few men of refined culture." And in broader terms, haunted by the synthetic vision of history as an organic evolution, Herder accustomed Goethe to the conception of forces universally and perpetually in action. Finally, he expounded the cult of the individual genius, which he conceived as " a cluster of the forces of nature." He admired Homer, Pindar, Aeschylus, Sophocles, Ossian, Shakespeare, and through him the young poet and all the " Sturmer-und-Dranger " discovered new literary gods. Because he failed to understand France, Goethe, too, was to turn away from her and her culture for a while.

Henceforth Shakespeare was to occupy the throne of Olympus. His fortune in Germany was strange [1]: unknown in 1740 to the extent that his name was spelt " Saspar," thirty years later he was raised to the height of fame. Between these two dates a most interesting evolution took place. Among the critics it was Lessing who blazed the trail, first with his *Letters concerning Contemporary Literature* (1759-1765), then with his *Hamburgische Dramaturgie* (1767-1768). In his view humanity had given rise to two great schools of drama: Greek tragedy and Shakespeare. It remained for the Germans to achieve the synth-

---

[1] On this important question, consult Gundolf's great work, *Shakespeare und der deutsche Geist*, 1914, and Benno von Weise's more recent study *Die deutsche Tragödie von Lessing bis Hebbel* (Hoffmann and Campe, Hamburg, 1948, 2 vols. of 351 and 503 pages). The same firm has also recently published *Gedachtnisschrift für Robert Petsch* which includes a contribution from P. Bockmann on *Der dramatische Perspektivmus in der deutschen* Shakespeare-deutung des 18. Jahrhunderts.

esis. Furthermore, Lessing did not accept Shakespeare en bloc, and he insisted on the artistic value of his work. The first " Stürmer " adopted a nearly opposite point of view, for they were influenced by Young and his *Conjectures on Original Composition* of 1759 which was translated into German in 1760.

This apologia for original genius was one of the mainsprings of " Sturm-und-Drang." Gerstenberg adopted it in his *Lettres sur les curiosites de la littérature* (1776-1770) and glorified Shakespeare for having created a true naturalism. After hesitating for several years, Herder presented a synthetic point of view in his famous *Essays on Shakespeare*. He saw in the great Englishman both a unique genius, capable of interpreting nature, and a great artist; he considered his work the product of a particular nation and period; finally, he attributed to him the great merit of presenting history, of carrying it to " the highest degree of theatrical illusion." Feeling himself closer to Shakespeare than to the Greeks, he advised imitation of him while preserving originality. Goethe, who had had some acquaintance with Shakespeare since Leipzig and admired him without knowing him well, had occasion to speak about him with Herder, and it was not long before he expressed his enthusiasm in his *Zum Shakespeares Tag* (1771). He was drawing closer to Gerstenberg, however, and his conception marked a withdrawal from Herder's. He and the " Stürmer " were to celebrate Shakespeare as a force of nature beyond the law.

Goethe arrived in Strassburg already richly endowed with ideas and examples, but still encumbered by social conventions, still the prisoner of the atmosphere in which he had grown up. His contact with Herder brought him into the sphere of a man who had delved profoundly into the principles of language, poetry, humanity, nature and art. Although he declared himself " still too embedded (befangen) in the midst of things to think of these sources and their ends," he found himself led back to nature. In this autumn of 1770, when Herder arrived in Strassburg, Goethe was taken to Sesenheim by Weyland. He knew by then what poetry should be, he had formulated new literary conceptions, and life offered him the experience of love which was to transform him into a poet.

The Sesenheim idyll inspired the beautiful pages of Books X and XI of *Dichtung und Wahreit* as well as some of his finest poems. The story has been told many times, particularly by Frédéric Massoul,[1] and has become, with *The Vicar of Wakefield*, one of the best known episodes of world literature. The scholars have taken possession of it and have reconstructed the facts, which are not quite as charming as the idyll. It matters little to us that Friederike had been a " gourgandine " —which is sometimes suggested, though without conclusive evidence—or a girl seduced and abandoned by Goethe, by whom she was to have a son. What does matter is that she aroused an authentic passion in the young poet, provided him with the character of the immortal Gretchen, and inspired the *Sesenheimer Lieder.*

The liaison of Goethe and Friederike began as a comedy, developed into an idyll and ended in drama. The young man, having first come to Sesenheim in disguise, returned many times, content to live the idyllic existence of *The Vicar of Wakefield* which Herder was at that time reading to his friends. For some time, remembering the curse pronounced by the dancing-master's daughter, he remained caution. But, as he was to write later about Lili, " love in vain flees love." Thus he found himself following the path of Herder and Jung-Stilling: that of marriage. He became alarmed, however, and consulted Salzmann, hesitating to sacrifice the greatness of which he dreamed to mere con-

---

[1] *L'amour du poète: Frédérique* (Mercure de France, 1942, 324 pages).

jugal bliss. The day that Friederike came to Strassburg and he saw her out of her romantic setting, he understood that she would never be able to accompany him in his eccentric existence, in his ascent to glory. He left her and Alsace at the same time.

He tried to justify this desertion in the story of the *Die neue Melusine*, whose hero accepts the status of a dwarf in order not to leave his love, then, one day, breaks the magic ring in order to become a normal man again. Goethe likewise broke his liaison in order not to burden himself with restrictions which could prevent him from fulfilling his potentialities. Feeling morally guilty towards his fiancée, he could tell himself that he had acted well, for he should never cease to " prosper according to the law under which he had been born." Paul Valéry [1] has observed how he " saves by flight the mysterious casket containing all possibility," convinced that life is essentially " the preservation of the future." This explains, yet fails to justify, his " sacrifice of all women to the Eternal Feminine." Considering love a means to an end, he sacrificed the love of all women to his unique genius.

No doubt there was no one who needed friends more than Goethe did; perhaps no one had a personality so determined, so ready to press into service the resources of the outside world for his own evolution and continual enrichment. At Leipzig it was Behrisch and then Langer, whose influence lasted into Strassburg days; at Strassburg, Herder exercised an important influence. Similarly, in the domain of love, Kätchen, preceded by Gretchen, was in turn replaced, on a higher plane, by Friederike. For three years illness, the influence of Susanna von Klettenberg, then, as he tells us in *Dichtung und Wahrheit*, the curse of the dancing-master's daughter, deterred him from amorous adventures. But during the months of May and June, 1771,

[1] *Nouvelle Revue Française*, June 1932, pp. 955-956.

his visits to the presbytery of Sesenheim grew more frequent and the flame of passion was ignited. It inspired the " *Mailied* " which, compared to the poems of the Minnesinger, shows what new resources this twenty-two year-old poet had to offer his country. Another still more striking testimony, which reveals the evolution of the poet himself, is furnished by a comparison between the Leipzig poem " *die Hütte* " and " *Willkommen und Abschied,*" a poem undoubtedly composed in March 1771, after the lonely ride to Sesenheim mentioned in *Dichtung und Wahrheit* and revised after his return to Frankfurt, that is to say, after the separation. It was no longer a case of artificial realism " ornamented " with mythological recollections and a fashionable pastoral setting, but of an actual experience, a tale of passion, which unfolds in a dramatic atmosphere where nocturnal nature and impetuous love are the principal protagonists. The teachings of Herder, who felt that poetry must come from the heart and reach the heart, and above all his passion for Friederike gave rise to these four strophes, which represented the first revelation of a new German lyricism.

If the " Münster " was the great stone image which dominated Goethe's residence at Strassburg, Friederike, in her Alsatian costume, seems to have been the personification of the " Magnificent Alsace " which the poet celebrated so lyrically. Whether from the cathedral tower or in the course of excursions, it was this Alsace which helped him to recover his health, perhaps above all because it turned him again towards Germany. Strassburg was to have been a stage on the road to Paris. However, on April 29, 1770, after admiring the Gobelin Tapestries (mostly executed after cartoons by Raphael) which had been brought from the French capital to decorate the queen's reception rooms, he wrote to Langer: " To Italy, to Italy! But not for a year. It is too soon for me: I have not yet the necessary knowledge, much is yet lacking. Paris shall be my college,

Rome my university. For it is a true university; when one has once seen that, one has seen everything. That is why I am in no hurry to go there." It was the first manifestation of his yearning for Italy. France was relegated yet further into the background by various experiences which Goethe enumerates in Book II of *Dichtung und Wahrheit*. He began with a general consideration, directed at biographers:

> Our lives, like the cosmos which surrounds us, are made up in an incomprehensible way of freedom and necessity. Our wills announce beforehand what we shall do whatever the circumstances. But these circumstances seize us in their own way. The What is in us, the How rarely depends on us, about the Why we have not the right to ask, and the result is that we are finally referred to the Because.

Next he explained that he was deterred by the French language, which he liked and had spoken since his childhood, because people corrected him with a haughty politeness, asserting at the same time that no foreigner could ever master it. It was therefore decided at Salzmann's " table d'hôte " to speak only German.[1] Goethe was disappointed by French administration compared to that of Frederick II, and was shocked by the frequent assertion that Germans had no taste. These young intellectuals, intoxicated with pleasure and freedom, found French literature " too loaded with years and with honors " (*bejahrst und vornehm*). With the exception of Diderot, a " true German," and Rousseau, no other French author escaped the reproach of age, not even Voltaire; the Encyclopedists stupefied them, and not one of them could read to the end of Holbach's *Système de la Nature*, where " what seems higher than nature, or what appears as an elevation of nature was transformed into a material, weighty nature, alive, it is true, but, with neither purpose nor form."

---

[1] There was at Strassburg a " Society for the Improvement of the German Language," which contributed to dissuading Goethe from his original plan: he renounced Paris and France.

Goethe summarized his development in this conclusion: "Thus, at the frontier of France, we rid ourselves at a stroke of everything French. We found the way of life too rigid, too formal, the poetry without warmth, criticism destructive, philosophy abstruse yet not satisfying." The consequence was a frightening void and the disoriented youth was in danger of giving way to brute nature, at least for a trial. One can understand that, lost as he was, he felt the need for a new master: he chose Shakespeare.

At the conclusion of his years of apprenticeship, Goethe returned to Frankfurt. He was not coming home to lick his wounds, as on his previous return. He was a young man of twenty-two, rich in health and talent, who had at last completed his legal studies and was ready to play a part in life. Above all he was a poet who had observed the outside world in two cities as different as Strassburg and Leipzig, and whom illness had awakened to an inner life. It is true that he had hardly begun to write, but he had discovered nature and love, the secret of poetry and the greatness of genius. It remained for him to find expression, and he was now ready to apply his powers to this task.

Chapter 3

Sturm - und - drang
(1771-1774)

Goethe was convinced of the underlying identity of the plant and human organisms. At the end of the first three parts of *Dichtung und Wahrheit* he explained that before even beginning to write them, he had decided to arrange them according to the laws of the metamorphosis of plants. In the first book he wished to show how the child pushes out tender roots in every direction, but develops only a small number of leaves; in the second, youth was to put forth branches of increasing variety; finally, the third would show the shoots surging with life and impatient to bloom. If the first sixteen years were in fact those of childhood, and the next five those of the youth opening out to receive love, in the last the young man emerges into the world and the young poet takes the stage.

Goethe filled his father with joy by passing his law examinations and seemed to be ready to crown his hopes by becoming a member of the bar in his native city, where, with his father's help, he actually pleaded twenty-eight cases. Was he to become an advocate, a Frankfurt official, a model bourgeois? The danger was not great. He possessed too much vitality and promise to condemn himself to such a prosaic existence. He was called " the Wanderer," an epithet which sprang from an instability which reflected his inner uncertainty. This new stay at Frankfurt (August, 1771-October, 1775) was interrupted by the months spent at Wetzlar, from May to September, 1772, and also by numerous journeys to Darmstadt, Giessen (August, 1772), Ehrenbreitstein (September, 1772) and the Rhine valley (July, 1774).

His relationships with his friends and with contemporary writers and intellectuals became very important at this time.[1] In Frankfurt he found Horn, Krespel, Riese and Schlosser, who later married his sister. He corresponded with his Strassburg friends Klinger, Lenz, A. L. Wagner, Jung-Stilling and Herder. In Darmstadt he met Merck, who was to be a model for Mephistopheles, at Wetzlar, Kestner, Jerusalem and Gotter. More important for the future were his meetings with Jacobi, Lavater [2] Basedow, Zimmermann and the brothers Stolberg, who came to visit the already famous young poet. Goethe wrote to a friend, " Frankfurt is the New Jerusalem where all the nations of the earth go in and out, the habitation of the just." [3] He returned their visits and traveled with them, gaining insight into the spiritual atmosphere of his time.

Despite his many activities he still found time to read and study important works and authors: the Bible, which led him to religious researches of some depth; Hamann, a complete edition of whose works he projected all his life; Shakespeare, in whose honor he organized a great *festival* on October 14, 1771; Ossian, from whose work he trans-

---

[1] In his *Goethe* A. Fuchs devotes a well-documented chapter to the poet's relations with his contemporaries, both men and women.

[2] For Goethe's relations with Lavater, see Guinaudeau's article in *Études germaniques*, Nos. 14-15, pp. 213-226.

[3] Quoted by Lichtenberger in his *Goethe* (Nouvelle Revue Critique, p. 46).

lated passages destined to find a place in *Werther*; Spinoza,
" that extraordinary man " who " was to exercise so great
an influence over my whole manner of thinkng " (*Dichtung und Wahrheit*, Book XIV); and above all, the Greeks.
" Pindar is now my domain," he wrote to Herder on
July 10, 1772, and " Since last I heard from you, the
Greeks have been my only study." He mentioned Homer,
Xenophon and Plato (for information on Socrates), Theo-
critus and Anacreon, and finally Pindar whose hold on
him was lasting. It was through Pindar that he came to
conceive of mastery and virtuosity as the art of dominating and driving four fiery horses. Until then he had been
merely casting about without taking hold of anything.
Herder had shown, in relation to sculpture, that the artist
who cannot work in a plastic medium is worthless because
" to grasp, to encompass is the essence of all mastery."
He had heeded so well the reproach in his Strassburg master's remark, " Everything with you is so much observation," that he had closed his eyes and groped. At the age
of twenty-two, no doubt on Herder's advice, he made the
Greek authors his sole reading, seeking the secret of their
art and finding it in the plasticity of their creations. The
lesson did not bear full fruit until later, particularly in
Iphiginia and in *Tasso*, but from 1772 onwards Goethe
knew the principles of classical art which formed a link
between the teachings of Winckelmann and the Italian
journey. His work did not yet reveal its influence, however.
It still remained the spontaneous outpourings of his tormented soul, unmediated by that emotional " distance "
praised by Hofmannsthal. [1]

The same letter to Herder provides us with valuable
information on the state of his soul. It begins: " I am
still riding the waves in my little boat, and when the
stars are hidden, I drift hither and thither with the winds

---

[1] On this subject, see his *Unterhaltungen über den Tasso*.

of destiny, and courage and hope, fear and calm alternate in my breast." While the rationalist enlightenment had accorded primacy to the mind, and eighteenth century sentimentality to the heart, Goethe seems to have discovered what may be called a new organ which was neither the " *Gemüt* " nor the " *Sinn* " of the romantics, but rather the organ of that human totality posited by Hamann. A new world opened for him on the day when he felt the force of the Greek words " *stethos* " and " *prapides* " [1] and he concluded: " Poor (is the man) whose head is his all." He was desolated by the reproach leveled by Herder against *Götz von Berlichingen*. " That is all fabricated." He wanted to free himself of all that oppressed him, and to cry, like Moses in the Koran: " Lord, make room in my narrow breast." He was to find freedom through poetic creation.

Among the works of this particularly fruitful period one may single out theoretical writings such as *von deutscher Baukunst* (1772) and *zum Schäkespeare Tag* (1771), articles in the " Learned Annals of Frankfurt," religious essays, farces or satires such as *Jahrmarktsfest zu Plundesweilern*, *Satyros* and *Götter Helden und Wieland*. Among the most important theatrical works were *Götz von Berlichingen*, *Clavigo* and *Stella*. There was also the famous novel *Werther*, and finally many poems among which one must mention " *Der Wanderer*," " *Wanderers Sturmlied*," " *Mahomets Gesang Prometheus*, " " *Ganymed*, " " *An Schwager Kronos* " and " *Der König in Thule*." Without pausing over the theoretical writings, whose principal ideas we shall have occasion to discuss, or the farces and satires which do not give full expression to Goethe's thought,

---

[1] Liddell and Scott's Greek-English lexicon mentions that the former, common in Homer with the meaning " breast " was later oftenest used metaphorically to indicate the seat of thought and feeling; as for the latter, it means the " diaphragm " considered as the seat of all the powers of the spirit.

3. Katherine Elisabeth Textor, mother of the poet (Portrait by J. Schmoll)

we would like to examine his masterpieces. There we find his true genius revealing itself through poetry, which was at once his refuge and his means of liberation, the mainspring of his being and his mode of action. In an important page of *Dichtung und Wahrheit*, Book XV, he describes his creative power as the very basis of his existence: " In seeking the means of assuring my independence, I found that the surest foundation was the fertility of my talent." Lichtenberger was right when he compared the young poet to a new Prometheus, in revolt against the gods and their laws, who was about to create his own universe. In this context the genesis of his first great work is particularly revealing, for it was the product of his entire life, of his mind and of his heart.

On November 28, 1771, he wrote to Salzmann: " My entire genius rests upon an enterprise which makes me forget Homer, Shakespeare and everything. I am dramatizing the story of one of the noblest of the Germans. I am vindicating the memory of a good man." How did he come to write it? The humdrum routine of life in Frankfurt had created the need for a pastime. His mother tells us that he discovered the name of Götz in a law book; he became interested and got hold of his autobiography, which he transformed into a play for reading (*Lesedrama*), entitled " Story of Götz von Berlichingen, dramatized." [1] Why did he choose such a subject? First, he was following the advice of Herder, who considered Shakespeare the great model for tragedians and attributed the merit of his works to his exploitation of history. He believed that it was necessary to select from history a great man rather than an event and to present him in such a way that the audience would cry: " That was a man! " Secondly, Goethe wished

---

[1] The chief work on *Götz* is by R. Wiessenfels: *Goethe im Sturm-und-Drang.*

to introduce an element of grandeur into an era which, with the exception of Frederick II, was lacking in outstanding personalities. Thus he searched history for men who might be held up as models to " a century of eunuchs " (Schiller, in The Brigands), men capable of leading it back to a normal, natural life as Rousseau urged. Among the subjects for plays envisaged by Goethe at this period, *Götz* was the only one to be completed. He found in his hero the qualities he considered specifically German and which he admired above all others: courage, independence, honesty and goodness. He made a sixteeenth century robber baron into a national hero, the champion of the oppressed and paladin of liberty; he was to become the mouthpiece of the Sturm-und-Drang's literary revolution.

There was a danger that the new work would be a fabrication of an armchair playwright, an arbitrary dramatization of a singularly undramatic subject. The life of Götz consisted of a number of unrelated raids and battles, the unsuccessful leadership of the peasants' uprising and an uneventful retreat to his castle to write his memoirs. Goethe had to give this story " a dramatic pulse." In order to find a solution he had to add to what he had learned from Herder and from Götz von Berlichingen's autobiography, from Weislingen and brother Martin, as well as the resources of his poetic imagination and the experiences of his own life. The feminine characters provided scope for the evocation of his idyll with Friederike Brion.

The young poet already possessed enough dramatic sense to realize that his play, an attack launched against the enlightenment, lacked sufficient conflict. He therefore invented the character of Weislingen, who is the antithesis of Götz and who functions as the archtype of his enemies. Weislingen was spoiled by " his wretched court existence " in luxury, idleness and duplicity, while Götz, in his castle at Jaxthausen, cultivated the ancient German virtues. The former is an imaginative dreamer, feeble and unfit for action, the opposite of the knight who is born for battle. If he does display a certain energy it is to conquer Adelheid, who says to him: " I expected to find a Titan and I find a melancholy poet." Thus he envies Götz. Like all the heroes of the " Sturm-und-Drang," he wants to develop his individuality, and in his desire to acquire " that greatness which is denied him " he takes the opposite course, seeking his fortune with the great, the bishop of Bamberg and the Emperor, whose instrument he becomes. His ambition is so strong that he hesitates at nothing to destroy the friend who has become his rival. Wishing to create a dramatic conflict by opposing Götz to an adversary who plays " the ever-necessary role of the antipathetic character " Goethe made Weislingen so important that one may wonder whether the play should not have been called *Adelbert von Weislingen.* Götz does remain the hero, however, but it must be admitted that although the unity of the play is safeguarded, the unity of action is not respected.

To the historical and the dramatic components Goethe added, as always, a lyrical element, a love story involving two women. Adelheid, the " *femme fatale,*" is opposed to Maria, just as her brother Götz is opposed to Weislingen. Love played no part in Götz's autobiography, but we know its importance in Goethe's life. It intervenes directly in the action of *Götz von Berlichingen* for the character of Weislingen bears witnees to the power of women. Indecisive, he wavers between Adelheid and Maria, the one drawing him towards the court, the other towards Götz. According to his friend, the causes of his fall were, first, court life, then women whose favors he sought, just as Goethe had done. The poet therefore imagined an unscrupulous siren, capable of driving men mad with love, including the good Sickingen and the young Bohemian. Opposite her he placed a pure young girl to whom he gave the Virgin's name, and we know that the decisive turn in

Weislingen's story was inspired by a heart-rending letter from Friederike Brion. The parallel between the play and real life is striking. First, the lyrical scenes with Maria are a transposition of the idyll of Sesenheim. Weislingen cries, " I must go... I cannot," just as Goethe wrote from Sehenheim. " Here I find myself between door and threshold. " Next, desertion is common to both, and Goethe, sending a copy of *Götz* to Salzmann to deliver to his abandoned mistress, said to him, " Poor Friederike will receive some measure of satisfaction at seeing the faithless one poisoned." Finally, there was forgiveness in both cases. Friederike's pardon, to be bestowed in the course of a journey in 1779, was already contained in Maria's words: " May God forgive you everything, as I do."

We have only examined the principal characters who bore the great ideas and the great passions dear to " Sturm-und-Drang ": Götz's high-mindedness, Weislingen's ambition, the fire of Adelheid, and Maria's love. We must add another essential although secondary character, brother Martin, a representative of Luther, who asserted his right to be a complete man, a man of flesh.

The form of *Götz von Berlichingen* is no less revolutionary tham its subiect matter. Goethe wanted it to be Shakespearean and true to life. The rules of classical composition prohibited both the representation of all of the important episodes in the hero's life, and the opposition of the two extremes represented by Bamberg and Jaxthausen. The poet therefore cast overboard the unities of time and place. Thus Act III comprises no less than twenty-two scenes set in twenty-two different places, creating a dispersal of the action. In his desire to follow nature he wrote in prose, making each character speak in the manner of his social rank. Both in construction and in language therefore, we find a living idiom. Thus conceived, constructed and written, the play was a real declaration of war on traditional literature, particularly on the classical drama of France. Such was indeed the poet's aim, if we may judge from the lines which accompanied the dispatch of the play to Merek in December, 1771.

We have paid particular attention to the original version which Goethe wrote in a few weeks at the end of 1771, thinking that it was no more than a sketch. He hastened to send the manuscript to Herder, whose judgment he respected and feared. He had written to him in October, 1771: " Herder, Herder, remain what you are in my eyes. I shall not let you go. I shall not leave you. Jacob wrestled with the angel of the Lord. Even if the result be paralysis for me." After several months of waiting, he received an answer which we know by his letter to Herder of July 10, 1772: " It is all fabrication " and " Shakespeare has entirely spoilt you." Goethe admits only the second criticism, a surprising reproach from an admirer of the English poet. He admitted it the more readily as his Greek studies had meanwhile substituted a different ideal. He therefore rewrote his play in order to reduce the exaggeration of the Shakespearean manner and also to attain greater naturalism. He concentrated the action, strengthened the characters of Götz and Weislingen, weakened that of Adelheid, reduced the role of love and fantasy, added two scenes and modified others, heightened the local color, and in fact raised the dramatic and historical tone. The work made a sensation and created a real vogue for Shakespeare, though Frederick II considered it a barbarization unworthy of the German stage.

We see that Goethe was inspired by his interest in a distant period of German history and by a desire to bring it to the stage following Shakespeare's example. He wished to immortalize an individual, as Lessing had tried to do, and to resurrect great men, as the " Sturm-und-Drang " sought to do. Thus, in feverish passion, he dramatized the story of Götz. At the same time he freed himself of remorse by inventing the character of Weislingen, the reflection of his own worst traits, and made him take poison to avenge Friederike. He created this play in a theatrical mould which was partly Shakespearean and partly his own, with no particular thought of writing a fine piece, but with the desire to create something sincere. A few months later the lesson of the Greeks and Herder's criticism sufficed to enable him to judge it objectively and to revise it. He finally admitted the existence of certain aesthetic laws to which he had to conform. While in 1771 his chief aim had been to treat a particular subject, a year later he was dreaming of realizing an aesthetic ideal. Thus he already carried within him the germ of the classic Goethe whom, for the moment, he still denied.

We must also consider *Clavigo* (May, 1774), although it is a much less important work. It too was inspired by a written document, a story of Beaumarchais, which tells of the vengeance he had wreaked on a Spaniard, José Clavigo y Fararado, who was guilty of breaking a promise of marriage to his sister. Goethe read it at a social gathering, and the pretty Anna Sibylle Münch, his partner in the game of mock marriage being played at the party, said: " If I were your sovereign and not your wife, I would demand that you turn that story into a play." The young poet answered that she should immediately be satisfied; a week later he read his play *Clavigo* which was at once printed and published in July, 1774. It is the very model of an impromptu play and one cannot but admire his literary prowess. But he could not have done it, as he wrote to Jacobi on August 21, 1774, if the character and actions of the narrator had not blended with his own. Already on the first of June, he had thus characterized his work to G. Fr. E. Schönbern: " A modern anecdote dramatized with the greatest possible simplicity and heartfelt sincerity. My hero, an unsettled man, both great and petty, the pendant of Weislingen or rather Weislingen himself, fully rounded out into a principal character." So Goethe invited us to link these two " dramatized stories " to each other and to see in their lyrical aspects the evocation of his love and betrayal of Friederike. But he went still further: he allowed us to link *Clavigo* with *Stella* and with the tragedy of Margarete, for he tried to justify his infidelity through the person of Carlos, who can be related to Mephistopheles and hence to Merck. In the very first scene, Clavigo, a true echo of Weislingen-Goethe, declares, " I cannot prevent myself remembering that I abandoned Maria, that I deceived her—call it what you will." And his friend, the echo of Mephistopheles—Merck—answers in these cynical words: " Extravagant. It seems to me that one lives only once in this world, that one has only once these powers and prospects and that whoever does not use them to the full or fails to go as far as possible is mad. And to marry! To marry just at the moment when life is at last truly about to blossom,—to set up house, to limit oneself when one has not yet made half one's journey, half one's conquests! For you to have loved her is natural, for you to have promised to marry her was folly; and if you had kept your word, it would have been insanity." Further on we seem to hear Mephistopheles in person: " Don't worry, she is not the first girl to be deserted, she will not be the first to get over it." Goethe may have put Beaumarchais, the avenger of his sister, on the stage, but he couldn't help opposing to him, however indirectly, the right of genius to stand " beyond good and evil."

This is the same problem of love and marriage which he was to pose and resolve a year later, in *Stella* (February-March, 1775). He was driven to write it by his love for Lili, and the necessity of choosing between two irreconcilables: his need of liberty, and the fact that marriage was the only possible fulfillment for his love. There was much of himself in its hero, Fernando, who tried to lead a three-cornered existence between his wife and mistress. With this work Goethe abandoned German history and Shakespearean drama, intending to create a "play for lovers," more personal perhaps, and at the same time more broadly human, less revolutionary in composition. It sets out to justify revolt against the law in the name of freedom to love and to fulfill one's destiny. Later Goethe had to appease a scandalized public by altering the plot and causing the death of both Stella and Fernando.

From the same period dates the first brilliant sketch of *Faust*,[1] the *Urfaust*, which Goethe probably began in 1772, continued in 1774 and showed to only a very few friends. Long unknown, it was rediscovered by Erich Schmidt in the papers left by Luise von Göchhausen, and published by him in 1887. It consists of 1,435 lines (the first part of the complete *Faust* numbers 4,612) and includes the night scene in Faust's study with the appearance of the "Earth Spirit" and the dialogue with Wagner, the scene between Mephistopheles and the student, in Auerbach's tavern, at Leipzig, and the tragedy of Margarete.

Here again we have an historical character, Dr. Faust, a German doctor and magician, who lived in the fifteenth century at the dawn of the modern world. To attain his ends he concluded a pact with the devil, who, after an agreed period of time came to claim his soul. The story

[1] The essential authorities on *Faust* are:

a) G. Witkovski's edition (9th edition, Brill, Leyden, 1936, 2 volumes of 591 and 590 pages).

b) E. Beutler's edition (Dieterich, Wiesbaden, 1940, 625 pages).

c) H. Richert, *Goethes Faust* (Tübingen, 1932).

d) In France, Lichtenberger's introductions to the bilingual edition in 3 volumes (Aubier).

The chief contribution of the "anthroposphs" who erected a theatre at Dornach near Basle called the "Goetheanum" is that of Rudolf Steiner with his two books *Das Faustproblem* (1931) and *Faust der strebende Mensch* (1931), both published by the Philo-Anthroposoph Verlag. Am Goetheanum, Dornach, Switzerland.

We would mention the recent works by F. J. Schneider (already quoted) and by Hermann Schneider: *Urfaust?* (Laupp, Tübingen, 1949, 110 pages).

has been popularized in a " Volksbuch " and used many times in literature [1] with a moralizing purpose, to turn men aside from the snares of Evil. The Age of Reason saw its hero as the champion of science and Lessing, as a savior, and opposed to the theme of the damnation of Faust, that of his redemption. Faust judged that his tireless and disinterested search after truth made him worthy of salvation. But Goethe, as we have seen, could not content himself with a hero who was a man of intellect only: he wanted a Titan, possessed by a superhuman *"Streben."* He also wished to make confession through his work, to liberate himself from that feeling of " innocent guilt " which had obsessed him ever since his desertion of Friederike. He thus juxtaposed two plays in the *Urfaust*, a drama of conscience and a love story, which are not completely unified. They remain two plays with a single hero: the first is simply a sketch; the second is finished, but not entirely satisfactory.

Faust, an austere savant, is not a specialist like Wagner, nor the representative of that " book-learning " which Goethe had met at Leipzig and which he ridicules in the dialogue between Mephistopheles and the student; he is the heir of those students of the occult whose works the poet had studied at Frankfurt. He wanted not only to study the outward form of nature, the " how," but also to explore the depths and scrutinize the " why." He therefore becomes a devotee of magic and, in a moment of illumination he conjures up the " Spirit of Earth " to whom he considered himself an equal. The spirit defines his sphere in these magnificent lines:

> In the billows of life, in the storm of action
> I undulate, I rise and fall
> And I weave my web!

[1] Consult G. Bianquis, *Faust à travers quatre siècles* (Droz, 1935, 370 p.).

> Birth and tomb
> A sea eternal,
> Weaving in and out
> A fiery life!
> Thus I work at the rustling fabric of time,
> Making the living mantle of Divinity.
>
> (Lines 501-509).

Then he rejects the despairing Faust.

Faust becomes the Devil's ally, following which he encounters a pure young girl, the counterpart of Maria in *Götz*, without the poet's establishing any connection between the two parts of the drama. He desires her, then, getting to know her better, is smitten by sincere love. He wins her heart and finally abandons her, condemning her to death for the justice of mankind does not pardon infanticide. This is the tragedy of Margarete made up of a variety of elements borrowed from reality. Its origin was undoubtedly the execution of Susanna Margarete Brandt in Frankfurt on January 14, 1772.[1] Next, Gretchen bears the name of the girl whom Goethe loved in early adolescence (but it was the second Christian name of Susanna Brandt), a character with all the charms of Friederike. Goethe-Faust doubtless pitied the girl, victim of bourgeois justice and in fact his own victim, but he did not make " The Tragedy of Margarete " into a violent protest against the laws of men, in opposition to the judgment of God. Furthermore, at the end of her drama he flees without knowing his destination, to an end revealed to us only in the second Faust.

Götz, Clavige and *Stella* were satisfactorily completed; *Faust* remained a grandiose fragment. Other subjects were to remain mere projects and synopses, and they form a singularly revealing collection: *Prometheus, Mahomet, Cäsar, Socrates*. They dealt with four superhuman persona-

---

[1] See Beutler, *Essays um Goethe*, 1, pp. 98-114.

lities: the rebel seeking to create a race hostile to the Gods, the prophet capable of founding a religion, the war leader, eager for domination, and finally the genial spirit, the " hero of philosophy " practicing the " divine profession of the education of man." For Goethe they were incarnations of the ideal in history. They answered his need to find forms in the outside world which would allow him to express his most intimate self; these heroes prefigured that superior being toward which his " *Streben* " was leading him. *Prometheus* (1773) got no further than the second act, but it contains the famous hymn, which is certainly the most extraordinary cry of disdain and defiance hurled by man at Divinity; of *Mahomet*, of which Goethe gave a detailed synopsis at the end of the fourteenth book of *Dichtung und Wahrheit*, we have scarcely anything except the great poem, already pre-classic in style, on the life and action of the religious genius. *Cäsar* and *Socrates* remain mere titles: they were too great, too distant, too foreign to the young Titan who was already working on *Werther*.

The origins of this celebrated pre-romantic novel, which made its author famous throughout Europe, are well known, yet they do not conform entirely to the account in *Dichtung und Wahrheit*. We know practically nothing of the growth of the work, written in one stream in only a few weeks (March-April, 1774). Goethe tells us that he did not begin to set it down until he had composed the whole work in his head; *Werther* is a magnificent illustration of this method. We must therefore trace the psychological growth of this confession in letters, and watch it maturing in the very soul of the poet, thus studying it as a lyrical novel. If we have no poems on the subject, it is precisely because the work itself is a vast lyric prose poem.

There is a certain unconscious humor and great psychological finesse in the letter in which Kestner announces the arrival, in the spring of 1772, of a " certain Goethe of

Frankfurt " who had come to Wetzlar ostensibly—for such
was his father's intention—to practice law at the Imperial
Tribunal, but in fact intending to " study Homer, Pindar, etc... and for such other pursuits as his genius, his way
of thinking and his heart might inspire." His heart was
soon lost to Kestner's fiancée, Charlotte Buffe. Goethe spent
many delightful hours in the countryside in the company
of these two young people. But whatever her feeling was
for the attractive poet, Charlotte remained faithful to Kestner. On Merck's advice, Goethe decided to flee on September 11, 1772, at seven o'clock in the morning. Distance did
not cure unhappy love and he returned, without, however,
preventing Charlotte's marriage to Kestner on April 4, 1773.
A full correspondence began between the young couple
and the poet, who was still desperately in love.

But to what literary use could he put the story of a
love who did nothing but run away? Fortunately for the
author there was Jerusalem, Councillor of the Brunswick
legation, who was also in love with an unattainable woman.
Weaker or more passionate than the poet, he committed
suicide, and it could be said that the bullet which killed
him saved Goethe. The latter asked Kestner for details
of Jerusalem's death and he used them for the end of his
novel. In the thirteenth book of *Dichtung und Wahrheit*
he even asserts that this event precipitated the necessary
concentration for the work, and inspired the plot, an error
of memory, for Jerusalem killed himself on October 30,
1772 and *Werther* was not composed until the spring of
1774. Yet this episode provided an important part in the
dénouement and in the attainment of an essential " distance." At this time Goethe himself had thought of suicide
and sometimes, before going to sleep, he tried to plunge a
dagger into his breast. "As that would never succed, I
finished by laughing at myself. I cast far from me all my
hypochondriac grimaces and resolved to live." The example of Jerusalem, who had chosen to die, disturbed him

deeply, allowing him to evoke the image of an unbridled
and hopeless passion and providing him with a dénouement,
based on life. On the other hand, a novel of passion could
not proceed directly from a passionate state of the soul;
it could become a work of art only if Goethe could detach
himself and, so to speak, treat the subjective element objectively. Jerusalem's suicide permitted him to withdraw sufficiently to see himself objectively and to crystallize in a
symbolic " hero " all of the forces that had been working
within him.

The poet now had the beginning and the end of his
novel as well as an essential part of the story, but the
work did not yet come forth. Goethe was not to work
on it until 1773, as if a new impulse were necessary before
he could find release. Then the third and final episode took
place. On fleeing from Wetzlar, he had gone to Ehrenbreitstein where he stayed a few days with Sophie de la
Roche and met and admired her daughter Maximilienne.
In January, 1774, aged seventeen, she married the merchant Brentano of Frankfurt, who was thirty-nine and
already the father of five children. This lovely and intelligent girl condemned herself to a life among oil casks and
herring barrels at side of a dull, homely husband. She
was delighted when the poet became an attentive friend
of the family, but her jealous husband became anxious,
doubtless as a result of domestic scenes, and Goethe was
invited not to return. At this moment, rejected like Jerusalem, he found himself in a favorable state of mind and,
combining the characteristics of several persons, he wrote
his novel. Afterwards he felt " as after a general confession, happy and free, with the right to lead a new life."

Yet the hero is not simply the poet's double. In his important letter to G. Fr. E. Schönborn of January 11, 1774,
Goethe tells him that he has depicted

a young man gifted with a profound and pure sensibility as well as
with true penetration, who loses himself in enthusiastic dreams, un-

dermines himself with speculation until finally, annihilated (*zerüttet*) by the intervention of unhappy passions and above all by a hopeless love, he blows out his brains.

And again, in the famous discussion on suicide, Werther speaks these prophetic words to Albert, the happy fiancé:

Consider man in his narrow limitations, see how impressions set upon him, how ideas become fixed in him to such an extent that finally a swelling passion deprives him of all possibility of peaceful reflection and annihilates him.

We are at a period where the ego dominates, where sentimentality overflows, where, in reaction to the "*Aufklärung*," the aim is less to suppress the passions to obtain happiness than to canalize them and use their power. Gundolf sees in *Don Quixote* the first novel of the individual and in *Werther* the first novel of the ego, with the latter marking the transition from individualism to subjectivism. Doubtless the poet expressed his own personality through this hero whom he might have called his lyrical double as he called Wilhelm Meister his dramatic double. But with a lucidity surprising in a young man of twenty-five, he deprived himself of individuality in order to envisage "Man," eliminating particular features and landscapes to such an extent that the whole world could recognize itself in Werther. Goethe had already risen, unconsciously and perhaps unwillingly, from the particular to the universal. While he revolted against imitation of France as did the whole "Sturm-und-Drang," he was faithful to French classical ideals and was already on the road to his own classicism. The result was that this enthusiast's portrayal of passion was also an indictment. Seeing the distress occasioned by his novel, he added to a later edition the advice to the reader spoken by the hero himself, "Be a man and do not follow me."

Werther is a young man who has not yet succeeded in coming to terms with the world. He is too talented to settle down to a commonplace existence, but he can give no proof of his gifts, for a superabundance of sensations prevents him from realizing a single work. His chief merit is his ability to feel, shown in relation to nature, woman, mankind, and God. He lives by his heart, and in this he is the representative of both the " Sturm-und-Drang " and pietism. But he also possesses what Goethe calls " *eine Wahre Penetration*," a sort of semi-intellectual, semi-sensual intuition which allows him to understand with the heart, to judge others, and above all to analyse himself, although without resulting in self-improvement. These qualities and gifts, which could produce a great artist, prove dangerous, encouraging only dreams and specula-tions. He dreams of love, but we feel that even if Charlotte became his, he would remain unsatisfied. He dreams of finding peace in nature, but he discovers a sepulchre instead. He dreams of comprehending God, but when his pettiness rises to the level of the sublime, he is annihilated just as Faust is annihilated by the Earth Spirit. His dreams of a great work of art produced nothing, while his dreams of an active and socially useful life lead to humiliating failure. He concludes in his letter of May 22 that " life is but a dream, we must seek in ourselves what escapes us outside and move through the world with a dreamer's smile."

His propensity for " speculation " is even more serious than the tendency to dream for it leads him to brood over past disappointments instead of enjoying the present. Later, Mephistopheles will give the metaphysician the following advice:

> I tell you; any speculative fellow
> Is like the animal which in a dry place
> Turns round in circles, led by evil spirits,
> When all around is green and pleasant country.

> *Faust I* (lines 1830-1833).

Haunted by the " problematic " of life, Werther forgets to live. Yet emotional suffering is needed before he can be led to seek release in death; thwarted ambition, a motive which Goethe tones down in later editions, and particularly his unhappy love for Charlotte, provide the motives.

It is really a play, despite the exterior form of an epistolatory novel inspired by the *Nouvelle Héloise*, and we need not seek far to find in it all the elements of the usual type of dramatic action. An exposition introduces us to the hero and his antecedents, to the place, the time and local populace; it creates the spiritual atmosphere and prepares the action, which will be determined to a great extent by the character of Werther. The action begins with the appearance of Lotte, and rapidly rises to a first climax on the night of the ball, then to a second between May 21 and July 30. The young man thinks himself beloved and has never been so happy. An anticlimax is produced by Albert's return, and the falling action is emphasized by the despair of Werther, who finally decides to go away. We then have "*ein retardierendes Moment*," in which outward action is halted, for the protagonists are separated. The inner action continues as the hero becomes a hounded traveler, finally returning to Charlotte. By his return, the action recommences; it is no longer a question of a love which suddenly appears and grows in joy, but of an explosive passion which destroys itself, provoking the final catastrophe.

If one wishes fully to understand the essential character of Werther, one must refer to the famous treatise which Schiller published in 1795, *On Naive and Sentimental Poetry*. In an effort to defend the Moderns against the Ancients and to justify his place alongside Goethe, he arrived at his formula: " Either one is natural or one seeks nature... ": in the first case we have the poetry of the Greeks, who felt naturally, and that of Goethe, a naïve poet; in the second case we have the poetry of the Moderns, who feel what is natural, and that of Schiller, a sentimental poet.

4. Self-portrait of Goethe in his room at Frankfurt (1768)

Werther is a " sentimental ": he feels nature, aspires to her and grasps her fleetingly, but remains outside her and can celebrate her only " sentimentally." There can be nothing more significant from this point of view than the letter of June 21, a finished composition which shows with what care Goethe drew up his revolutionary manifesto. In an early passage, Werther evokes man's dual leaning: to expand his ego to the limits of the universe and, on the other hand, to content himself with his cottage where, surrounded by wife and children he can find the " felicity vainly sought in the vastness of the world." Next he rejoices at having discovered his " dear Wahlheim," where he picks, shells and cooks his peas like a simple gardener. Yet we are not taken in by this: although the gardner, a simple soul, can live naturally and know innocent happiness, Werther can no longer live a simple life in the bosom of nature without affectation. A " sentimental," he is capable only of seeking nature, and can never be a part of it. Without wishing to classify the characters in the novel from this point of view one may yet say that Charlotte is a naïve being, satisfied with the narrow life of a housewife. When she sighs the name of Klopstock in the moonlight she is merely expressing the sentimentalism of the whole period. Although Werther may disturb her he does not turn her from her banal existence as an ordinary wife and mother. Yet this heroine of the novel who forgets the world for a moment in his embrace surely shares his " sentimental " emotion.

After *Götz*, a play of action and freedom, *Clavigo* and *Stella*, dramas of love, and *Faust*, a drama of the understanding, Goethe gave his enthusiastic public this drama of unhappy passion unfolding within the soul of Werther.[1]

---

[1] Max Herrmann in his introduction to *Werther* in the " Jubiläumsausgabe," XVI.

The lyricism in these works is a series of fleeting manifestations, like the explosions of a spirit in perpetual turmoil; Goethe's creative power is to be seen only through a continual series of poems. It is not possible to examine them all here; yet it is only right to point out, as Gundolf has done, the essential part which Goethe played in the evolution of German poetry.

What is a poet? Goethe laughed at the aestheticians who tried to formulate an abstract definition, and said to Eckermann, on June 11, 1825: " Why have they this need of definitions? What makes a poet is a vivid sense of situations (*zustände*) and the ability to express it." Besides, as we have seen, he called his poems " poetry of circumstance " (*Gelegenheitsgedichte*), born from an event or a state of mind. But if this provides the subject matter (*Stoff*), it is the ego of the poet, using the subject as a vehicle for self-expression, which constitutes its tenor (*Gehalt*). Poems may be compared to stained-glass windows; they may be admired from the outside, but their striking coloring, their rich ornamentation and wealth is only revealed to whoever enters the chapel,[1] that is to say the poet's mind, at the moment of conception. Nature and God, love and friendship, life and death, joy and sorrow, all that goes to make up man, the " *Stimmung* "[2] dear to Novalis, these are the " situations " expressed by the poet.

The young Goethe found, at his debut, two types of poetry. He first imitated them, and then surpassed them, enriching them with the emotion of folk poetry revealed to him by Herder, and with the power of his genuis. There was on the one hand anacreontic poetry, slight and af-

---

[1] *Gedichte sind gemalte Fensterscheiben*, a poem translated into French in *Pages immortelles de Goethe*, p. 102.
[2] This is imperfectly rendered by " state of the soul." For its importance to Novalis, see Charles Du Bos: *Fragments sur Novalis* in the special number devoted to German romanticism by *Cahiers du Sud*.

fected, represented by Uz, Hagedorn, Gleim, etc., and the more genuine but still feeble poetry of a Brocker or a Haller. On the other hand there was the poetry of Klopstock which laboriously attempted to scale the heights of Parnassus. They can be compared in French literature to the minor poets of the Plèiade and to Malherbe, although Klopstock had greater breadth. He was less preoccupied with limiting and analyzing the poetic flux than with providing German poetry with new meters and a new idiom in an age of creation and progress. It is to Goethe's great merit that he did not remain satisfied with the rococo anacreontism in which he had grown up, and that he profited from Klopstock's contribution.

Three groups of poems date from 1765 to 1771 [1]: *Annette*, the *Songs of Leipzig* and the *Songs of Sesenheim*. The first, found among the papers of Luise von Gochhausen, was published in 1896. It forms a collection of nineteen poems, chosen partly by Behrisch [2] whose only real worth lies in its studied poetic form.

The second appeared anonymously under the title: *Neue Lieder in Melodien gesetzt von Bernhard Theodor Breitkopf.* It comprises twenty poems still full of anacreontism, in which Gleim's influence is combined with Wieland's. Yet Gundolf chooses six: *Die Nacht, Der Schmetterling, Hochzeitslied, Unbeständigkeit, Das Glück der Liebe* and *An den Mond* [3] which, while still in the tradition of erotic anacreontism, have a partly new sound,, whether due to subject or to form. Gundolf [4] observes that for the first time in Goethe's work and in German poetry,

---

[1] For all the poems of this period, Eugen Wolff's *Der junge Goethe. Goethes Gedichte* is indispensable. The first volume of the " Hamburger Ausgabe," while giving a wide selection, is particularly valuable for its very important notes, references and explanations by E. Trunz.

[2] Wolff, *Goethes Gedichte*, p. 272.

[3] Wolff, *Goethes Gedichte*, pp. 58-59, 60, 63-64, 67-68, 68-69.

[4] Gundolf, *Goethe*, pp. 62 et seq.

instead of speaking of love, love itself becomes a living experience, and is made to speak. It is not yet a question of passion but of a more gentle emotion which finds its place in this rococo setting, and without creating new channels of expression remains content with the old. A new sensuality also makes its appearance. As to the carefully chosen form, metrical rather than rhythmical form had predominated since Opitz. Meter expresses foreseen movement and general order, while rhythm is the expression of an entirely personal interior movement. By creating new words, as Gundolf observes, Goethe combined different spheres of feeling, forcing the reader to pass from rational representation to re-lived sensation. In *An der Mond*, for example, the new composite word " shiver of silver " appears. He elicits a magical rather than logical understanding by destroying the partition which separates the domain of silver from that of shiver. Although in the poem *Die Nacht* one still finds the gods and the moon and the zephyrs so dear to the rococo, Goethe revitalized the old themes with a fresh naturalism in such a line as " the moon snaps the darkness of the pines." He pursued this course further in the *Sesenheimer Lieder*.

Three important factors intervened: the cult of the folksong promoted by Herder, a new feeling for nature discovered in Alsace, and his passionate love for Friederike Brion. All three are combined in *Heidenroslein*, which may have been inspired by an authentic " *Volkslied*," the *Stimmen der Völker in Liedern*, in *Willkommen und Abschief*, and above all in *Mailied*, an extraordinary outpouring of lyric poetry in which man is depicted as a bough of nature, a bird of the forest, who shares a single vital force with all animate nature. This is no longer the language of the rococo period, but the voice of a child of nature. This poem, dating from May, 1771, is transitional, and marks the limits of a stage which Goethe had already surpassed. He moved from minor to major poetry, he undertook great subjects and eventually became the inspired successor of Klopstock.

With Klopstock, says Gundolf, German poetry left behind both the " *Aufklarung* " and anacreontism and entered the realm of feeling and " pathos." Living experience, that " *Erlebnis* " which Dilthey, in his well-known book *Das Erlebnis und die Dichtung*, makes the very mainspring of poetry, influences literature alongside of logic. Language expresses movements of the spirit as well as ideas and concepts. Yet Klopstock still confined himself to the great themes of infinity, God, death and the immortality of the soul. Like Schiller later, he deserted the ideal to descend to the material, and religion and ethics remained his sphere. " It is true he no longer dwelled on his thoughts about his emotions as the rationalists had done, but almost exclusively on the emotions provoked in him by his thoughts " (Gundolf). The first collected edition of his *Odes* appeared in 1771. Goethe had previously read some of them in reviews, and the name of Klopstock figured early in his letters. Without attempting to exaggerate Klopstock's influence as a precursor, one must recall that in 1767 Goethe wrote three odes to his friend Behrisch which surpass all his other contemporary work, and that from 1771 onward his poetry rose to an extraordinay level in both content and form.

Gundolf, whose remarkable study we are following here, singles out the master ideas of these poems: at the center is the man, of course the superior man or genius, who is always active and creative. He wanders through life and through storm (*Der Wanderer; Wanderers Sturmlied*): his whole existence is a road to the beyond (*An Schwager Kronos*); he is the benefactor of humanity (*Mahomets Gesang*) and a rebel against God (*Prometheus*), for he thinks himself superior to God. The great divinity is nature, and man is a part of her (*Mailied*). Nature is imnipresent and omnipotent, she is the living and organic body of God to whose level she rises through universal love (*Ganymed*). Little does it matter whether she wills our happiness or our suffering. We need only inhale her " sad delight." [1]

Gundolf states that from this point on Goethe identifies himself with his poetry. " He does not explain his situation (*Zustand*) like the naïve poet, nor does he discuss his situation, like the sentimental poet; the situation itself is expressed, becomes language, becomes rhythm and color, and assumes all the particular symbols of the loved one of the Divinity..." The poet is but an instrument which vibrates and sings, just as the Aeolian harp [2] is no more than " the vibration of the wind that moves and becomes song." With Goethe there is no longer any distinction between poetic creation and the event which set it in motion.

Gundolf's third assertion is the most subtle. Earlier poets had not known the world of life. Herder had taught that nature was the product of divine evolution. Goethe, while himself in a state of becoming, began to celebrate the world of action. He gave his favorite expressions (*Schwingen, Atmen, Reifen, Welken, Drängen, Schwellen, Wirken, Weben, Quellen, Fliessen* and *Streben*) poetic consecration and used them to express a new mode of feeling. He discovered and threw open to poetry the world of " becoming," where constant change is all important.

How did Goethe bring this new world to light? First by breaking away from fixed forms in favor of the ode, the dithyramb, the hymn, and by using blank verse to express interior rhythm; next by coining new words, an important process which endowed German poetry with new means of expression. Gundolf distinguishes three aspects of this

---

[1] Wolff, *Goethes Gedichte*, p. 183.
[2] Mörike has written a fine poem on this theme: *An eine Aeolsharfe*. Goethe himself wrote a love-duet in 1792 entitled; Aeolsharfe, inspired by Ulrike.

process.[1] First, he used epithets which represent actions rather than qualities; he also used past and present participles as independent adjectives (*ein getürmter Riese, schwebende Sterne, reifende Frucht, fruchtende Fülle, der ewig belebenden Liebe vollschwellende Tränen, heilig glühend Herz*). And again, following Pindar's example, he activated adjectives or verbs of direction (*Berge Wollkig himmelan, entlangrauschen entgegenbeben, abwärts schweben*). Finally, as if the established world had dissolved into swirling chaos, Goethe seized the scattered elements of the language and regrouped them at will. Thus appeared combinations like *Muttergegenwart, Flammengipfel Sternenblick, Nebelglanz, Bruderquellen, Gipfelgang, schlangenwandelnd, silberprangend,* etc. From this also sprang the formation of words uniting verb and preposition (*umsäuseln, anglühen, hinaufwiegen*) or adverb and adjective (*heiligglühend, leisewandelnd, leichtempfangen, tausendschlangenzüngig*) or the use of verbs with unexpected objects (" *Rettung dank dem Schlafenden glühn* ": " *Mässigung dem irren Blute tropfen,*" etc.). Through these processes which he introduced into poetry and general usage, Goethe followed the examples of Herder, of Pindar, of Shakespeare and of Luther in creating a new poetic world. He is the father of modern lyricism.

At the year 1774 we should pause and cast a backward glance at the world of " Sturm-und-Drang," which Goethe was about to leave behind.

Goethe contributed to this revolutionary movement to a greater extent than any other contemporary writer. While the thinkers of the " *Aufklärung*," influenced by English deism, were creating a cold and rational God, while the pietists strove to reach God by an impulse of the heart,

---

[1] Gundolf, *Goethe*, pp. 103 et seq.

the young Goethe tended to reject the idea of a personal God. He placed the impulse of the heart at the service of man and, a hundred years before Nietzsche, he proclaimed the gospel of the Superman. Instead of God to whom, he says, children and the mad offer their sacrifices, he erects Titans of action (*Götz*), of thought (*Faust*), of the heart (*Werther*), of denial (*Prometheus*); without proclaiming that God is dead he says " No " to him, in order to say " Yes " to the man of genius, for genius is the manifestation of divinity. Goethe does not go as far as Zarathustra and Nietzsche in making man the keystone of the bridge leading from the monkey to the superman, but he wanted to free man of all bonds. He wanted to let him develop his personality to the maximum, placing him " above good and evil." He preached revolt against God (*Prometheus*), against authority (*Götz*) against the conventions of society (*Faust* and *Werther*) and against marriage (*Clavigo*). In short, he favored liberty against every law.

He is equally repelled by all conventions in the literary field. He had but one principle, the imitation of nature. Werther's letter dated May 26 is a lyrical argument brilliantly summarizing the new theory. On his arrival in Wahlheim he found there only a group of two little boys which he drew, adding " the hedge nearby, a barn door, a few broken wheels, all the details such as they were on every plane "; he observed that he had made a well-composed and very interesting drawing without putting into it the smallest part of himself." From this he drew a double conclusion which is both ethical and aesthetic.

This confirmed me in my resolution to adhere henceforward rigidly to nature. She alone is infinitely rich; she alone can form the great artist. One can say much in favor of rules, much the same things as one can say in favor of organized society. A man who conforms to the rules will never produce anything absurd or bad, just as he who models himself on the laws and on propriety will never be an unbearable neighbor nor an outstanding rascal; on the other hand all rules, whatever may be said, will tend to destroy true feeling and expression of nature.

In the letter of May 30 Werther confirms his judgment: " What I said recently about painting holds equally true for poetry."

If nature had truly become a new idol it is because, like the man of genius, she was divine.   Two influences acted upon Goethe; that of Rousseau, preaching the doctrine of the good savage, and that of Spinoza, whose exact role is difficult to determine, but whose " *Deus sive natura* " became a dogma of the " Sturm-und-Drang."   The famous *Fragment* (1781) a grandiose hymn to the goddess Nature, is doubtless not by Goethe, but it expresses exactly his personal feelings and those of his period.   And again in 1786, Schiller published these revealing lines in the *Rheinische Thalia*:

> God and nature are two great powers exactly alike (*die sich vollkommen gleich sind*). The whole sum of harmonious activity which exists, concentrated in the divine substance, is found again in nature, a copy (*Abbild*) of this substance, diversified (*Vereinzelt*) to an infinite degree in size and plane. Nature (if I may be permitted this imagery) is a God infinitely divided; just as by the prism a ray of white light is broken (*spaltet*) into seven darker rays, so the divine ego is split into innumerable perceptible substances (*empfindende*).

Werther was a triumphant success not only because of its love story but also because of its poetry of nature. The hero is justified in wondering, in the letter of May 12, whether the paradisal charm of a landscape does not spring from the ardent and divine imagination of the one who inhabits it. He projects upon it the radiance of his own spirit and the rhythm of its seasons, like that of the hours of the day, is the very rhythm of the heart, keeping time with the pulsations of a love which springs up, grows, becomes exalted, darkens and destroys itself.   Nature's year is that " year of the spirit " which Stefan Georg was to use as the title of a collection of poems.

The burning summer which transforms Werther's love into a flaming passion inspires the letter of August 18 in which a complete revolution in his conception of nature, now seen as a devouring monster, is made manifest.

Werther represents a turning point in the history of feeling toward nature in Germany. The famous " *Einfühlung in die Natur,*" an essential trait of the German spirit, is sustained by a true metaphysic. The rationalists had looked upon nature simply as an object of study and the anacreontic poets as a setting for love. Nature plays hardly any part in Goethe's first works: *Die Laune des Verliebten, Die Mitschulding, Stella, Götz* or in *Faust,* where the human problem carries him away. On the other hand she appears very early in the poems and is the real heroine of *Werther.* There nature becomes man's partner. If the same laws hold sway in the world of physics as in the world of man, it is because nature is, as Herder had taught, a living and moving organism, both creative and destructive, whose secret forces Werther feels and perceives. These forces, whose secrets Faust sought to understand and which are symbolized by the Spirit of Earth, can be thought of as the gigantic shuttle of a divine weaver. This is not simple pantheism, as some have lightly asserted; it is already almost a Nietzscheian dionysism. But, it is also a projection of the material world into God using man as an intermediary, and Korff is right in defining this " religion of nature " as " naturalism irradiated in God." [1] The immanent God is transcended by a personal God embracing the whole universe. Is it not precisely this Spinozan conception which led Goethe, in his famous letter of June 9, 1795, to Jacobi, to proclaim that " existence is God " and to seek the Divine " *in herbis et lapidibus* "? A continual

---

[1] Korff and Linden, *Aufriss der deutschen Litteraturgeschichte,* p. 132.

wave of love flows from the creator to creation and to creature and carries the modern Ganymede toward God.

What poet of twenty-five would not run the risk of
being spoiled by the fame of *Werther*. Yet Goethe was
not satisfied, for he felt that he had reached an impasse.
Frankfurt was certainly an important center—thanks to
him a cultural center also—but already in his letter to
Salzmann on November 28, 1771, he had called his native
town a nest for hatching birds and " a shocking hole,"
adding " May God save me from this misery! Amen."
His " *nisus verwärts* " was so strong that he could not bear
to exhaust his powers in the bourgeois confines of his family circle and within the limits of his native town. The
year 1775 was to be decisive.

Chapter 4

At the crossroads (1775)

On October 18, 1775, Goethe wrote to Bürger that the first three-quarters of the year had been " the most diverse, the most confused, the completest, the fullest, the emptiest, the strongest, the most inept " of his life. In fact, 1775 was a crucial year in Goethe's development and Charles Du Bos is right when he writes that at this stage of his life " all takes place under the sign of the *daimon*, and has the maximum of demonic *tempo*." [1] The young poet, now attaining his twenty- sixth year, had sown his wild oats and proved his genius in *Götz, Clavigo, Werther, Prometheus, Faust*. Would he continue in the same direction and find the tragic fate reserved for most of the " Sturmer "? Or would this man of the Titans and revolution become another Prometheus enchained? He found himself truly at the crossroads; in the course of this year, in which he was to write *Egmont* and become engaged to Lili Schönemann, he was to know the most critical months of his life, before obeying the voice of Destiny which called him to Weimar.

[1] Charles Du Bos, *Goethe*, p. 255. For the " demonic " see pp. 95-96 and 277-278.

If one wished to classify the dramatic works written by Goethe in the preceding years according to their content, one could distinguish one nationalistic historical play, *Götz*, the amorous confessions in *Clavigo* and the tragedy of Margarete, and the philosophical plays expressing his most profound thought, *Prometheus* and *Mahomet*. To these should be added his plan for a *Cäsar*, in which he hoped to represent a " conscious son of chance," which is exactly what his new hero was to be. All three categories may be found in *Egmont*. It is an historical drama or rather, as Goethe said of *Götz*, " dramatized history." (Schiller contested this description on the ground that the foreground is less an affair of state—the antagonism between the Low Countries and their Spanish masters—than a private affair.) Even more, Egmont is the poet's mouthpiece, the lyrical expression of his demonism. Finally one finds in the new work a love of freedom which relates to " Sturm-und-Drang " and a cult of " *Sittlichkeit* " (morality), which links it to *Torquate Tasso*. But the three themes are not always fused together, for the work, begun or at least projected in 1774, was completed only in 1787. By then Goethe had passed from youth to maturity; as we have no manuscript earlier than the one which Goethe sent to Weimar from Rome on September 6, 1787, we cannot date the different scenes.

The poet borrowed the main subject of his drama, not to mention numerous details and even whole episodes, from the book of the Spanish Jesuit, F. Strada, *De bello belgice*. Count Egmont, governor of Artois and of Flanders, was executed by the Duke of Alba for not having repressed the revolt of the iconoclasts with enought severity. Thus we have, as in *Götz* or later in Schiller's *Wilhelm Tell*, two contesting forces: the people, and their Spanish masters. The first appears in the course of three lively scenes, in which first the people express their gratitude and loyalty to Egmont, then their anxiety en feeling themselves threatened, finally their cowardice, when Clara tries to provoke them to revolt to free their hero. On the other side, Spain is represented first by the conciliatory and tolerant regent Margaret of Parma, then by the bloody and pitiless Duke of Alba, whose natural son Ferdinand is the link with Egmont. Yet despite this conflict, Goethe has not created a political and social drama: Egmont does not perish for placing himself at the head of the revolution, but for having neglected the warning of William of Orange, who plays a part comparable to that of Antonio in *Tasso*; he succumbs because he put his faith in his luck, and trusted his enemy. It was a drama of liberty in the manner of Götz that Goethe started to write, but it became a drama of the individual in the course of its elaboration.

There has been much discussion about the passages in *Dichtung und Wahrheit* where Goethe expressly declares that he wished to represent a " demonic " hero in Egmont. Delaying a fuller examination of the question until later we may simply refer to him as a hero impelled by his " demon." The poet has been reproached for retrospectively introducing into this work an element which was not originally there, and which would never be found there but for his remarks. But in general it is a mistake to consider his autobiography written in his sixties as more poetical than true. Goethe ended this phase when he left the Rhineland for Weimar in 1775, expressing himself through the lips of Egmont himself in a passage which must date from before 1787, and may well date from 1775.

Child, child! It is enough! As if goaded by invisible spirits, the fiery horses of time rush on, dragging the light chariot of our destiny; all we can do is to hold firmly to the reins, calm and courageous, and to turn the wheels, sometimes to right, sometimes to left, here from a stone, there from a precipice. Where does this flight lead us? Who knows? We can hardly even remember from whence we come. (Act II, Scene 2).

The hero therefore believes in his destiny, has faith in his star, or in what Goethe, who had not yet fully conceived its demonic character, currently called the Spirit (*Geist*) or Genius. He constantly strives to attain new heights, aided by the hope, the courage and the strength he feels within himself (Act II, Scene 2). But in the end he has to recognize that while man believes that he is directing his own life, in reality " in his deepest self he is irresistibly drawn towards his destiny." (Act V, 4). Such, then, is the fundamental argument of the play: no one has any power against his " demon." The highest morality will be shown by a " demonic " hero who submits to his destiny.

In a very thoughtful book,[1] Greta Schaeder cites a suggestive idea of Ernst Beutler's, who connects the three plays of Goethe's youth, *Götz*, *Faust* and *Egmont*, showing that in all three we find the transition from " demonic " to moral freedom. The first is liberty against the law, the second is that liberty within the law which the classical Goethe is to discover. Götz dies anxious about the future of his people, Egmont foreseeing his country's revolt, Faust hoping that his work will serve mankind. At the moment when their " demonic " pride deserts them, each is confronted by anxiety, which in *Faust* takes human form; the selfish cult of the ego gives place to altruism, at first anguished, then calm. This process is demonstrated by the evolution of Egmont in Act V, which was probably written later. The hero of so many battles is immured in a cell, where sleep eludes him; he addresses Care as if it were an apparition, anticipating the end of the second *Faust*: " O Care, O Care, you who began to assassinate before time began, loose me." (Scene 2). A moment later they come and announce his sentence of death. Then Ferdinand, who has an affectionate admiration for him, begins a conversation; death is an involuntary boon from his enemy, which " frees him from anxiety and suffering, from fear and all

[1] *Gott und Welt*, p. 102.

Die Leiden

des

jungen Werthers.

Erſter Theil.

Leipzig,

in der Weygandſchen Buchhandlung.

1774.

5. *Title page of the first edition of* The Sorrows of Young Werther

other feeling." A gentle slumber then overcomes him and in a dream he sees Liberty, bearing the features of his beloved Klärchen who has just taken poison; she invites him to happiness, makes him understand that his death is the price paid by the Low Countries for their independence. She hails him as a conqueror and holds out to him a crown of laurels. He feels no further anxiety and declares proudly: " I die for Liberty for which I have lived and fought, for which now I suffer and sacrifice myself," and in his last words he invites others to imitate him, " as I show you an example." The circumspect William of Orange will fulfill his wish.

One could see in Klärchen another incarnation of " demonism," if one recognizes that for her the " demon " consists of willingness to love. She reminds us of Gretchen, but while the latter gave herself to Faust timidly hoping to bind him to her and to find happiness, Klärchen freely sacrifices herself to the happiness or the greatness of her lover. In her eyes Egmont is a hero, whom she would follow to the death had she the luck to be a man. Since there is not room on earth for such greatness, she precedes him in death. She is exactly what he needed: a woman who, in Nietzsche's brutal phrase, is made for the relaxation of the warrior. She is certainly also the type of woman who attracted the young Goethe, and type which, like Christiane, was able to hold the mature man. She is the humble and loving companion of the man who is too great for her. What confident abandon in the delightful scene (III, Scene 2) where he declares that he is not " Count Egmont, the great Egmont "... for there are two Egmonts: the official personage, formal and sour, respected and envied, loved and hated; and another Egmont, Klärchen's, who is the real one, " calm, open, happy, loved and understood by the best of hearts which he also knows through and through and presses to his own, full of love and confidence! "

Besides this duality, historic and dramatic, personal and demonic, there is also an ideological element. First there is love of liberty. Egmont makes himself its champion and herald; it is, as we have seen, an integral part of his being. There is also a conception of life which may be summed up in the formula, " Live and let live," a maxim of value to the individual and to all peoples. It is a good expression of the temperament of a spoiled child of fortune whether he be Egmont or the Goethe of 1774 and particularly of the years from 1775 onwards. It is not the attitude of an impetuous " Stürmer " nor yet that of a " twenty-six year-old poet " as Du Bos calls him. It grew out of the torments which plagued him in the year 1775 when he risked his future in the Schönemanns' drawing-room, and it is significant that certain scenes of *Egmont* should have been written in that summer of 1775 when destiny appeared again in the form of Lili.

The romantic loves of young poets and well-born ladies have often been told, and their glamorous aspects exploited. It is most important, however, to point out their serious and sorrowful side. For the first time Goethe fell violently in love with a girl who could only become his wife. He found himself engaged and ran away, first to Switzerland, then to Weimar. On March 5, 1830, he confided to Eckermann: " She is in fact the first I deeply and truly loved. I can equally say that she was the last, for all the inclinations which moved me in later life were, compared to that, but light and superficial." One can understand the young poet's perplexity; his wish to remain at her side where he found happiness, and also his need to escape from her, for his " demon " never ceased to whisper in his ear that this happiness in love was a danger. His love for Lili is the only one of which it could be said, according to Goethe, that it contained something of the " demonic ": he was forced to choose between poetic " demonism " and the " de-

monism " of love. We have direct evidence of his anguish
in the famous *Letters to Augusta von Stolberg*,[1] superbly
commentated by Du Bos.

The girl, a great admirer of Werther, had written to the
author, probably through her brothers, about the middle
of January, 1775. This letter " gripped " him: " You ask
me if I am happy? Yes, my dearest friend, I am, and
if I am not, at least there is within me every deep feeling
of joy and of suffering." He was about to begin with this
unknown girl (whom he was never to meet) an affectionate correspondence, in which he confided in her the joys
and sufferings of his love.

In the fourth part of *Dichtung und Wahrheit*, which he
considerately did not publish until after the death of Lili
(1817), he related his idyll. At the beginning of January,
1775, he was taken by a friend to the banker Schönemann's
house, and came to know his daughter, Elisabeth (Lili,
Belinde), seventeen years old, blonde, charming and co-
quettish. His feeling for her was soon reciprocated, which
did not cease to worry the poet; in February he composed
the poem *Neue Liebe, neues Leben*.

> What is it then, my heart
> That so oppresses you?
> What strange new life is this?
> I hardly know you now.
> For all that once you loved,
> For all that troubled you;
> Gone is your work, your peace —
> How did you come to this?

and he finished it with this line:

> O Love! Love set me free!

Accustomed to a modest bourgeois life, Goethe became
alarmed, for he had to adapt himself to the sophisticated

---

[1] A very convenient German edition is the well-known Insel-Bücherei
collection (Insel-Verlag, Wiesbaden). In the relevant chapter of his
Goethe (pp. 255-296) Du Bos reproduces a large part of it.

ways of the Schönemann household; he expressed his state in the poem *An Belinden*, and especially in the famous letter of February 13, to his " dear unknown " (Auguste von Stolberg, whom he familiarly called Gustgen):

> If, my dear, you can picture a Goethe in braided coat and get up from head to foot in the height of fashion, surrounded by the meaningless splendor of chandeliers and sconces, among people of all sorts, riveted to the gaming table by two bright eyes, (a Goethe) who, for a change of distraction, lets himself be dragged from a reception to a concert, and from there to a ball, who with all gaiety and determination courts a little blonde, then you will have the present Carnival Goethe... But there is another Goethe, in a gray beaver coat with a brown silk scarf and boots, who, caressed by the February air, already feels the coming of spring, sees his dear great universe opening once more before him, who, always alive within, aspiring and laboring, tries to express in his own way the innocent feelings of youth in little poems, the stronger fare of life in dramas, who draws in chalk on gray paper his friends' faces, the lines of his favorite places and of his house, who asks neither to left nor to right what people think of what he is doing, because by working he is always raising himself to some degree, because he does not wish to reach his ideal in one bound, but by struggle and play to raise his feelings to the level of faculties...

So there were two Goethes, just as there were two Egmonts; which would win? The one who, in the same letter, rejoiced in his dealings with the best men of his time, and was conscious of bearing a whole world within himself? or the one who wastefully spent all Shrove Tuesday night dancing, far from nature, far from his work, far from himself. " Save me from myself! " Such was the cry for help he sent to Gustgen on March 25.

The first decision came from the outside world. Neither family encouraged this inclination; the Goethe family was bourgeois and Lutheran, the Schönemanns were partician and Calvinist. But in April a Fräulein Delph from Heidelberg appeared, a woman who adored matchmaking. The poet tells us in *Dichtung und Wahrheit* (Book XVII) how, after obtaining their parents' permission, she one evening asked the two young people to join hands. Goethe found this a strange design of Providence. She had decided that

he should experience the feelings of a fiancé! He discovered that this state was in no way disagreeable, and even
found in his lovely fiancée deep qualities of which she was
to give proof in later life. Yet he gave the impression of
being caged. In the poem *Lili's Park*, composed no doubt
in the first half of May, he described with infinite humor
this zoo, which was Lili's " menagerie," and depicted himself a bear. Trapped in the dark forest and held on a
silken leash, he acts the gallant bear, kissing not the hand
but the shoe of his sweetheart, and growling with satisfaction when she strokes his back with her foot or when, on
days of special favor, he is allowed to rub against her
knee; he is tame to the point of servility when ordered in
French:

> Allons tout doux! eh la menette!
> Et faites serviteur,
> Comme un joli seigneur.

But let Lili be in no hurry to play and laugh!
The bear is dreaming of his liberty:

> And I? — O Gods, it is within your power
> To bring this dark enchantment to an end;
> What thanks I'll render, if you set me free!
> And yet from you no help is granted me.
> But 'tis not without hope I stretch my limbs:
> I feel strength still within me, that I swear.

Already help was on the way in the shape of Gustgen's
brothers, Counts Christian and Friedrick zu Stolberg, born
in 1748 and 1759, both poets, and, like their sister, admirers
of *Werther*. Their fellow-student Kurt von Haugwitz had
invited them to travel in Switzerland. On May 9 they
arrived in Frankfurt. Goethe, who wished to escape his
state of confusion, immediately called upon them and declared himself willing to join them in their travels. This
was the second intervention from the outside world. On
May 14 the four friends set off. They visited Darmstadt,
Mannheim, Heidelberg and Karlsruhe, where they meet

the young duke Karl-August of Saxe-Weimar, who invited the poet to visit him in his capital, Strassburg, Emmendingen, where his sister Cornelia formally advised him not to marry Lili.   They continued to Freiburg, Schaffausen, Constance, Winterthur and Zürich, where Goethe stayed with Lavater.   Guided by another friend, J. L. Passavant, he embarked on the lake on the fourth of June.   The brief journal which he kept contains the well-known lines in which he expressed his double love for nature and for Lili, and his torment:

> Dear Lili, if 'twere so I loved you not,
> What happiness this sight would then inspire!
> And yet, dear Lili, if I loved you not,
> Where then, O where would be my happiness?

The voyagers got to Einsiedeln and Schwyz and finally reached St. Gothard, finding themselves at the gates of Italy. Did they give in to the appeal of the South, as Goethe's father had hoped?   No, for it was Lili's seventeenth birthday, and her fiancé remembered the little golden heart which she had given him, to which, probably during that winter, he was to dedicate his poem: *An ein goldenes Herz, das er am Halse trug.*   He could not leave her, for she held him in leash (*an deinem Band*), like the bird, which, having escaped to reach the forest, drags after it the remains of its bonds, the shame and memory of its imprisonment. " Italy's time has not yet come," writes du Bos: " though mortally wounded, it is still Lili's hour; and slowly Goethe heads north once more." [1]

On July 22 the bear returned to his gilded cage.   He returned to Frankfurt and to Offenbach, where, from his fiancée's desk, he wrote Gustgen a letter signed " The Anxious One."   In the girl's room, surrounded by her dresses and frills, he described himself as " limited as a parrot on

[1] *Goethe*, p. 283.

its perch." Lili welcomed her wandering fiancé with a certain reserve, yet, despite the warnings of her family, she was ready to marry him, even to go with him to America. But the long letter to Gustgen written in fragments between the 14th and 19th of December reveals a Goethe on the way to freedom. He compared himself to a rat, who, having swallowed poison and wishing to extinguish a devouring interior fire, looks all round for a way out. He flirts with another girl and sees Lili without saying a single word to her. His long letter ends with an " Amen 1775 " which seems to set the seal on a period of sorrow.

While awaiting the coach which was to take him to Weimar, he blockaded himself at home, and worked feverishly at *Egmont*. He rejuvenated his hero, who in reality was forty-five and had eleven children; and made him instead a young man beloved by all in order to identify himself with him. It was probably at this time that he wrote those scenes in Act II which contain what E. Beutler calls " The problematic of the Lili period." [1] On the one hand, he felt faith in genius which longs to rise ever higher, and on the other hand, fear of feminine influence which drags him down. It is a question of the regent, to whom Egmont is not indifferent. He describes her thus: " She is a woman, and would therefore like to subdue all men to her gentle yoke; she would like each Hercules to doff his lion's skin and join the court around her distaff." Tired of waiting for the ducal carriage, and irritated by the nagging of his father, who continually tried to put him on his guard against the Great, Goethe fled to Heidelberg where he met Fräulein Delph. When she too tried to turn him away from Weimar, he answered her in Egmont's words about the horses of time.[2] He thus confirmed us

[1] E. Beutler, *Essays um Goethe*, II, pp. 148 et seq. (Dietrich-Verlag Wiesbaden).

[2] Id. ibid., II, p. 149.

in the belief that there was a link for him between the Lili affair and the play *Egmont*. He needed several more years and his stay at Weimar before continuing his work. He did not forget Lili, but his feeling for her slowly declined in proportion as his love for Baroness von Stein increased. The young patrician of Frankfurt was merely a forerunner of the great lady of Weimar; it was reserved for the latter to civilize the bear, to make him progress, like his heroes, from the " demonic " to the civilized world.

Later, Goethe was to tell Eckermann, with a tinge of regret, that he had never been so close to happiness. And yet the works inspired by Lili show the same disorder as his letters of the period. First there are the poems, which do not stream forth happiness, like those inspired by Friederike; they do not express the joy of an intimate communion of souls, as those of Weimar do later. They are monologues evoking the charm of a lovely woman, and reverberating with the Mozartian tone, profound and gentle, of a lover's soul. Lili can also be traced in *Erwin und Elmire* (1775) and *Claudine von Villa Bella* (1775), pendants to *Die Laune des Verliebten* and to *Die Mitschuldigen*, and especially in *Stella*, whose heroine has the age, blond hair, beautiful eyes, charm and goodness of his springtime fiancée. Thus Goethe sent her a copy bearing this dedication:

> From me in gentle vale, on snow-clad height,
> Your face did ne'er depart!
> I saw it in the drifting clouds of light;
> 'Twas ever in my heart.
> Here you may feel how, held in iron fee,
> My heart to yours is driven;
> That love in vain to flee
> From love has striven.

He offered homage to her with this work in which we have seen the poet expose the " problematic " of marriage. It was also an excuse for his desertion, for, almost at the moment when he became engaged, he made Fernando say;

" I would be mad to allow myself to be enchained. This state (marriage) stifles all my powers, robs me of all my spirit's courage, diminishes me. I must get away into the great world."

The year 1775 was a year of suffering and sorrow as are all periods of decision in which man is exposed to temptation. In this case it was the temptation of happiness. In *Egmont* Goethe was still close to " Sturm-und-Drang," although he wished to surpass its limitations and could even describe it as a disease, as he was later to describe romanticism. His love for Lili threatened him with a sterile, mundane existence in a city which no longer offered him adequate scope. As he had shown at Strassburg, he wanted no new Melusine. He felt himself growing and wrote to Gustgen on September 19 that: " In the midst of all this emptiness so many restrictive layers are lifting from my heart," that the tension inside him was relaxing, that his outlook on the world was gaining in serenity, and his dealings with men in assurance, firmness, breadth. In his innermost self he still felt entirely devoted only to the " sacred love," which little by little was eliminating every foreign element through the spirit of purity, so that in the end his soul might be " as pure as refined gold." While composing *Egmont*, he had already inwardly moved beyond his play; it released him from himself and carried him on towards a new destiny. He referred to all of his works, as " fragments of a great confession," for each one of them was a release and was left behind by its creator who was continally impelled onwards by his vital force. He then denied all that he had previously produced, to the extent that in his letter to Frau A. L. Karsch on August 17, 1775, he said: " I have written all sorts of things, yet in one sense very little, and fundamentally my work is nothing. On our prows we gather the spray of the great wave of humanity, and we imagine we have captured fleeting islands... Perhaps the invisible whip of the Eumenides will soon drive me from my country."

When the ducal carriage finally came to fetch him, he was ready to receive the lessons of Weimar.

Part II

Towards an ideal of humanity
1775-1794

Chapter 1

The lesson of Weimar (1775-1786)

From the " Stürmer " of Strassburg and Frankfurt to
the Sage of Weimar there was a long evolution, a series
of metamorphoses.   Goethe was shortly to undertake to
write *Wilhelm Meister*, the story of the formation of a
human being, and he was able to do this because he himself
hoped for and expected to be transformed.   His arrival at
Weimar in 1775 marked a break with the past, just as
his friendship with Schiller in 1794 was the prelude to
the flowering of German classicism, prepared for in the
course of these nineteen years which make up the second
period of his life and work.   This period may be seen as
a triptych, whose central panel is the famous Italian journey.   The three panels owe their unity to love; Charlotte
von Stein, from 1775 to 1786, and Christiane Vulpins, from
1786 onward, are both linked and separated by the sensual
Italians.   As we have seen Goethe had certainly not been
ignorant of love, nor was it to be absent from his later years;
but from 1775 to 1794 his life was enacted entirely under
the sign of love, of love in all its forms, whether for the
great lady, the courtesan or the wife.   The young bourgeois,
the traveler and the ennobled minister each in turn knew

and loved different types of women, each of which was to enrich and transform him.

Goethe's destiny seems to be inscribed in the five strophes which he entitled *Urworte, Orphisch*. The poet himself commented on these five Orphic pieces, as if inviting us to explain him through them. Everyone has his astral " demon " which determines him, and by individualizing him distinguishes him from other individuals. But " chance " intervenes in the form of a particular education; it acts chiefly upon youth, which " with its passions, its pleasures, its sociability and its frivolous behavior, casts itself first in one direction then in another, finding nowhere stability and contentment." Disturbance and longing arise; the young man awaits a new God, Love, in which the individual " demon " and seductive chance are united. Eros encompasses all inclinations, from gentle affection to flaming passion. Man thinks himself free, yet chance leads him in the path of error towards destruction. There is only one means of escape: " to dedicate himself to the unique being." Then the egoistic " demon," advancing through the world with absolute will and seeing with distress its way barred here and there by " Tyche " feels that he can " possess with an eternal imperishable love another being as he possesses himself." Renouncing freedom, two souls join in a single body, two bodies fuse into a single soul. Then child is born, the family is set up, the tribe is formed, caprice and fickleness are overcome, stability acquired. We can see how far this evocation surpasses his liaison with Kätchen or the idyll with Friederike, raising love to the level of the eternal, recalling the union of souls achieved with Charlotte von Stein, the physical union which Goethe knew in Italy, and the conjugal union with the woman who was to be the mother of his children even before she became his wife.

From 1749 to 1775 the poet's evolution continued in three cities. Duke Karl-August, eighteen years old, invited him to pay a visit to Weimar, a little town of six thousand inhabitants, but the capital of a duchy, and soon, thanks to Goethe, the intellectual capital of Germany. When the fugitive from Frankfurt arrived there on November 7, 1775, it was for a short stay. We know that he led a wild life with the duke, which scandalized court circles and earned him a rebuke from Klopstock. This was not, as at Leipzig, pleasure for the sake of pleasure; it was a matter of accepting hospitality. The prince, who was still a very young man, wanted for companionship a " Stürmer " of genius, not a wise mentor but a competitor at the table and on horseback, in the hunt and in the dance; they became excellent friends, and it was precisely this carefree intimacy which was to offer Goethe an important opportunity and which would orient his life.

His letter of November 22 to Johanna Fahlmer reveals at the same time his state of mind and his doubts; he compares his existence to a sleigh-ride, then he immediately continues: " God knows what destinies yet await me that I am put through such a schooling." God, or destiny, was often a subject in the letters of this period, always with the idea that this visit to Weimar might easily become a permanent stay. " What destinies yet await me that I am put through such a schooling? It is certainly intended to set me in a place where the usual torments of humanity cannot possibly reach me. And even now I consider everything as a preparation " (to August von Stolberg, May 18, 1776). On February 14, 1776, he had already announced to Johanna Fahlmer that he would doubtless remain at Weimar, where he would play his part as well as possible and for as long as he liked, or destiny allowed. Instead of leading an inactive life at Frankfurt, he would become the duke's auxiliary, and make himself useful. On July 9, 1776, he wrote to the Kestner family that he was staying and that his intimacy with the duke had become a marriage of minds. The duke appointed him to the state service and gave him a seat in his secret council with the title of " *Geheimer Legationsrat.*" He made him minister, and to impose him upon certain aristocrats who, like Herr von Fritsch, refused to sit with a commoner even made him a nobleman.

Thus the poet became harnessed to affairs of state. Would he be Pegasus under the yoke, as Schiller represented him? Doubtless the task was a thankless one; in this tiny duchy, Goethe had to occupy himself with such mundane affairs as tax-gathering, the development of quarries and forests, the construction and maintenance of roads, the uniforms of the troops, etc. But it was just this contact with reality that the " Stürmer " needed. Practical work made him feel useful and gave him no chance to bluff. While the young refugee from Lili's menagerie fluttered between Pharaoh's table and the ball, the minister of Weimar discovered the miserable life of the Apolda weavers, and learned his first lesson in humanity. The tortured, taut genius who had preached revolt in the name of nature found himself plunged into the life of a state, and discovered that there are natural laws stronger than man. Destiny had led him to the school where he was to discover human realities. What is more, forced to undertake frequent journeys, he learned to observe the stones of the quarries and the trees of the forests with new eyes, and the poet, the creator of dreams, became the man of science.

It would be impossible to overestimate the importance that this activity as the high administrator of a little state had for Goethe. As a " Stürmer " he had been up to 1775, to quote Alain's well-known formula, " the citizen against the powers ": as a minister he was now a power against the citizens, at least he could have been, but he used the power in the service of the citizens. Did not Goethe try to prevent the exploitation of labor by capital, propose fiscal reform to ease the burdens of the poorer contributors, foresee the division of great properties for the benefit of those

6. *Goethe's wife, from a pen drawing by Goethe*

who worked on them, and joyfully accept the "ministry of war" because it was there that the greatest economies could be made? It was Goethe's privilege to have seen the life of a state not only from the point of view of the governed, but also from the seat of power, and to have seen the uselessness of disorder and revolt. His aim was to introduce justice into order. His attitude towards the French Revolution, and his famous dictum (from *Belagerung von Mainz*) which earned him so many critics, "My nature is to prefer to commit an injustice rather than to tolerate disorder," [1] are explained by the fact that he was a minister, and knew that order is sometimes the result of injustice. A day was to come when he would no longer be interested in power and would wish to free himself just as he freed himself of Friederike by abandoning her, of Lili by flight, of his family and of Frankfurt by installing himself at Weimar. His faith in himself, a manifestation of faith in his destiny, would demand that he cease to be a minister so as to resume his freedom as a man, after having first assumed the responsibility of power.

This ministerial activity was a major cause of the metamorphosis which Goethe underwent at Weimar. None the less, its influence cannot rival that of Charlotte von Stein. The love of these two beings was the central, the essential event in the life and evolution of the poet. One can imagine another Friederike, but one cannot imagine another Charlotte von Stein. Goethe bestowed immortality upon her through his poetry, while she was responsible for his development (as Charles Du Bos [2] says about the famous *Wanderers Nachtlied*), "from the 'demonic' to the divine, from genius entangled to genius sublimated, from violence to peace." In this passage from youth to matu-

---

[1] *Belagerung von Mainz.*
[2] Du Bos, *Goethe*, p. 296. The part devoted to Baroness von Stein is from p. 296 to p. 327.

rity which marks the first twelve years at Weimar, Charlotte von Stein was the star whose gentle, calming light guided the poet. Thus, while Kätchen, Friederike and Lili seem to have played their parts as episodes, she who lives on in *Zueignung, Die Geheimnisse,* in *Die Geschwister,* in *Iphigenie* and *Tasso,* in Natalia and even in Makarie of *Wilhelm Meister,* was the very substance of a Goethe who had finally found peace.

No poet ever burned more incense at the altar of his beloved. Yet there will always remain a halo of mystery about this " marriage of souls." After the breach Charlotte von Stein destroyed the letters of her " lover," and Goethe, though he had laid bare and commented on the other phases of his life, always remained silent about this love, as if wishing to stop at the steps of a sanctuary. Neither her husband nor the court nor the citizens of Weimar criticized or suspected ill of this liaison. Yet literary historians discuss it, and wonder if it went to the length of a physical union.

The story of this love, one of the most " classic " in literature, began with the meeting of the two protagonists, for which " chance " had no doubt deliberately prepared Goethe. In the course of the year 1775 he had the opportunity to study a silhouette of Charlotte von Stein twice; first in Zurich he assessed her physiognomy for Lavater, emphasizing her yielding firmness (*nachgiebige Festigkeit*) and ending with these prophetic words: " She conquers with a net "; at Strassburg he declared to Zimmermann, " It would be a magnificent sight to see the world reflected in this soul. She sees the world as it is, yet through the medium of love. Hence the general impression is of gentleness." These were flattering words which Zimmermann, a doctor at the baths at Pyrmont where he had Charlotte von Stein under his care, did not hesitate to repeat to her, adding that Goethe could not sleep for three nights because of what he had learned about her. The object of this eulogy was the daughter of a stern Scotswoman and of Herr von Schardt. Charlotte, born in 1742, had married Herr von Stein, stablemaster to Karl-August and more fit to busy himself with horses than to understand his wife. She had seven children by him, four of whom were dead and one sick. She had never really known the joys of either marriage or motherhood; her precarious health forced her to live away from the court at Kochberg, and she regretted wasting her spiritual resources in paltry tasks. Perhaps she also awaited Goethe whose *Werther* had visited her in her solitude and had possibly disturbed her. Indeed, in an impromptu piece she had described Goethe (under the name of " Rino ") arriving at Weimar, and through the lips of Gertrude she thus expressed her thoughts:

> He is not quite indifferent to me.
> Yet I know not if 'tis him who speaks or Werther.

She was attracted by the young poet to such an extent that in January 1775, Zimmermann had put her on her guard. He had written to her in French: " *Mais, pauvre amie, vous n'y pensez pas, vous désirez de le voir et vous ne pas à quel point cet homme aimable et charmant pourrait vous devenir dangereux.*" At the same time, however, he cut out a plate from Lavater's *Physiognomy* to offer her " this Eagle's head." We do not know what she thought of it, but we may suppose that she awaited a conqueror with ideas of conquest of her own.

It is probable that their first meeting took place at Kochberg on December 6, 1775. Goethe was still obsessed by the memory of Lili, and the gay life which he led with the duke in the company of lovely women might have set him against this recluse, whose mild beauty would not have fascinated him had he not had a presentiment about her. In his letter of January 22, 1776, he already calls her " Besänftigerin " [1]; on January 28, she is no longer his " dear

---

[1] Literally " the appeaser."

lady " but his " dear angel ": a word he overworked, an
angel who does not understand " how " he loves her. To
Johanna Fählurer he wrote on February 14 that she is a
" splendid soul," to Auguste von Stolberg on May 18 that
she is " an angel among women." In a short poem which
he sent her without comment on February 12, 1776, he
gives us the key to his attachment. The *Wanderers Nachtlied*, composed on the slopes of the Ettersberg, is one of
those works in which the subconscious appears on the surface of the mind:

> Thou, who art from the heavens,
> Easing all pain and suffering,
> Filling with double comfort,
> Him who feels double sorrow.
> Ah! I am weary of this unrest!
> What are complete pain or pure joy to me?
> Sweet peace,
> Come, ah! come into my breast.

This is not, as in the poem of the same title of September
6, 1780, a matter of the peace of the world outside slowly
conquering his tired body and mind, but of inward peace,
to which he aspired while not yet knowing from whence it
would come. In this " *Treiben* " he no doubt included the
wild gay life he had led for the previous three months
in Weimar. This " double distress " referred to his double
love for Lili and for Charlotte. A storm-tossed genius, he
longed for tranquility and it was to Charlotte von Stein that
he addressed his plea as if, more or less unconsciously, he
saw in her the source of peace and begged her to defend him
against himself.

But she remained on her guard. She confided her first
impression to Zimmermann: " I feel that Goethe and I
will never become friends: besides I do not care for his
manner with our sex; he is what in France they call *coquet*:
there is not enough respect in his behavior." More precep-
tive than Klopstock, she had understood that in sharing
the life of Karl-August he was not following his own incli-

nations, but was seeking to win his favor in order to influence him in the future. She waited without rebuffing him but she was intolerant of any eccentricity. Thus she relates that on March 6-8, 1776, when she corrected him for addressing her as " *du*," he lost his temper and left the house without taking his leave. She punished him by not going to Weiland's on the May 7, to avoid meeting this " barbarian." This was Goethe's last misdemeanor. Charlotte was determined to make him a man of the world: she had conquered him, and held him in bondage. In the following weeks, and particularly during the course of a journey to Leipzig, where he saw Kätchen again, an interior force was at work in him, bearing witness to the influence exerted, unknown to him, by Charlotte von Stein.

On April 14, 1776, he sent her a magnificent poem, whose new tone permeates all the works in which Charlotte appears: *Warum gabst du uns die tiefen Blick?* This poem includes the famous lines:

> Ah! You were, in times loved long ago,
> My sister or my wife.

We find the same idea repeated in a letter to Wieland in April, 1776; " I cannot explain the importance, the power of this woman over me except by the transmigration of souls. Yes, we were once man and wife. Now we recognize each other, veiled in the atmosphere (*Duft*) of the spirit. I have no name for us—the past—the future—all." In April he also wrote to Charlotte: " Henceforward I shall see you as one does the stars," and again, " Farewell, dear sister, since it must be so.". She was to be the sister, the Cornelia of his childhood, the Iphigenie who would cure him. Goethe was to describe his relations with her as the purest, the most beautiful, the truest he had ever had with any woman, except perhaps, with his sister. Charles Du Bos poetically described the following years as the first circle of the stellar union, the second being the " marriage of souls." Goethe referred to these five fraternal and tranquil years as his " noviciate." By the end of 1780 a new tone had appeared. What had happened? Just as he had finally taken leave of Kätchen in 1776, so in 1779, in the course of his journey to Switzerland, he saw again both Lili, now become Frau von Turkheim, and Friederike. who forgave him. If one may employ so brutal an expression, he had " liquidated " his past love-life, and was left face to face with his " only love." He realized her exceptional importance for, in the letter of September 20, 1780, after telling Lavater of his will to continually build up the " pyramid of his existence," he immediately adds: " Besides, the talisman of this great love, with which Frau Stein leavens my whole life, has a strong effect. Little by little she has inherited the place of my mother, of my sister and of all the women I have loved; there has been woven between us a link as strong as nature's." No doubt he asked more of his " only love " than he had when he regarded her as a " sister," and what else could it have been but the total surrender of herself? On December 16, 1780, he sent her a short poem which is a cry of joy; he feels the need to tell the trees the full extent of his love for:

> Her, who answers with so fine a love,
> Which gives him back, and purified,
> The purest of his impulses.

So he had received some pledge of love; he knew that she had become his. On March 12, 1781, he wrote to her: " My soul is strongly attached (*angewachsen*) to yours, I don't make pretty speeches. You know that I cannot separate myself from you... I wish there were some vow or sacrament which would make me visibly and legally your property." Lacking this, he encircles his arm with one of her ribbons, as he addresses his prayer to her. But we possess even more decisive poems, whose importance was pointed out in 1878 by Ernest Lichtenbenger in his *Etude sur les poesies lyriques de Goethe*. On September 29 and

October 1, 1781, he addressed two poems to her: *Nachtge-danken* and *Der Becher* which he proposed to publish with the note " imitated from the Greek." In the first he pities the wandering stars, which have no knowledge of love; and finished with:

> What journeys have you not completed
> Since, resting in the arms of my beloved,
> I forgot you, and the hour of midnight.

In the second he explains that he was drinking from a fine goblet when Love came in and promised him an even more beautiful beaker containing a quite different nectar. Love kept his word; he offered to give Lida (Charlotte von Stein) to him " who had long aspired to her."

> When your beloved body I embrace,
> And on your lips, incomparably loyal,
> I taste the balm of love so long withheld,
> Then say I to my soul, in blessedness:
> No, never any other God but love
> Has owned so finely made a cup as this...

After this hymn of gratitude one can understand that on October 9, 1781, he sent her these lines which amount to a vow:

> 'This with good right, dear Lotte, you demand
> The only one you love should be all yours.
> Yes, he is yours alone.

It is hard enough in any case to suppose that at the age of thirty-two Goethe, once so in love with freedom, could submit to a union which was only " a marriage of souls." It seems obvious that by this time Charlotte von Stein was no longer merely a sister to him but had become his wife as well, just as in *Die Geschwister*, Marianne, child of the deceased Charlotte, grew up as a sister to Wilhelm and eventually became his wife. The letters of this period are more impassioned and indicate a more complete bond: " Your love is to me as the evening and the morning star, setting after the sun and rising before it. Nay! Like the pole star, which, never setting, weaves a crown of eternal life above our heads " (March 22, 1781). " You appear to me, transmuted, in every object: I see all things well, and yet I see you everywhere: I am neither absent-minded nor distracted, yet I am always with you, always thinking of you " (from Osteim, April 10, 1782).

We dwell on this secret only because it explains the cooler tone of Goethe's letters in the following years and the renewed desire for freedom which eventually led to his Italian journey. Between the two extreme solutions of consent and denial, there is room for a third very plausible hypothesis. May one not imagine that at the end of 1780 or more likely at the beginning of 1781, Charlotte von Stein gave in to Goethe's entreaties either to bind him more securely and forestall a possible escape, or to give him the decisive proof of her love by sealing their " marriage of souls " with a physical union? Did this union last? Probably not, and one may suppose that it was a disappointment for both of them. We can now more readily understand Goethe's discovery of purely sensual love in Italy and his liaison with Christiane Vulpius.

Despite protestations of love, despite the " you are loved as you wish " of October 2, 1783, we sense a certain lassitude and yearning for escape. He wrote at Christmas, 1782: " O dear Lotte, had I not you, I would set off into the wide world." He was continuing to rattle his chains when he sent her these lines on August 28, 1784:

> Surely ere now would I have traveled far,
> Far as the wide world had permitted me,
> Were I not ruled by those more powerful stars,
> Which with such force have linked my fate to yours
> That 'tis through you alone I know myself;
> Yearnings and poetry, desires and hopes,
> All these bind me to you and what you are;
> My life depends upon your life alone.

Despite his protestations of fidelity, provoked perhaps by Charlotte's jealousy, their love merely endured; it was threatened by Goethe's need to leave Weimar. Charlotte had become an obstacle. Thus, when he left Carlsbad for Italy, he was careful to conceal his destination from her. She sensed that he was about to flee and sent reproaches which only offended him. On his return, the rupture was inevitable. Goethe's " demon " was the final victor in this trial of love, which was the vital core of his Weimar experience.

That a woman was able to exert such great influence upon him is perhaps easier to understand if one recalls the early instance of Fräulein von Klettenberg, a woman who played a significant role in his development even without any bond of love. Goethe had known and written about love, but he had not yet submitted to it. He had never met a woman who could be his equal through the beauty of her soul and her power of intuition, who could surpass him in strength and serenity, in the art of living and suffering, a woman who could merit this astonishing eulogy: " You, the Unique, to whom I need contribute nothing, finding all in you " (letter of March 21-22, 1782). It was his destiny and his good luck to find at this moment a woman who was both similar and opposite to him, who knew how to be at once a wise mother, an understanding sister, and a demanding mistress. Kätchen and Friederike had had only their bodies and youthful passion to offer; Fräulein von Klettenberg, the " fine soul " cut off from the world, had turned him towards that " *Natur-frömmigkeit* " which shines through the works of his youth, and towards a symbolism which was to enrich the works of his old age. Lili Schönemann had offered him the prospect of an easy life in worldly surroundings. Charlotte von Stein offered him all the love of which her husband had proved unworthy, the exclusive love of a woman who realizes that she will know no other. She was not only a contemplative soul, but a woman who, before withdrawing into an introspective life, had known the world and the court. The complete woman, she was the first whose love could play a formative role in the " Sturmer's " evolution. His prior experiences, whether with Friederike or with Charlotte Buff, had exercised only the impulsive action of a force of nature. If Herder had supplied Goethe with the basis of universal culture and the forms of folk poetry, to Charlotte von Stein must go the credit for enriching him with a new conception of life and of art. She contributed powerfully towards setting him on the way to a new ideal of humanity.

She accomplished a significant feat in refining his manners and making him a man of the world. The affectations which he had assumed in Lili's drawing-room now became the outward sign of an inner revolution. But Goethe learned far more from the concrete example of her life, together they read and studied ethics, and she led him to the realization that the rule of life cannot be merely the unrestrained development of one's individuality. " Whatever pleases is allowed," said Tasso, who inscribed this maxim over the entrance to the earthly Paradise, as did Rabelais over the portal of the Abby of Thélème. " Whatever is seemly is allowed," replied the princess, Charlotte von Stein's mouthpiece. Baroness von Stein was the symbol and the guardian of an ordered world, to whose laws even genius had to submit. The rebellious Titan bowed to an ideal of harmony which precluded revolt. Charles Du Bos [1] quotes this happy metaphor from Emil Ludwig: Charlotte is " the lake into which Goethe pours all his waters and draws them forth purified," and connects the masterpieces of the Charlotte period to those which he himself called " *les cristallins.*" He says that they are, like Gide's *Strait is the Gate*, " clear waters which have been crystallized through the power of poetry." Unconsciously he follows Alain who wrote of Goethe: " He loves the solid; I would almost say that

[1] *Goethe*, p. 324.

liquids are his true enemies. He eliminates what is fluid in himself. He hopefully awaits the moment of crystallization and fixed understanding." [1] So Baroness von Stein served as the model for those serene heroines who were to illumine his classical dramas: Iphigenie, the princess in *Torquato Tasso* and Natalie in *Wilhelm Meister*. Henceforward Goethe's heroines were to find salvation according to how well, guided by an idealized Eros, they could integrate themselves into a cosmos under the rule of law.

This harmony became the rule of poetry as well. The " Stürmer " who worshipped Shakespeare dreamed of equalling Greek drama, and sought to rival Euripides in *Iphigenie*. He created a new Werther in *Tasso*, a play whose formal perfection recalls Racine. He elevated his mistress to the level of the divine woman who, in *Zueignung*, invites the poet to receive " the veil of poetry from the hands of truth."

Goethe did not dedicate his great mystical and masonic poem to Baroness von Stein; but apart from his great classical works he left two tributes which are the finest any woman could desire. In the great poem which he sent her on April 14, 1776, be already admitted what influence she had over him, and what mission he assigned her:

> You knew me in each feature of my being
> Watching each nervous quiver of my soul,
> And with one look you read me through and through,
> Though hardly else by mortal was I read.
> You cooled by heated blood with soothing calm
> And guided my impulsive, errant course;
> Within the circle of your angel's arms
> My stricken breast found peace and strength renewed.

He had a presentiment that by the grace of the " *Besänftigerin*," the storm-tossed " Stürmer " would find peace. In 1820 he had printed the short poem *Zwischen beiden Welten*

---

[1] *Propos de littérature*, p. 188 (Paul Hartmann, 1934).

in which he immortalized Lida (his name for Charlotte) and acknowledged his debt to her and to Shakespeare. If Rudolf Hildebrandt is correct, the first six lines were written in about 1780; it was at the age of seventy that the poet added the last three, reconfirming his earlier thoughts:

> By belonging to one woman only,
> Revering only one man,
> Thus are the senses and heart reconciled!
> Lida! Most intimate happiness,
> William! Highest of stars,
> To you I owe all that I have become.
> Though years and days are departed,
> Yet on those hours is based
> All value I have attained.

To the lessons in reality and the experience of an ideal love, one must add a third element which has been inadequately appreciated up to now. The letters of this period show us that Goethe was not only the companion and minister to the duke and the lover of Charlotte von Stein; he was also the philosopher who meditated in his garden, enjoying the serenity of the countryside. On May 17, 1776, he wrote to Augusta von Stolberg: " I have a charming garden before the gates of the town beside the Ilm [1]; beautiful meadows in a valley. There is an old house which I am having put in order for me. All is blossom, every bird sings." He is so happy to be in his garden that his only thought is to be rid of the masons so as to spend his first night, May 18-19, in solitude. At eleven at night he added: " It is a wonderful feeling to be settled all alone outside the town, in the fields... Everything is so peaceful. I hear only the ticking of my clock and the roar of the distant weir." He loved to feast his eyes on the verdant green, to watch the countryside bathed in moonlight (to which we owe the poem *An den Mond*) and to plant and

---

[1] A litle river, some 75 miles long, which rises in the Thuringian forest, flows through Weimar and empties into the Saale.

prepare for the following year. One need only compare the *Mailied* (1771) with these letters of May 1776, in which the theme " in my garden " constantly recurs, to understand the depth of the transformation which took place in Goethe. When he was twenty-two, spring had been an explosion of vitality, and led him, as Hebbel was to write, to burst the limits of his ego and drive forth towards the infinite; now it became the course of a tranquil joy which seems hardly in tune with nature's effervescence. In *Werther* he still longed for the distant and the unattainable; now he would have approved Charles Louis Philippe's admonition to Gide, who craved the exotic: " I shall teach you the fruits of the orchard."

The lesson of the garden seems to have been confirmed on the journey to Switzerland,[1] where Goethe went with the duke during the autumn of 1779, after passing through Frankfurt. Indeed, at the beginning of December he suggested to Lavater an idea which he had much at heart: to set up a monument in the ducal park intended to commemorate a journey marking the beginning of a new period in the life of Karl-August, and, he added, " in ours." What did he have in mind? On the front was to be Fortune, on the right, Genius, inviting and indicating the way, on the left, " Terminus, the thoughtful, calculating adviser, pointing with his wand to the boundary-stone." Is this not a figurative representation of the two Goethes, the " Stürmer," with his " *nisus vorwärts*," and the classic poet, acknowledging the need for order and moderation?

He wrote to Charlotte von Stein on April 8, 1777, that destiny had transplanted him to Weimar, just as the nurseryman cuts off the uppermost branches of the linden to give it new strength. His instability had disappeared; he now urged Kestner to seek greater stability (September 28,

---

[1] See Hügli's article on Goethe's voyages in Switzerland in *Études germaniques*, No. 14-15.

1777). The genius, who once dreamed of high adventure, now experienced within his own house the feeling of the navigator, secure in his ship upon the sea; the Titan who had accepted no limitations, wrote this vital passage to Baroness von Stein on July 22, 1776, where we already find the word " *Beschrankung*," prelude to the famous " *Entsagung*."

One thing remains eternally true; to limit oneself (*Sich beschränken*). Really to need one thing, or a few only, to love them truly, to attach oneself to them, to examine them from every side, to be united to them, that is what makes the poet, the artist, the man.

By 1780 Goethe had already passed through a process of evolution which had made a new man of him. A new orientation appears in his lyric poems, which again form an intimate confession, especially in *Gesang der Geister über den Wassern* (October 9-11, 1779), Limits of Humanity (1780-1781) and *Der Geistliche* (1781). He composed the first after seeing the falls of Lalterbrunnen and no doubt borrowed an idea of Mme. Guyon's for this analogy between the human spirit and water and their movement between heaven and earth: "Man's spirit is like water, which comes from heaven and returns there, drawn towards earth in an eternal cycle." We are far from the concept of the Titan whose genius transports him to the level of the Gods, and near the man whom Lamartine describes as "a fallen god who remembers heaven." A human being, such as he perceived in the image of Charlotte von Stein, is both earthly and divine and is moved by destiny as the wind "mingles and confuses the foaming waves." In the second poem he finally denies the superman and humbles transient human life before the immortality of the gods.

In 1774 when he wrote Prometheus he contrasted the wretchedness of the gods to the greatness of Promethean men. Now man is only worthy to humbly "kiss" the lowest hem of the mantle of the Holy and Eternal Father.

But he was not an orthodox believer. We know that he had read Spinoza, " the most Christian," with Baroness von Stein (to Jacobi, June 9, 1785), and *Des erreurs et de la vérité* by Claude de Saint-Martin. He considered himself a pagan: " Your thirst for Christ grieved me deeply. You suffer more than we pagans, whose gods seem to us in distress " (to Lavater, January 8, 1777). He also referred to himself as a " decided non-Christian " (to Fr. V. L. Plessing, July 29, 1782). In his third poem, *Die Geistliche,* the gods have become the Immortals, the divine appears as the terrestrial transcended, and the world's heirarchy is now complete. The scale leads from inanimate Nature to the " beings we know," that is, to the lower animals, from which man is distinguished only by his qualities of nobility, charity and goodness, by power of justice or poetic genius. It then progresses " to the superior beings of whom we have some presentiment," that is, to the Immortals, who resemble men who " would do on the grand scale what the best of us does, or would like to do in miniature."

The evolution in his thinking about Nature was less radical. His characterization of Nature as a living being was perhaps accentuated as is expressed in his " *Natursymbolik.*" In *Wanderer's Nachtlieder* (February 12, 1776, September 6, 1780) and in *An den Mond* (Summer 1777) he treated landscape as a source of peace. In *Der Fischer* (1777) and in *Der Erlkoning* (1782) nature is a redoubtable power, whether found in the coolness of the wave that attracts the sun-scourged fisherman, or in the fevered imagination of a sick child that leads him to mistake the willows in the autumn mists for the king of the elves and his daughters, a vision which makes him die of fright. The source of this dramatic and lyrical poem in perhaps less the Danish ballad *Le Chevalier Alaf,* translated by Herder, than the lines which the poet sent to Baroness von Stein on October 13, 1760: the moon was infinitely beautiful, the night celestial, and " the elves were singing." In this romantic ballad he expressed all the charm of a beautiful nocturnal landscape, bathed in soft moonlight.

For the years from about 1781 to 1786, it would be more correct to speak of enrichment than of evolution. Goethe had consolidated his position as a minister, he traveled often and deserted his garden to inspect the duchy, always familiarizing himself further with state affairs, or to revisit Leipzig, or to go to the baths at Carlsbad.

Two new elements which were to have important consequences in the future completed the Weimar experience: his introduction to Freemasonry and his scientific studies.

We have already remarked his interest in the paramasonic society called the " *Arkadische Gesellschaft zu Phylandria* " in 1764. F. J. Schneider [1] asserts that in 1772, at Wetzlar, he was admitted to a table-d'hôte which had all the appearance of a lodge of knights. He was given the name " Honest Götz von Berlichingen." How could he have stood aside from a Freemasonry in love with " *Bildung* " when all cultivated Germans of his century were members, when Leibniz had been secretary of the Rosicrucians, and when Herder, a Protestant pastor at Konigsberg, had joined it to " enlighten " and educate his fellowcitizens? [2] It is more surprising that he had not sought admission earlier. It may be supposed that he feared a rebuff such as he had experienced at Frankfurt, which is easily understood when we learn that he had to address his request on February 13, 1780, to Baron von Pritsch, the man who had refused to sit with him in the ducal council. In his letter he says that he has long wished to become a Freemason, that his recent journey to Switzerland had underlined the necessity, for he had lacked only the " title " of Freemason to enter into close relations with people for whom he had the highest regard; it is, he added,

[1] *Die Freimaurerei*, p. 114.
[2] Haym, *Herder*, I, p. 105.

7. Goethe's home at Weimar

" this feeling of sociability alone which makes me beg admission." Recalling the part played by the " Society of the Tower " in *Wilhelm Meisters Lehrjahre,* we may wonder if this was his only motive, but it is significant that he emphasized the aspect of sociability which makes us think of Baroness von Stein, of certain lines of *Torquato Tasso* or of the second of the orphic strophes: *Nicht einsam bleibst du, bildest dich gesellig.* Goethe was admitted, fulfilled his obligations, and by March 31, 1781, he considered himself worthy enough to request promotion to the grade of Master. This was only the beginning of his masonic activity. The Amalia lodge died out two years later, but he worked personally for its reopening in 1808, and it was he who recited Wieland's eulogy in 1813. To be completely objective, however, let us point out that in 1807 he advised against the formation of a lodge at Jena, but chiefly, it seems, because it would have been attached to Gotha and Berlin and not to Weimar [1].

The first expression of masonic thought, without which no full understanding of *Meister* nor of the second part of *Faust* is possible, is to be found in the great epic and mystical poem undertaken in 1784. Here Goethe wished to proclaim the moral and religious truth he had acquired by glorifying Charlotte von Stein, the " sublime being " who had inspired him. We have only two long fragments, *Zueignung* and *Die Geheimnisse,*[2] of this unfinished masterpiece in which the formal beauty of the stanzas, in imitation of Ariosto, equals the grandeur of the ideas; he conducts the reader " through a sort of ideal Montserrat "

---

[1] This important text may be found in the *Gedenkausgabe,* XII, 760-763.

[2] They appear in *Pages immortelles de Goethe* (103-106) and 133-144) as does a résumé of the sequel which Goethe planned (144-145). Consult also G. Bianquis, *Étude sur deux fragments d'un poème de Goethe,* where suggested links with Claude de Saint-Martin, the " unknown philosopher," may be found.

to a sacred place where the world's best men would be grouped around a mediator with the symbolic name " Humanus." The action takes place during the course of Holy Week, beneath the sign of the cross encircled with roses.

At the same time scientific researches attracted the poet more and more, sometimes interrupting his literary creation. We have already pointed out that he was led to the natural sciences by affairs of state. The supervision of the forest and quarries opened to him the world of botany and geology. On August 5, 1778, he wrote to Merck that he reopened a quarry which had long been closed. With the voluptuous feeling of a sculptor he described its stone which was hard yet allowed of delicate craftsmanship, of a fine gray color, halfway between ordinary stone and marble. He began to live " body and soul, among rocks and mountains." and the world took on a new aspect. With joy he struck the rocks with his hammer, and devoted himself to a study of granite (to Baroness von Stein, September 11, 1780), a study which produced, in 1784, pages which were to become a classic. On October 11, 1780, he informed Merck about his " mineralogical researches "; he devoted himself to this science " with complete passion " and found in it " a very great pleassure." On November 14, 1780, he sent him J. K. W. Voigt's " *Voyages Minéralogiques* " which contains a geological survery of the Fulda country. He would have liked to ask Voigt to do a similar survey for the rest of Thuringia and perhaps for the Harz mountains. In November 1782, he sent him a long letter which was almost entirely devoted to these questions; he confided his " great wish " to initiate " a mineralogical survey of the whole of Europe."

While he was a pupil, in this domain, in osteology he proved himself a master. He practised assiduously in the academy of drawing and with the anatomist Lodeg at Jena; he followed the the work of Merck, his adviser (letter of October 22, 1782) and studied the skull of an elephant (to Baroness von Stein, June 7, 1784). He also undertook some "speculations upon rocks," and discovered "some fundamental principles of formation," which he was keeping secret (to Charlotte von Stein, June 17, 1784). On the other hand, on June 27, 1784, he announced his discovery of the inter-maxillary process in man, and sent Herder the news the same day, telling him of his "inexpressible joy." It was less a question of a chance discovery, afterwards confirmed by the scholars, than of the confirmation of a fundamental idea; a single type was the progenitor of all living beings, the "Urtypus," which was to become the foundation of Goethe's thought. The scientific hypothesis harmonized with the religious philosophy which had inspired the hierarchy of being in his poem *Der Geistliche.*

In Goethe's evolution it is impossible to distinguish his life from his works, but we must never lose sight of the fact that the man is always greater than his works and that none of them can express his personality entirely. For the Weimar period, however, one must try to make this distinction, because of the formative significance of his many activities. One can imagine the poet continuing in the course he had followed from 1771 to 1775, just as one may imagine what French literature would have produced had the renaissance not spread, or had Malherbe not harnessed the luxuriance of the Pleiades. But this would be to fall to understand Goethe's need to continually surpass himself, his desire to shape his own nature, his need to move away from the form achieved in search of the new. Weimar was the scene of his greatest metamorphosis; it was his spiritual home.

That is why these eleven years did not see the birth of as many important works as the four years at Frankfurt. On the one hand Goethe was much absorbed in business and journeys, by his scientific studies and his love for Baroness von Stein; on the other hand, while formerly he had experienced an extrovert urge to express his ego, he now felt an opposite necessity; he needed to enrich and renew himself by contact with the outside world. Man's metamorphosis, like that of every living being, is the result of a ceaseless exchange, of struggle and acquiescence, between himself and his surroundings. This necessity led him to undertake *Wilhem Meisters theatralische Sendung*, which is still bathed in the atmosphere of " Sturm-und-Drang," but which ultimately became the model of the educative novels. On the other hand, Charlotte von Stein was the true inspiration of his classical dramas, *Iphigenie* and *Torquato Tasso*, completed later, but conceived in the atmosphere of Weimar.

Chapter 2

The humanism of Weimar

The three masterpieces undertaken during the first ten years at Weimar suggest the image of Janus, with one face looking towards the past, while the other is turned towards the future. The *Theatralische Sendung* is no longer entirely a work of the " Sturm-und-Drang " although its roots lie in that movement. It is not a work of the " period of genius " but it still employs the concept of the genius to which is attributed the mission of a Shakespeare. Besides, the Goethe of Weimar did not finish it; he awaited his return from Italy before substituting for his young man in search of the theatre a young man in process of development. It was not until the last decade of his life that he confronted his hero with the social problem. On the other hand, the two plays in which he expresses his ideal of humanity, *Iphigenie* and *Torquato Tasso*, were brought to conclusion either in 1779 or during the course of his Italian journey.

The first mention of the *Sendung* is in February 1777, but in the *Tag-und-Jahreshefte* of 1819 Goethe states that its origins were earlier, in the form of cotyledons. He tells us that he saw the germ of his work in the idea that man

117

sometimes undertakes things for which he is not fitted and appears to waste his life, although in reality he reaps " a great harvest." It is thus that the *Lehrjahre* finish, and one may suppose that Goethe in 1819 attributes to himself ideas which he certainly had in 1796, but not in 1777. Gundolf,[1] on the other hand, establishes a link with *Werther*, where it was a question of " a being, and the resultant sufferings " while here we have " a becoming, and the resultant effort." On the one side there was disintegration of a Titan of sentiment, on the other, the mission of a superior being. Wundt [2] goes so far as to admit that *Meister* and *Werther* were conceived together, complementary to each other, for they represent the two aspects of genius as understood at that time; one, the sensitive personality, which we would call introverted, the other the creative personality which does not reject reality but instead shapes it at will. The *Sendung* is a belated product of the " Sturm-und-Drang," whose completion was at once prompted, influenced and thwarted by the stay at Weimar.

All the young authors of the years from 1770 to 1775 were attracted by the theatre. It seemed to them that creating a world in the image of their dreams was the easiest and surest means of escape from mediocrity and of reaching the public ear. But despite its passion for the drama, Germany had as yet no permanent theatre, nor even a permanent company; in fact all the authors were in search of a stage from which to expound their new ideas. Goethe was one of the young innovators. He busied himself with the drama not only as an author but also as a producer, and the demands of the medium modified his ideas. He now dreamed of a national theatre as a professional dram-

---

[1] *Goethe*, p. 339.
[2] Max Wundt, *Goethes Wilhelm Meister und die Entwickelung des modernen Lebensideals* (De Gruyter, Berlin, 1902. 509 pages). This is the indispensable authority.

atist, not just as a writer of plays. He called Wilhelm Meister his " dramatic double " (to Baroness von Stein, June 24, 1782) because he had finally gained the " distance " which allows one to judge objectively. Goethe observes Wilhelm Meister who is, like him, author, manager, actor and producer. Another motive attributed to weimar probably played its part; after his cold welcome by the nobility of the court, he wanted to find a means to impress them and raise himself to their level.

By January 2, 1778, Goethe had successfully completed the first book, but, as business forced him to work only by first and starts, the second was only finished in August 1782, the third in November 1782, the fourth on November 12, 1783, the fifth on October 28, 1784, and the sixth on November 6, 1785. By December 8, 1785, he had planned the six following books; yet he was only to realize this project in the shape of the *Lehrjahre*, the second verion of *Wilhelm Meister*. The six completed books remained unknown until 1910, when Barbara Schulthess's copy was discovered. Thus *Wilhelm Meister's theatralische Sendung*, called " *Urmeister*," was published in 1911.

The young Meister is no longer a rebellious Titan, but a gifted idealist. His ambition is to develop his talents, and to bestow a great theatre on his nation. He is also stimulated by his passion for the actress Marianne. Sent on a business tour by his father, he meets and joins a troupe of strolling players. Performing with this group, he takes part in a play of his own composition. The group is welcomed at a castle where he meets Jarno; together they are then attacked by brigands and saved by the intervention of persons of high rank, a mysterious Amazon and her uncle. He finally reaches a town which boasts a properly organized theatre, and he sees the chance to realize his dream of an ideal production of *Hamlet*; he enters the theatre. This romantic story is full of youth and vitality.

We do not know what dénouement Goethe had in mind. Must we admit that the pretended *Sendung* was a mistake, and consider the title as irony, or was Meister to succeed in creating a national theatre as Shakespeare had done? We prefer the second hypothesis. Goethe seldom used irony, and certainly not in this case. The title is no more ironical than *Hans Sachsens Poetische Sendung*: it is difficult to suppose that he would have mocked his own hero, that is to say, himself. He was so passionately attached to the theatre that he wrote in his journal on May 13, 1780: "It is one of those few things in which I still find a childish and artistic joy." He showed Meister's rise from Guignol to established theatre with a logic which demands the final "Yes." In any case the intervention of the Amazon, destined to play an important part in the definitive work, would have brought in the Society of the Tower and presupposes an inspired ascent in which the dramatic stage would have been at least a first step.

If Goethe did not finish the *Sendung* it was perhaps because it was conceived in the state of mind of "Sturm-und-Drang" which he had already left behind. It was a magnificent expression of a period when poets proclaimed the pre-eminence of the artist, whose mission was to rise ever higher in order to raise society with him. But in 1782 and certainly 1785, Goethe no longer believed in this primacy of aesthetics; a man of the world, a scientist, a minister, he was moving towards a much broader concept of humanity, which he was to express in two plays, *Iphigenie* and *Torquato Tasso*.

While *Wilhelm Meister's theatralische Sendung* is a prolongation of the "Sturm-und-Drang" period, *Iphigenie* is the first great classical work. With the *Sendung* Goethe freed himself of a past he had outgrown, with *Iphigenie* of a recent experience which had turned his thoughts to-

wards a " spiritual drama " in which he could portray
the grandeur of humanity.

This work is a confession once again. His experiences
led him to choose this subject and to enlarge upon the ancient tragedy. Did he not write: " The tragic poet has no
other duty or task than to set out a psycho-ethical phenomenon taken from the past, presenting it in the form of
comprehensible experience "? [1] The two poles of the psychological experience which gave rise to *Iphigenie* were the
letter of August 17, 1775, to Frau A. J. Karsch and the
lines written on April 14, 1776, in which he predicted
the influence of Charlotte von Stein. Between these two
dates the Frankfurt Orestes, scourged by the invisible whip
of the Eumenides, found his spiritual home. There was
the psycho-ethical phenomenon; it remained to find the
story from the past capable of expressing it. Goethe was
ready to turn to Greek mythology and Attic tragedy, which
he had been studying assiduously since Strassburg days.
He had already borrowed the Prometheus myth from antiquity and he now took from Euripides the subject of his
Iphigenie auf Tauris, the story of Orestes the matricide,
ordered by Apollo to seize the statue of his sister Artemis
from the Taurian barbarians. The young Greek would
have paid for this attempt with his life if Athene, playing
the part of a *Deus ex Machina*, had not ordered Thoas to
let him go. Goethe found this a suitable subject and dramatized it, but not in the manner of *Götz*; he gave each
of his characters his own feelings or the characteristics of
his friends. Thus he recreated himself just as he recreated
Charlotte von Stein in Iphigenie. During the months of
February and March 1779, either at Weimar or on his
travels, he wrote the first version in prose. It was produced
at the duke's theatre on April 6, 1779, with Karl-August

---

[1] Quoted by Benno Von Weise, *Geschichte der deutschen Tragödie*,
I, p. 506.

as Pylades and Goethe himself as Orestes. It scored a great success. He revised it in 1780, 1781, and particularly in 1786-7, during his Italian journey, trying to make it more coherent. This fourth version, in iambic pentameters, appeared in 1787.

Korff [1] has most ably demonstrated the value of the work as a "*Humanitätsdichtung*." It is this concept of humanity, dear also to Lessing, Herder and Schiller, which makes the work so important. It is necessary to differentiate between the two expressions "*Menschlichkeit*" and "*Humanität*"; the first has to do with commonplace humanity, the second with the pure humanity of superior beings. The latter is only for the ideal soul, and is attainable only after a long process of evolution. In the family of the Tantalides, which shares the curse of Tantalus, superior humanity appears first in Agamemnon, next with Orestes, and comes to full bloom in Iphigenie. But the first falls back into inhumanity through pride when, to obtain favorable winds, he sends for his elder daughter to sacrifice her on the altar of Diana. The second falls when he kills his mother to avenge his father. By her purity, faith and sincerity, by her superhuman qualities, Iphigenie is to redeem her race. She has not been sacrificed, but saved and carried by Diana into Tauris to become her priestess. There she performs a first miracle; she wrests King Thoas and the Taurians from barbarism; she procures for them a period of peace and happiness, and she secures the suppression of the royal decree condeming to death all strangers cast ashore. Such is the background of the drama.

The action begins when the king puts this barbarous decree into force again after Iphigenie refuses his offer of marriage. The priestess finds herself forced to sacrifice two Greeks, her brother Orestes and his companion, the

[1] *Geist der Goethezeit*, II, pp. 164 et seq.

faithful Pylades. Pursued by the Erinnyes since the execution of his mother, Orestes can only find peace, as promised by the oracle of Apollo at Delphi, after bringing back to Greece " the image of the sister who reigns in Tauris." He has therefore come to seize the statue of Diana. Without a second miracle from Iphigenie, he would perish. The priestess persuades Orestes to reveal his name, then in a weird trance she enables him to see his father and mother reconciled in hell. He then understands that the gods require not blood, but forgiveness, not hatred, but love. He feels a great sense of liberation, for remorse, personified by the Erinnyes, has left him. All that remains is for the two Greeks to return to their own country, taking with them the statue of Diana and Iphigenie. The priestess has her part to play in the plot divised by Pylades; she must lie and deceive the king. This is the too human temptation, the temptation to return to Greece and the palace of her fathers, perhaps to found a family. By giving way to it for a moment, she loses her pure humanity and her radiance. But she recovers; at the risk of her life and those of the two Greeks, she confesses the truth to the king. Thus she brings about her third miracle; Thoas rises to her level and renounces his claim on her, for it was she, not Diana, whom Apollo had demanded through his oracle. It is she who will purify the palace of the Atrides.

What E. Beutler said of *Götz*, of *Faust* and of *Egmont* is even truer of *Iphigenie*; the principal character, the family, even the relations between races, mark a transition from demonism to morality.

L. Leibrich [1] has pointed out the modernity of the work and revised our conception of *Iphigenie* by examining it in the light of contemporary personalism and existentialism. In fact the play deals with the problem of the individual

---

[1] Iphigénie en Tauride à la lumière de la philosophie d'aujourd'hui in *Études germaniques*, nos. 14-15, pp. 129-138.

and his " engagement.". We could also speak, to add a religious connotation, of his calling, and of the contrast between Iphigenie's humanitarian vocation and Meister's theatrical vocation. The girl lives in a world of sincerity, purity and piety, but she yearns to live in Greece among her own people, and to found a family. This is expressed in certain lines of her first monologue. When Thoas offers her marriage she might be tempted to accept, thinking that this surrender would allow her to strengthen her humanizing mission with royal authority. Yet her only thought is to preserve the integrity of her soul from this intrusion of the outside world. Then remaining faithful to herself, she continues her work of pacification, this time for the benefit of Orestes. She will find herself involved in action and will be forced to deny herself by becoming the instrument of the crafty Pylades. Then there arises the problem of " unclean hands ": she has to chose between purity and effectiveness, either to remain herself while sacrificing her brother or to save him by perjuring herself. The famous *Song of the Parques* expresses the horrifying doubt which plagues her. In the well-known tirade in the fifth act, however, she rises to a height of feminine heroism never before equalled. Here is a " witness " in the fullest sense of the word; at the risk of perishing and of involving the two young men in her doom, she renounces effectiveness, represented by the plot of Pylades, to preserve the purity and integrity of her ego. She accepts the sacrifice of these three lives in order to save her soul. By a true miracle, purity proves its effectiveness, and the spiritual value of the human personality is triumphant.

By saving her soul and preserving her idea of herself, Iphigenie redeems her family, which is also the subject of the play. In 1802, Schiller, who had long wished to write a drama " in the Greek manner," wrote *Messina's Fiancée*, a play with a chorus, in which Destiny makes use of a young girl to destroy the royal family of Messina.

It is the antithesis of *Iphigenie*, which might also be called a " drama of destiny " (*Schicksalsdrama*), were Destiny not thwarted and overcome by the intervention of the priestess who redeems all the members of her family except Tantalus, the guilt-stained grandfather. The story of the family of the Tantalides, which Goethe cleverly makes Iphigenie relate to Thoas, is the transition from the demonic to the moral. Only Tantalus himself remains condemned in the lower regions, enchained in a Promethean hell. This is a problem which has given rise to much discussion; why was Tantalus not saved? Is he the sole victim of the curse; his descendants being thus absolved of all hereditary responsibility? Dalmeyda [1] gives several explanations, some valuable, some subject to criticism. It certainly seems that Tantalus had committed the unforgiveable sin in the eyes of Goethe, who was then writing his *Limitations of Humanity*. The Titan tries to pass the boundaries imposed on man, to make himself the equal of the Gods; he thus became guilty of that *hubris* which was an inexpiable offence for the Greeks. He is, in Spinoza's term, a " blinded being " and must be condemned. One can imagine another explanation; there is a dual conception of the Divinity in Iphigenie. On the one hand we have religion based on fear, on the other, religion based on reverence, the *Ehrfurcht* which assumes such great importance in *Wilhelm Meisters Wanderjahre*. The first, represented in varying degress by all the characters save Iphigenie, is the belief in cruel, tyrannical gods, jealous of their superiority and greedy for the blood and suffering of man. This faith gives strength to Orestes, agent of the divine law according to which murder can be avenged only by murder. Yet the young man already has an inkling of a new moral law, that unwritten law for which Antigone sacrifices herself. While he knows

---

[1] *Goethe et le drame antique.* Paris, Hachette, 1908, 430 pages.

he is innocent in the eyes of the gods, he yet feels guilty according to the conscience of man, which reproaches him for killing through lust for blood. He experiences remorse, personified by the Erinnyes. Could one not interpret his expedition to Tauris as a pilgrimage of penance? The second concept of religion is represented in Iphigenie, whose faith may be compared to that expressed in Lessing's *Nathan der Weise*, and recalls the faith of Goethe's mother; it is based on confidence in the goodness of the gods, and submission to their will. The priestess knows that they demand not blood but adoration, and that they love men. In her monologues she is shown passing from childish confidence to religious doubt when, from her childhood memories, a lullaby reminds her of that terrible song in which the Parques glorify the ancient gods.

Finally we find in this inexhaustible work the contrast between the Greek world and the barbarian. L. Leibrich interprets this contrast as the antagonism between open and closed societies, as defined by Bergson. We are at one of those periods when two civilizations meet and clash, and which, as Hebbel was to show later, offer eminently dramatic subjects. The Taurians, a closed society, are protected against strangers by putting to death, by order of the gods, all who land on the coasts of Tauris. It is really a messenger of peace from the open society who comes to them in the person of Iphigenie. She has the blood-thirsty decree abolished, temporarily at least. Her work is destroyed by the spite of the kin disappointed in love, but she gains her greatest victory by securing her return to Greece and the liberation of the two Greeks. Tauris has thus become an open society, and the last words of Thoas are pregnant with meaning; they represent not only a sad farewell, but also the beginning of a new era, which will see the establishment of friendly relations between Tauris and Greece. Thus Iphigenie has saved her soul, her family and the peace of the Aegean.

By looking upon this work of Goethe's as modern and emphasizing its Christian character, we set it at a distance from Greek tragedy. We here agree with Bodmer, who wrote a criticism of it in 1782, contrasting its sententious and almost metaphysical character with the mythological works of the Greeks. The question has been frequently discussed, and it is not difficult to show what the play owes to Attic tragedy; but what interests us, and what matters, is precisely what it does not owe to that example. Goethe was himself conscious of this, at least towards the end of his life, for he was to tell Eckermann that had he known the Greeks better he would not have written his play. Schiller, who also wrote a critique of it, placed it above its antique original, precisely because the modern poet had been able to draw on the further experience of two millenia of western civilization of Christianity. In *Werther* the action takes place in the hero's heart, in *Iphigenie* it is set in the soul of the heroine. There are two actions: one is on the surface, the expedition of the two friends to seize the statue of Diana, and their return to their own country; the other is within, and takes place entirely in the soul of Iphigenie. The first would have led to a catastrophe but for the intervention of the pure soul of the priestess. It is only necessary to contrast Goethes's denouement with that of Euripides to realize that the modern has absorbed the gods, that the voice of God has become the voice of man, or, if one prefers it, that God expresses himself through the best in man. This " drama of the soul " is no longer Greek, it is Weimarian Goethe.

In his essay *Shakespeare und kein Ende* which dates from 1813-1816, Goethe contrasted Greek tragedy, based on the conflict between man and necessity, with the modern drama. where human will is the ruling force. Further, he wondered whether it was possible for him to create a true tragedy, and he even wrote to Zelter on October 31, 1831: " I was not born to be a tragic poet, for I am by nature conciliatory. Thus I can take no interest in a purely tragic case, where, in fact, all possibility of conciliation must be excluded, and besides, in this extraordinarily calm world, what cannot be reconciled seems to me quite absurd." [1] This conception was not simply an old man's idea, for on June 6, 1824, he told Chancellor von Müller, " All true tragedy depends on irreconcilable antagonism. As soon as a solution appears or becomes possible, the tragedy disappears." [2] Benno von Weise, who makes an exhaustive study of the question in his important work on German tragedy, admits that Goethe has given the tragic the name " demonic "; it is this " demonic " which creates the tragic conflict and which drives Goethe's heroes to disaster. In *Iphigenie* for the first time the result is happy because the hero is a woman, and because Goethe had undergone the influence of Baroness von Stein. It is impossible to attach too much importance to a confidence of November 24, 1809, reported by Riemer. He tells us that Goethe declared " that he saw the ideal in feminine form, that he did not know what man was like, that he could show man only biographically with an historical basis." [3] There can be no finer tribute to Charlotte von Stein and to the " eternal feminine " exalted by the poet at the end of the second *Faust*.

By 1779, therefore, Goethe had come far from the masculine Titanism of *Werther, Götz, Faust* and *Egmont*. He had expressed his faith in an ideal of humanity. In restoring man to his position beneath the gods, he at the same time places him beneath woman, whom he makes the foundation of his new concept. We shall find similar ideas expressed in *Torquato Tasso*.

[1] See Colleville, *Goethe et le théâtre* in *Études germaniques*, pp. 148-161.
[2] Flodoard von Biedermann, *Goethes Gespräche*, 1909, III, p. 119.
[3] Ibid., II, p. 56.

DON DOMENICO CARACCIOLO

de' Duchi di S. Teodora, Marchese di Villa-
maina, Cavaliere dell' Infigne Real Ordine di S. Gen-
naro, Gentiluomo di Camera con Efercizio di S. M.
Configliere di Stato, e Segretario di Stato di Cafa
Reale, affari Efteri, e Siti Reali, Soprintendente
Generale delle Regie Pofte, e Segretario di S. M.
la Regina.

Partendo *per Roma Mons.ʳ Giovanni de Goethe di Weimar,*

Te dyco i

*Per ordine di S. M. impongo a tutti li Miniftri fuoi, e Officiali di Giuftizia, e Guer-
ra, e a quelli che non lo fono dimando in fuo Real nome che non gli diano moleftia,
ne impedimento alcuno nel fuo viaggio, anzi gli preftino il favore che gli fia neceffario
per efeguirlo. Napoli primo Giugno 1787 —*

Il Marchefe Caracciolo

Gratis

Vaglia per *Dieci* **giorni.**

The passage from the country of King Thoas to the court of the Duke of Ferrara, from Greek antiquity to the Italian renaissance, is not simply a change of time and place. It also constitutes an advance from a civilization hardly free from barbarism to a period distinguished by the highest learning and refinement of culture. Goethe owed this new orientation to Weimar, and especially to Baroness von Stein. It is not surprising, therefore, that Goethe had the idea of *Torquato Tasso* while on his way to her house on March 30, 1780. He found this idea so attractive that he was to speak of the " day of discovery." But the poet could not pause on his journey, nor interrupt an evolution which, from the end of 1781 or the beginning of 1782, was leading him away from Weimar and from Charlotte von Stein. The completion of *Torquato Tasso* took almost as long as that of *Egmont* and the finished work shows a similar duality.

It is very possible that Goethe considered a play about Tasso before March 30, 1780, for he had read Kopp's translation of *Jerusalem Delivered* in his youth, and the *Life of Tasso*, published by Hanse in the review *Iris* in 1774, may have inspired the idea. But when he began his play he had been living for four years at the court of Weimar, like the Italian at the court of Ferrara, and he had been in love with Charlotte von Stein, just as his famous model had loved the princess Eleonora d'Este, the sister of Duke Alphonse II. Thus in the first two acts, which correspond to the two acts in prose composed in 1780 and 1781, he shows us the poet who offers his prince the manuscript *Jerusalem Delivered*, is crowned by his beloved, and finds himself at the summit of felicity. That was exactly Goethe's own situation at the time when Baroness von Stein doubtless made her final surrender, a hypothesis confirmed by his letter of March 25, 1781: " Do you notice how love takes care of your poet? A few months ago, the next scene (the great love scene, the first in Act II)

9.

would have been impossible. How easily it will now flow from my heart." He worked vigorously at *Tasso*, happy to be able to express his love, his relations with the duke and the courtiers, and his own concept of poetry. He worked at it in communion with Charlotte; his *Tasso* is a daily correspondence, a hymn to woman, an act of adoration, a joyous invocation, as his letters bear witness. " In the silence of the morning I have composed a panegyric on woman, especially on you " (March 27, 1781). " As you wish to take to yourself all that Tasso says, I have already written much to you today " (April 19, 1781). " What I have written (Tasso's monologue in Act II) is good, if it is remembered that I am invoking you " (April 23, 1781). With these two acts completed in the autumn of 1781, the poet was brought to a standstill, no doubt by the difficulty of leading up to and motivating the rupture between Eleonora and Tasso while Charlotte and Goethe remained united. He faced a further difficulty; how was he to justify Tasso's exile while he himself was in great favor at Weimar, and in fact was made Prime Minister in 1782?

We have seen that by 1782 his liaison with Charlotte von Stein was beginning to become a burden to him; we shall see later on that he was also beginning to desire a lightening of his administrative duties and an escape. He decided to go to Italy and to take his unfinished play with him. On March 11, 1788, he planned it out, but other work kept him away from it. However, his journey provided him with a precise picture of the places where his hero had lived, and the sorrow he felt on leaving Italy gave him a better understanding of Tasso's distress when replused by his patron and forced to leave the woman he loved. He also discovered a *Life of Tasso* (1785) by the Abbé Serassi, which provided him with much important information. Let us add that on his return to Weimar he soon broke with Baroness von Stein, and came to enjoy a far from platonic relationship with Christiane Vulpius. He could therefore smile at the passion of a princess so chaste that she punishes a single kiss with eternal exile. He returned to work, having begun a complete edition of his works, and in July 1789 he completed *Tasso*. He spoke of it to Eckermann, who had asked him on May 6, 1827, what ideas he had in mind:

> An idea? None that I know of! I had Tasso's life, I had my own life, and while I was combining the characteristics of two such curious people there was born in me a vision of Tasso, to whom I opposed Antonio to produce a prosaic enough contrast; I had no lack of models for him either. The other conditions of life, love and the court, were the same at Weimar as at Ferrara, and I could truthfully say of my evocation; it is bone of my bone and flesh of my flesh.

He thus confirms Herder who, having hardly finished reading the first scene, declared to his wife: " Goethe can do nothing but idealize himself and say what is in him." He also justifies Baroness von Kalb, who in the first three scenes thought she could distinguish the voices of the poet, the duke, the duches and Baroness von Stein.[1]

In this subtle and complex work we find the story of Goethe's love and the story of Tasso closely interrelated. The first act is the apotheosis of poetic genius; this can be no surprise to us for in 1783, in the famous ballad *Der Sänger*, Goethe chose one of the Homerides as hero, a true emissary of the Gods, who made an apostleship of his art and proudly cried:

> I sing as sings the bird,
> I, who live in the branches;
> The song which pours from my throat
> Is rich enough reward.

In the play the four other characters are, to different degrees, lovers of poetry. Leonora Sanvitale evokes the greatness of Tasso in terms which make one think of the poet as conceived by Novalis.

---

[1] Bielschowsky, *Goethe*, p. 450.

> His gaze but rarely lingers on the earth,
> His ear's attuned to nature's harmony;
> Both history and what life has to offer
> He gladly gathers to his poet's breast;
> His soul assembles all that is dispersed,
> And animates, by feeling, what is dead.
> Often he raises what we had deemed low,
> And humbles former objects of our praise.

(I, 159-166).

In a very fine article on " The Tragedy of a Creative Artist " [1] Miss E. M. Wilkinson points out that Goethe succeeded in bringing to the stage " the drama of artistic creation " by showing us four examples of poetic creation: the evocations of the Elysian Fields, where the crowned Tasso believes himself to have been transported (I, 3, 527-557): of the Golden Age (II, 1, 978-994): of his future arrival at Sorrento (V, 4, 3140-3162) and of the garden which he dreams of maintaining for the princess (V, 4, 3190-3211).

In fact, however, it is less a question of the drama of creation than of the tragedy of the poet involved in life. Goethe himself pointed out to Herder that the key to this work is " *die Disproportion des Talents mit dem Leben,*" that is, the conflict between genius and life, a romantic theme par excellence. We can readily understand how *Torquato Tasso* gave birth to de Vigny's *Chatterton*, and led him to exalt in the preface those inspired beings who were " unfit for anything but the divine work." Leonora Sanvitale explains this idea in a tirade where she sums up the violent antagonism between Tasso, the poet, and Antonio, the courtier and diplomat:

> These are two men, a long time now I've felt it,
> Bound to be enemies, for of the pair
> Nature's not made a single entity.

(III, 2, 1704-1706).

[1] *The Tragedy of a Creative Artist* in *Publications of the English Goethe Society*, New Series, vol. XV, 1946, 96-127.

Thus we meet again, on a higher plane, the problem posed in *Werther*, that of the artist who shows himself unfit for life in society. But this is no longer, as in the novel, an assemblage of mediocre aristrocrats and bourgeois who wish to expel an alien element; it is a group of superior beings, whose judgment the poet cannot reject, and whose sentence is thus all the more serious.

On May 3, 1827, Goethe read J. J. Ampère's articles in the *Globe* with the liveliest interest and approved of his calling Tasso " an intensified Werther." If we go back to the sentence in which Goethe analysed Werther's character for Schönborn, we can explain Tasso. He is not as young, but he has more genius and creative power; he is the author of *Jerusalem Delivered*, and he creates genuine lyric poetry before the spectator's eyes, which always springs from personal feeling or intense emotion. Like Werther, he loses himself in enthusiastic dreams, aspires to be an heroic warrior, a man of action, his duke's adviser. When his princess has placed upon his brow the crown which had adorned the bust of Virgil, he is moved to such transports that Leonora has to recall him to reality. Later, victim of his sickly anxiety, he comes to consider all those about him as his enemies, including the princess. He nurses an " unhappy passion " for her. Every time she sees him on the point of giving way to despair she is adroit enough, with a cleverness not without coquetry, to risk a word of love which inflames him. Finally, like Werther, he takes a mistress who is so like Baroness von Stein that he inevitably asks more than she is ready to grant. In the novel, Charlotte, who is still partly naive in Schiller's sense of the word, contents herself with flight, though not without having enjoyed the heady passion of a kiss; the princess, a sentimental being, a " fine soul," whose feelings are naturally attuned to moral laws, rejects and condemns him in one word: " *Hinweg.*" Tasso had not understood that his transport of love was sacrilege; he collapses.

He could not understand, for he was a poet of genius, not a politician or a man of the world like Antonio; he was still, in the sense of German classicism, " inhuman." For Tasso, the Golden Age is the world of love and liberty. The princess, however, considers this Golden Age the poet's chimera, and she herself lives under the rule of law. If he wants to learn " what is proper," he need only ask noble women, for while man aspires to liberty, woman aspires to decorum, and the expression " *Sitte* " dominates the whole play. While genius is developed in solitude, decorum can only be acquired in society, by contacts with people:

> Talent is formed and molded in retreat,
> But character is shaped by wordly torrents.

> (I, 2, 304-305).

These lines of Leonora are re-echoed at the end of the play when the duke exhorts Tasso, to come out into the world:

> Whate'er the bard may lose, the man will gain.

The complete man must possess not only genius but also that " humanity " which Tasso has not acquired and which Goethe found in Weimar. It was at Karl August's court that Goethe, the " Stürmer," became a statesman like Antonio. It was through his tortured love and his renunciation that he finally became a true man.

How far we have come from Werther, unhappy victim of society and conventional morals, from Egmont, whose over-confident demon led to his destruction, from Wilhelm Meister, a great artist, but in the final analysis only a comedian, of whom Goethe, even as he finished *Torquato Tasso*, was preparing to make a man, through the theatre, certainly, but also by the example and society of an elite! To the original and imagined characters which filled the works of the " Sturm-und-Drang " period there now succeeded, whether borrowed from Greek antiquity or the Italian renaissance, heroes and heroines who represent what one call the Weimar humanity. The superior persons is no longer the genius, but the human being fashioned by an élite society whose laws and conventions he accepts. Yet it would be false to apply to *Torquato Tasso* the reproach later hurled by the romantics at *Wilhelm Meister's Lehrjabre*; that it is "a *Candide* directed against poetry." Genius may succumb, but it retains one thing:

> And if, in all his torments, man is silent,
> God granted me the gift to cry my pain.
>
> (V, 5, 3423-3433).

In 1823 Goethe still considered these lines so important that he set them at the head of his *Marienbader Elegie*, in which he described the sufferings of an old man rejected in love.

We are also far from the " Stürmer's " conception of nature as the heart's country and the true model of art. The Belvedere, where the action takes place, without being as insipid as the sheep-pens of the rococo period, harmonizes with refined beings whose conversation has the aristocratic charm of the dying eighteenth century. The characters are no longer copied from nature; they are already, in part at least, human types, and in this *Torquato Tasso* marks the evolution of Goethe's ideal since 1779, finding its place between *Iphigenie* and the later *Hermann und Dorothea* and *Die naturliche Tochter*. If Antonio and Leonora Sanvitale seem to be individuals taken from real life, the duke and the princess represent types of the enlightened prince, and of the great lady as known to Goethe in the person of Baroness von Stein or the duchess Louise. As for Tasso, he must evidently be the type of the poet himself, whose specific characteristics are individualized by exaggeration. One may say, borrowing a later remark of Goethe's, that here nature and art, which seemed to shun each other, meet in perfection.

Torquato Tasso is a play for the connoisseur; Hoffmannsthal called it unfathomable, comparing it to a Greek torso whose marble is alive yet infinitely remote from ordinary life.[1] For this reason it could never be a success on the stage, nor even much of a spectacle. If in *Iphigenie* the surface action was reduced, here one may wonder where it is to be found at all. Even more than in the Greek play, everything takes place in the hero's soul, or springs from it. Goethe was disappointed by its lack of success, and confided to Eckermann, on March 27, 1825:

> I once genuinely cherished the idea that it was possible to create a German theatre. What is more, I had the illusion that I might be able to make a contribution, and bring some stones to the foundations of such an edifice. I wrote my *Iphigenie* and my *Tasso*, and with childish confidence I supposed that all would go well. But nothing stirred, there was no excitement, all remained as before. If I had produced any effect, had any success, I would have written you a good dozen of plays like *Iphigenie* and *Tasso*. There was no lack of subjects. But as I told you, there were not the actors to present such plays with spirit and life, there was no public to appreciate and welcome them.

With these " dramas of the soul," Goethe took his leave of the stage, and never recaptured his youthful enthusiasm for it, even when he was director of the Weimar theatre.

In studying the three great works undertaken between 1776 and 1780, we have had to anticipate the future, as we did before wih *Egmont*, and allow the Italian journey to intervene; it seems that Weimar was not enough to bring them to fruition. In *Torquato Tasso* we glimpse a desire to put some distance between the poet and the court on which he depends, as if he were shaking his chains. Goethe had fled from Lili Schönemann to Switzerland, but he had resisted the temptation of the promised land; now we shall see him flee again, this time reaching Italy.

[1] *Unterhaltung über den Tasso.*

Chapter 3

The Italian journey
(September 3, 1786 - June 18, 1788)

> I count a second birth, a true renais-
> sance, from the day I first trod the
> soil of Rome. (to Herder, December,
> 1786).

Goethe himself invites us to consider his Italian journey
as the starting-point of a new era in his life, and it has
been long regarded as the beginning of his classical period.
We feel that this assertion is unjustified, and that a certain
rancor caused the poet to be unfair to the ten years at Weimar, or at least to the first five; it was there that he broke
with " Sturm-und-Drang," not at Rome. From 1775 to
1780 a real revolution took place in him, while the months
in Italy, important though they may be, mark only an
evolution, a consolidation of what had already been
achieved, and a source of further progress. The years which
followed his return to Weimar did not produce a new Goethe, as would have been the case had they brought the
revelation of a new truth. We would like to quote again
an expression he used to describe his liaison with Baroness
von Stein, and say that the years from 1775 to 1780 were
his novitiate; the Italian journey " confirmed " it.

Between 1780 and 1786 a complex period confronts us. The poet seems to have hesitated between Weimar, which inspired his dramatic masterpieces, and the country whose splendor had been revealed to him by his father. His " demon " told him that the ups and downs of " chance " had served him well, that " Eros " had been kind to him; it also whispered that he had taken the best that Weimar had to offer, and should seek new nourishment elsewhere. It is right that we should understand the reasons, becoming ever more imperious, which drove Goethe southwards, how he saw Italy, what lessons he expected from her, what he in fact learned there.

From the crucial year 1780 we possess a document whose vital importance we have already pointed out. On September 20, Goethe wrote to Lavater that he was becoming more and more attached to the task imposed upon him, in which he desired to become the equal of the greatest of men, " and in nothing greater." He goes on:

> This wish to raise as high as possible the pyramid of my existence, whose base is given me (*angegeben*) and firmly assured (*gegründet*), takes precedence over everything, and scarcely permits a moment's forgetfulness. I have not the right to delay. I am already getting older and perhaps Destiny will crush me on the way, leaving my Babylonian tower in the state of an uncompleted trunk. At least it must be admitted that the plan was a bold one, and if I live my strength will allow me, God willing, to reach the summit.

This passage reveals pride, but also a deep humility. The poet was thirty-one years old; he was thinking of the famous " *nel mezzo del cammin di nostra vita* " of Dante, who was allowed the time to build the cathedral that is his *Divine Comedy*. He had the sense of a mission which would allow him to become the rival of the greatest men of all time. He knew that his apprenticeship was over, that he must, without waiting, starting from this firm foundation which he felt beneath his feet, reach ever higher. But if he made out the balance sheet of his achievements and counted his progress, he could be satisfied.

On the other hand, Merck and his friends who could not follow this interior ripening and had seen from him only one important work, *Iphigenie*, in five years, were getting worried about him. They gave the alarm to Frau Rat, him mother, and she passed on their fears in a letter to him dated June 19, 1781, but finished only on July 19. They had advised her to bring him back to Frankfurt, for " the infamous climate of that place " did not suit him. He had successfully finished his task, the young duke's education; " as for that other filth (*Dreckwesen*), any one can do it, Goethe is too good for that," etc. She asks him to reflect before choosing " what is best." The poet took time to think it over and on August 11, 1781, he sent her his reply, which is an apology for Weimar. Merck and his friends see only his sacrifices, not his gains, " they cannot understand that I become richer daily by giving myself." He had to leave Frankfurt because " the disproportion between the narrowness and slow movement of the bourgeois circle and the width and rapidity of his being would have driven him mad ": if not, he would never have known the world, would have remained in a perpetual childhood. At Weimar he found himself in a situation larger than himself, which put him constantly to the test, corrected his faults and provided him with hundreds of examples of which he stood in the greatest need for his development. And now again, he could not imagine a happier state than his which holds for him something of the infinite. For, " even if every day new faculties developed in me, if my ideas became clearer, if my strength increased, if my knowledge grew, if my judgment became sounder, if my courage became higher, I would yet find the occasion to employ these faculties every day, now in great matters, now in small." His duty was to stay, his interest was to wait for what had been planted to grow.

In fact, at this date Goethe was at the apogee of his Weimar period. He was the friend and chief collaborator

of his duke, and he had also received the total love of
Charlotte von Stein; he was working actively at the second
act of *Torquato Tasso*, and he did not yet know that he
would be unable to finish it. The recent past and the promise of the present seemed to guarantee that he really
was where he wanted to be. Why should he wish for a
change? A year later his disposition had changed completely; now he shared his friends' apprehensions, for on
July 29, 1782, he wrote this disillusioned sentence: " Of
myself I have nothing to write, save that I am sacrificing
myself to a profession from which I have nothing to gain
as if it were the aim and object of all my thoughts." A few
days later, on August 10, he told Charlotte von Stein of
his joy at finishing the chapter of *Meister* whose beginning
he had dictated to her, and added: " In fact, I was born
to be a writer." This idea developed in him to such an
extent that in the same year he complained: " I was made
for a private existence, and I don't understand why it should
have pleased destiny to force me into a government and
a princely family." [1]

Thus it is from 1782 that we must date this desire for
escape, this need to flee to Italy, whither, had he followed
his father's advice, he would have gone in 1775. This
became little by little a painful yearning or, as he wrote
to the duke from Rome on November 31, 1786, " a sort
of sickness," of which he could only be cured by the sight
and presence, such an obsession that he admits that before
his departure he could not bear the sight of a Latin book,
nor a picture of an Italian landscape. How can such an
obsession be explained?

We have pointed out Goethe's desire to escape from his
heavy ministerial tasks, from the duke and from Baroness
von Stein; he was also disappointed at not being allowed

[1] Quoted by Lichtenberger (Editions de la Nouvelle Revue Critique,
p. 87).

to carry out certain reforms which we would call democratic, and which displeased the sovereign. His letters from Italy show that he remained faithful to his Weimar friends, despite an apparent infidelity, for what really mattered was to be faithful to himself, to obey his " demon " among the tribulations of " chance."

First, it seems to us quite certain that his writer's vocation was incompatible with his duties as a minister. His outer life did not harmonize with his inner life; he had to separate Goethe the Privy Councillor from the true Goethe, just as in Frankfurt he had never linked the practice of the law with " the seeing of visions," and he had remained faithful to himself " only in his most intimate plans, projects and enterprises " (to Kaebel, November 21, 1782). He could assert that since 1783 he had produced no important work, and then again, Weimar was still, to use the terms of Mephisto in *Faust*, only the " small " world, a stage on the way to the " great " world. Why limit his horizon to the affairs of a large village, and to the business of a country which had no past, which could have no future except through him, while in other regions the treasures of several millenia awaited him? The same *nisus vorwarts* which had pushed him out of the petit-bourgeois circle of Frankfurt inevitably also forced him from the aristocratic circle of Weimar. In Italy he hoped to become a new man and, in the proper sense of the word, be re-born. He wanted to remain eternally a student; he knew that his destiny would impel him from school to school, so that he might make new skins and slough the old, remaining the man of metamorphoses. From Rome he wrote to the duke on January 25, 1788: " The principal aim of my journey was to cure myself of the physical and moral ills which plagued me in Germany and finished by rendering me useless: next, to appease my thirst for true art." His letters from Italy show the justice of these views;

he did not cease to repeat that he has come to put himself to school, and that he was making progress.

Why did he choose to go to Italy? He had said that Paris should serve as his college and Italy as his university. Rilke was to express the same idea in almost the same words, but Clara Warthoff's arrival at Worpswede on her return from Paris where she had met Rodin, and the commission fom the publisher Muther for a book on the French sculptor, turned him instead toward Paris. Goethe had grown up in a household where a journey to Italy was traditional. He needed to see the originals of those old masterpieces whose reproductions hung on the walls of the house of his birth. These images, which had watched over his childhood, remained imprinted in his mind.

When he set off on September 3, 1786, he intended to stay only a short time, but he did not return to Weimar until June 18, 1788. One cannot help being amused and touched, and at the same time a little irritated by his letters. In some he explains the need to prolong his absence; in others he begs the duke's permission not to remain a little longer. Without lingering over the details of his journey,[1] let us mention that from Carlsbad he hastened to Rome by way of Ratisbon, Munich, the Brenner, Trento, Verona, Vicenza, Padua, Venice, Ferrara, Bologna, Florence and Perugia. In the Roman capital he spent the months of November, December, January and February, living with the painter Tischbein, who painted a well-known portrait of him. On February 22, 1787, he set out for Naples and Sicily, returned in June, and did not leave Rome again until he started back to Germany at the end of April 1788. He fled all honors and society, living as a simple Roman student and traveling under the name

---

[1] It may be convenient to refer to L. Sauzin's abridged and annotated edition of the *Italienische Reise* (pub. Belin), or to R. Michéa's thesis *Le voyage de Goethe en Italie* (Aubier).

of Jean Phillipe Moeller, supposedly a painter. Tischbein has left us this impression of the life he led in Rome:

> What pleases me most about him is the simplicity of his life. All he asked of me was a little room in which he could sleep and work undisturbed, and simple food, which I have had no difficulty in providing, for his needs are so few. There he works every morning until nine, finishing his *Iphigenie*; then he goes out to look at works of art. He scarcely visits the great at all, and receives no visits except from artists.

Among the latter should be mentioned Hackert, with whom he studied drawing, Angelica Kaufmann and Alexander Trippel, who made respectively a portrait and a bust of him, and particularly Karl Philipp Moritz. He wrote to Baroness von Stein, on December 14, 1786, that he regarded Moritz as " a younger brother of the same sort, but neglected and slighter, while he himself had been favored and preferred."

What did Goethe learn from this country, where he found the realization of all his desires and all his dreams, the only country on earth which could be Paradise for him (to Kayser, July 14, 1787)? First, he discovered the beauty of the sky, the countryside, the architecture, the masterpieces of painting. For Goethe it was the revelation of that harmonious beauty lauded by Winckelmann. Next, he recognized its grandeur: " Nothing small here," he wrote to Herder on November 10, 1786, " even in what is damnable and lacking in taste, all share in the grandeur of the whole," and to Knebel, on November 17, 1786: " Whoever has not seen these ruins (of Rome) can have no idea of grandeur." He was vastly impressed by the duration of Italian civilization, which permitted him to feel that he was in contact with past epochs. In his letter of November 10 to Herder we find this magniloquent sentence: " When one contemplates an existence more than two thousand years old, which has continued through the chances of time, so varied, and fundamentally so unshakable; when one realizes that this is still the same hill, very often the same column, the same wall, and that one still finds among the populace traces of the ancient character, then one becomes a contemporary of the great decisions of destiny." The result was a lesson in *Solidité*; it is not without reason that this French word, which to the Germans has the sense of authenticity, frequently came from the poet's pen. On November 7, 1786, he wrote to Baroness von Stein: " Whoever casts a serious look around him and has eyes to see must become *solide*, must acquire an idea of *solidité*, never so vivid to him before "; to Herder on November 10, 1786: " The effect which I already feel in my soul is an inner *solidité* which, so to speak, stamps its impress on the soul." Finally, on January 27, 1787, using a bold metaphor, he writes to Baroness von Stein: " My existence has now acquired a ballast which gives it the necessary weight; I no longer fear the phantoms which have so often made sport of me." Thus Rome was for him, as for many of his compatriots, as Paris was to Rilke, the example of an authentic, enduring and beautiful existence. Eager to become, and bitten with the idea of metamorphosis, the Germans are none the less afraid of change, which means imbalance, and they are lured by a vision of stability, which always escapes them. The *Fragment* of 1780 praises nature for creating this imbalance which is always the prelude and the occasion of a new equilibrium. Yet the human being cannot be satisfied with this imbalance; Goethe, the man of metamorphoses, never ceased to strive for equilibrium, that inner equilibrium of which Italy was the model.

Goethe was on a triple quest; he went there as a man, as an artist and as a scholar. He was approaching forty, by which time he wanted to have completed his education (to the Herders, November 10, 1787) and his *Meister* (to the duke, February 10, 1787). He felt the need to renew himself; he dreamed of adding new stratum to the already solid foundations of his ego; he desired the death of his

past, and to live for what he was to become. This was
the dream which haunted him. He had scarcely set foot
in Italy when he wrote to the Herders, on September 10,
1786: " I hope to come back re-born." By November 4,
1786, it was no longer just a hope but a certainty, and
he wrote to his mother from Rome that he would return
a new man and would be a source of joy to his friends.
To Baroness von Stein, who would have some reason to
fear such a transformation, he explained on January 6,
1787, that he had gained much inner enrichment, that he
had rejected many firmly held views which had made him
unhappy, and that he was much freer: " Each day I slough
another skin, and I hope to return a complete man."
In Germany he had known the bourgeois life of Frankfurt
and had registered his protest by his behavior at Leipzig;
then a conventional life had aroused his youthful spirit
of rebellion; finally, he had experienced the stilted court
life of Weimar, and the demands of an aristocratic mistress
more interested in the soul than in the body and the senses.
Like all German writers he had been dogged by anxiety,
haunted by the problems called God, genius, love, nature,
theatre, rules, freedom; he had pondered too much upon
life instead of living simply and unaffectedly. Italy supplied the same answer that Rodin later gave Rilke when
the latter asked him how to live: not to puzzle incessantly
over the problem of life, but to live, letting no chance of
joy pass by. Edmond Jaloux, writing of this Italian journey
(he wrote also of the journey to Switzerland) as one who
has himself known and loved this chosen land, had in mind
this initiation into the joys of living when he wrote:

What Goethe seeks in Italy, I suppose, is what Italy especially has
to give him: that is, an immense possibility of pleasure in every minute. The word pleasure has acquired in the Northern countries a
meaning almost always pejorative. Who says pleasure indirectly says
sin. But this pleasure of the southern lands, which is made up of
nothings, a pleasant idling, the picturesque grouping of three people
in a street, the sudden coolness of the air, the sight of a perfect fruit

or a luxuriant flower, the humor of a remark overheard by chance,
kindness without self-interest, the fullness of life provided by a blue
sky or the struggle of two clouds; this pleasure belongs essentially to
the southern races.[1]

Goethe might have added the pleasure of living in love,
whether with the beautiful Milanese, Maddalena Riggi,
who was already engaged but who broke off her engagement for him, or with the earthier love of pretty girls
of easy virtue, like Faustina the Roman, who opened their
arms to the young and handsome " barbarian " of the
North, showing him that love is not only the offering of a
soul but the gift of a body, " the Alpha and Omega of the
good things of the world." What a difference between
Baroness von Stein and the indulgent mistress on whose
back Goethe scanned his hexameters! Everywhere Goethe
discoverd a sensual joy in life, which even succeeded in
removing death's hideous mask, covering the Neapolitan
child's corpse with flowers. He knows a joy, an intoxication, from which the *Römische Elegien* will benefit:

> How happy I feel in Rome, when I think of the time
> When there in the northern grayness I was enclosed
> When, sad and oppressive, the sky loured over my head,
> When the colorless, shapeless world spread about my pain,
> When to search the dark paths of my dissatisfied spirit,
> Sadly, silently introspective, I inward plunged.
> Here a far brighter sky illumines my brow;
> The great God Phoebus evokes new colors and forms.
> The night, star spangled, resounds with love serenades,
> And the moonlight shines yet brighter than northern day.
>
> (*Römische Elegien*, VII).

Goethe'e remark, " I feel myself once more an artist,"
has attracted much comment. Karl-August's minister might
have believed himself made for the life of a statesman and
man of the world. He had now only one desire: to escape

[1] Ed. Jaloux, *Goethe*, p. 143 (Éditions Arthème Fayard), 1949,
pp. 161-162.

the slavery of the public service, to give up the position of a " great officer of state " in order to devote himself to art, which did not, however, prevent him writing to Karl-August on August 16, 1787, that he wanted to devote himself to the administration of the country " for a certain length of time " as he was now devoting himself to the arts. He wanted to pay for his Italian journey, and, with this aim, to tour the duchy of Weimar with the observant eye of an artist so as to suggest certain improvements to the duke. On the other hand Baroness von Stein cannot have read without bitterness the letters of the first days of June in which the poet praised the Marchese Luccesini as the model of a man of the world, concluding: " I see clearly why I cannot be such a man." This is a singularly revealing confession at the moment when Goethe is about to complete *Tasso.* He now knew what was his proper function: it was, as he had tried to show in *Wilhelm Meisters Theatralische Sendung,* to produce a work of art which would raise him to the level of, not set him above, the nobility. That was his destiny.

Goethe has discovered, besides, that he was made not for the plastic arts but for poetry. In the preceding years he had not ceased to draw; he had begun to paint in oils, and it has even been asserted that at the time of his departure for Italy he was still hesitating between poetry and art. In fact, he always seemed dissatisfied with his drawings. On July 22, 1776, he wrote to Baroness von Stein: " I have drawn a great deal, but I see only too clearly that I shall never become an artist." He explained that his drawings go from the eye to the pencil, without passing through the heart. On September 14, 1777, he wrote that drawing is a comforter (*Saugläppgen*), which quietens children, and gives them the rest of an imaginary nourishment. On April 9, 1782, he admitted his inability to draw ruins, but saw in the mechanical exercise of drawing an outlet for what was in his mind. In Italy he drew

incessantly, especially during his second visit to Rome
(more than a thousand landscape sketches). He also
painted and practised modeling. He discovered that his
real vocation was for poetry, creation through the word.
From then on, practising that " limitation " which he was
already praising, he gave up drawing and painting. He
would be a poet, but he owed the art of observing people
and things to the company of artists and to his own
experience. Thus he was the ancestor of that line of writers
who tried the pencil and color first, like Keller, Stifter and
Hermann Hesse.

The Italian journey was no less important from the
scientific point of view. Yet, it must be observed, the letters sent by the traveler are much less rich, from this point
of view, than the *Italienische Reise*, a real repository of
observation on the sky and clouds, vegetables and minerals,
the mountains and the sea. Everything seems to have been
the object of a methodical investigation, impelled by a
desire to discover the laws which govern nature, and the
" types " which are its basis. What profound joy we find,
like that which followed the discovery of the inter-maxillary process, when Goethe was able to write to Charlotte
von Stein on June 8, 1787:

> Tell Herder that I am hot on the trail of the secret of the creation
> and organization of plants, and that it is the simplest thing imagi-
> nable... The original plant (*die Urpflanze*) becomes the most aston-
> ishing (*wanderlichste*) thing in the world, and nature herself must
> envy me it. With this model and the right key, one can go on to
> invent an infinity of other plants which must result, that is to say
> which, even if they don't exist, yet could exist and are not mere
> shadows, figments of a pictorial or poetic imagination but have an
> inner truth and necessity. The same law may apply to all living crea-
> tures (*auf alles übrige Lebendige*).

In the botanical gardens at Palermo he had the vision of
an archetypal seed, the original cell from which all the
elements of plant life were formed by multiplication and
differentiation, in which they were all united. From this

it was not difficult, applying the same law to all living beings, to build up the idea of an immense and intoxicating cosmic unity. From now on Goethe possessed a magic key which would allow him to relate the phenomena of nature, of science and of art. All reality had its perfection and its origins in a profound, necessary and divine truth: " In the face of it, all that is arbitrary, all that is imaginary dissolves, for there is necessity, there is God." It was the scientist in him that allowed Goethe to establish the link between nature and art. To the blazing naturalism of " Sturm-und-Drang," to the disciplined naturalism of the 1770's there now succeeded an artistic naturalism, which was a new step towards the stylized naturalism of his classical period. The letter of November 12, 1786, to the duchess Louise, wife of Karl-August, is an essential document:

I cannot here remain silent about a discovery I have made; the knowledge that it is more convenient and easier to observe and appreciate nature than art. The least of nature's works has within itself the circle of its perfection, and if I only have the eyes to see, I can discover its proportions (*Verhältnisse*); I have the certainty that within a small compass is enclosed (*beschlossen*) a whole and true entity. On the other hand, the perfection of a work of art is outside itself, is the " *meilleur* " in the artist's conception, which he rarely if ever attains; except in these rare cases, the work will have perfection according to certain accepted laws, springing, it is true from the nature of the art and from technique, but nevertheless not as easy to understand and decipher as the laws of living nature. Works of art owe much to tradition, while the works of nature are always, as it were, an original statement from God.

On December 29, 1786, he declared to Baroness von Stein that his assiduous and profound study of nature was equally helpful to his understanding of art. On October 3, 1787, he informed Knebel that he had happily discovered " a means of combining art with his manner of representing nature." This was his " general formula," applicable to all plants, which had already provided him with a method of relating and explaining the most diverse forms, such as

the pasque-flower and the arum. This nature-art liaison
he had now acquired: its influence on him never ceased,
and from it he evolved his classical aesthetic ideal.

His internal evolution had naturally outstripped the production of works of art. Goethe had taken with him several manuscripts: *Iphigenie, Tasso, Faust, Egmont, Meister.*
If we neglect the minor works, such as *Erwin und Elmire,
Claudine von Villa Bella* (second version), *Lila, Jery und
Bately*, we find that he had revised *Iphigenie*, finished *Egmont* and made some progress with *Faust*. In September
1787, he was working hard at *Iphigenie*, intending to tran-
scribe it in verse. On January 13, 1787, he sent it to Herder,
though he was not entirely satisfied with it. At about the
same time he started work again on *Egmont*, which he
finished in 1788. He wrote three scenes of his *Faust : Forest and Cavern, The Witch's Kitchen* and *Walpugiesnacht*.
As for *Meister*, how could this expression of " becoming "
progress in the world of " being " in which Goethe had become another man? It stayed as it was.

Goethe returned to Weimar on June 18, 1788, cured for
life of his Italian " fever." But was he not renouncing an
even wider horizon by this act? Would the same impulse
that had driven him to Rome and to Sicily not lead him
to new countries? He was already planning another journey to Italy, and in March, 1790, he went to Venice to
await the duchess Anna-Amelia, whom he was to bring
back to Weimar. His short stay in the city of the Doges
disappointed him, and the *Venetianische Epigramme* are
as strong in criticism as the *Römische Elegien* are in praise.
In Venice he was homesick for Weimar, for Christiane
Vulpius and his son August, born in December 1789. Perhaps there is more than a formal appearance of submission in this sentence written to the duke dated May 27-29,
1787: " I have seen such a great and beautiful part of the
world; the result is that I now wish to live solely with you

and in your country." He had found his way and his law as a man, as a poet and as a man of science; he had no need to annex the outside world, for he had to busy himself with the work for which he finally felt ready. He could do this more easily in the solitude of Weimar.

Chapter 4

After the Italian journey
(1788-1794)

When he came back from Italy, Goethe no doubt believed
that a new era was dawning for him and for his work.
For himself, he was no longer to be the minister, but simply
the first subject of his duke; he was to rearrange his relationship with him and with Baroness von Stein. He foresaw
neither the French Revolution, which would take him into
Champagne and to Mainz, nor the eruption into his life
of Christiane Vulpius. For his work, of which he was preparing a collected edition, the first four volumes had appeared in 1787, the fifth in 1788, but there was a delay over
the remainder explained in his letter of August 11, 1787,
in which he asked the duke's permission for an extension
of his stay. Egmont was finished, and with Tasso and Faust,
he was coming to the end of " his first (or in fact, his second) period as a writer." At the same time he was going
to finish the " little things " which were to fill volumes five,
six and seven, and on his return he was to assemble the
eighth. He would then be free to think " of something
new " and of Meister. Reviewing his earlier writings was
very useful for him. He thus undertook a " recapitulation
of his life and of his work " which helped him to know

himself by obliging him to compare " his new style with
the earlier " (the classical manner of *Iphigenie* with the
" Sturm-und-Drang " manner), and to put into execution
what were at the moment only plans. If we consider this
letter together with others in which he expresses his intention to complete his formation and *Meister* by his fortieth
year, we realize that he hoped, in 1789, to have reached
the end of a period and to have begun a new stage of his
literary career, probably with *Meister*, which was still a
theatrical novel. The eighth volume appeared in 1789 and
the sixth (with *Torquato Tasso*) and the seventh in 1790,
but the latter contains a Faust which is only the *Fragment*,
Urfaust, augmented by the scenes written in Italy, com-
prising 2,133 lines in all. *Meister* was far from complete.
It seems that from the age of forty to forty-five, Goethe did
not fully profit from all the experiences of his Italian journey, but had to await the friendship of Schiller before entering his third period. The years 1789-1794 seem to
have been years of marking time, a pause rather than a
period of expansion and progress.

By now Goethe felt like a stranger in Weimar. He recalled the lines of Ovid:

> Cum subit illius tristissima noctis imago,
> Quae mihi supremum tempus in urbe fuit.[1]

His letters of this period are colorless and lacking in interest. It seems that life had suddenly lost meaning for him.
But as he had often written that he would offer his friends
the benefits of his experience, he tried to force his new self
back into the old frame. Although he was no longer Karl-
August's minister, but retained control only of the arts and
the theatre, he did remain his friend and adviser. But he

---

[1] It was in a letter of December 27, 1788, to Herder then in Rome,
that Goethe evoked, in Ovid's words (Elegies I, 3) his last night there,
which was infinitely sad.

broke with Charlotte von Stein the day that Christiane Vulpius entered his life.

She was the daughter of an employee of the Weimar records office. When her father died in 1786, she had been forced to take a job in an artificial-flower factory where Goethe had noticed her. He met her on July 12, 1788, in the course of a walk, which she interrupted with a petition on behalf of her brother who was then out of work. She was twenty-three years old, small, plump and fresh, with that peasant charm which so pleased the poet. He installed her in his house, to the scandal of Weimar society which laughed at the Privy Councillor and his little " Mamsell." He also provoked the great resentment of Baroness von Stein, who saw herself ousted and insisted that the poet choose between herself and Christiane. He answered with two very dignified letters severing their relationship. Whereas previously he had recognized her right to demand anything, he could not now permit this jealousy, which confirms our belief that she had indeed given herself to him and could not endure his preference for a low-born uneducated girl, endowed with youth and provocative prettiness. Baroness von Stein, in her desire for revenge, even wrote a play called *Dido* in which she lampooned him. Her weakness is perhaps excusable if one considers the life in store for this woman of forty-six, condemned to live outside the sphere of the genius whom she had inspired, never again to be more than one friend among many.

Such a liaison is surprising. Goethe, who had always defended his freedom, who had deserted Friederike and broken with Lili Schönemann, attached himself to a woman incapable of understanding him, and made her his life companion. One might explain it as a desire for a comfortable household, and this motive may have played its part for Christiane was a good housekeeper. Yet we think that the true motive was different and belongs essentially, as it should, to the domain of love. From 1775 to 1786 Goethe had lived through a great love with Charlotte von Stein in which they had found spiritual union. In Italy he had known a purely physical love which produced an ecstatic union, and which revealed to him a new aspect of the human Eros. If Christiane had presented herself to him before his departure for Rome, would he have borne her off to his retreat? We believe not. She might have been the object of a passing fancy, but she would have been no match for her aristocratic rival, and could not have satisfied the needs which then tortured the poet. She would quickly have become an obstacle to be eliminated. She had the good luck to offer herself to him at a time when a long absence had kept him from a resentful Charlotte von Stein, when he had acquired a taste for easy conquest and voluptuous love, and when his inner resources allowed him to isolate himself in his own world and to ward off external intrusions. Thus he found himself alone, himself and his " bedroom treasure " (*Bettschatz*) who offered him little, but who at least did not bother him, who could renew for him those joys of Italy which he describes in his *Römische Elegien*, who was, under the gray skies of Weimar in the midst of a conventional society, the representative of the free, easy, passionate Italian life.

Another factor came into play later: on December 25, 1789, Christiane bore him a son, Julius August Walther, the first of five children and the only one to survive. Goethe was deeply grateful to her, and his letters reveal a tender solicitude for his son. His paternal feelings were aroused. Goethe was forty years old and a father; he knew that his life had changed in every direction. Through this son, Christiane became permanently involved in the poet's destiny. This ill-assorted household consisted of the union of two separate existences, rarely meeting except in the intimacy of love or over a cradle. It was a union of two beings who were happy apart, sending each other loving letters, but a union which none the less lasted until Christiane's

death in 1816. He married her in 1806 thus consecrating
a liaison which one can scarcely call an unqualified success.

We owe the twenty *Römische Elegien* to his love for
this " creature of nature." These poems were probably conceived in Italy and composed between the autumn of 1788
and the spring of 1790, and first bore the title *Erotica Ro-
mana* (1788); they could with equal justice have been called
Roman Idylls.[1] Their heroine may indeed bear the poetic
name Faustina, which recalls the amorous Italians, but she
is also called Christiane, and Goethe cleverly mingled past
and present. Three main themes appear in them: love,
Rome and the gods and heroes of the ancient world. Here
we no longer find the passion of youth, nor the spiritual
marriage of Weimar, but the ardent, exulting love of a man
still young, living without shadow of care in the happiness
of the moment, who has discovered the unselfconscious sensuality of the Ancients. This happiness is framed by the
Eternal City, with its churches and palaces, its historic past
and its legendary grandeur. Love and Rome enhance each
other. Mythical antiquity lives again, for what the poet fulfilled is truly a hero of old, worthy to appear before Jupiter.
As E. Trunz points out,[2] one need only compare the seventh elegy with the Leipzig poems, where Phoebus and
Luna already appear, to measure the distance traveled between the early anacreontism and the classicism of Weimar

For this first cycle of poems, Goethe adopted a composi-
tional form which may be called musical, for the themes
—one might already use the term " leitmotiv "—come
and go, are developed and combined as in a symphony.
Instead of a progression of action, we find the creation of
an ever-intensifying atmosphere of sensual intoxication and
spiritual joy. This musical character is happily combined

---

[1] For the question of ' elegy ' versus ' idyll ' consult Schiller's great
treatise, *On Naïve and Sentimental Poetry.*

[2] Hamburg edition, I, p. 491.

with a plastic grandeur which allots Goethe's elegies their place beside those of the classical world. Their great "poetic beauty" persuaded Schiller to publish them in his *Horen* in 1795.

The idyllic atmosphere of the *Römische Elegien* contrasts strangely with the political atmosphere in which Goethe was living. Hardly had he returned from Italy and established his life on a firm basis when the French Revolution broke out, the single great event in this short period, and the only one to find echoes in his work. Germany, as we know, was enthusiastic [1]: Klopstock, Herder, Fichte, Kant, Arndt, Johannes von Müller, Wieland, Stolberg, Kuebel, Görres and many others dreamed of a universal law code to be bestowed by the French rationalists, and entertained the idea of a German revolution. Goethe alone remained indifferent, if not actually hostile, and tried to build a wall around himself excluding everything but friendship, art and science. This attitude is surprising, and shows to what extent he had changed in fifteen years. At the time of "Sturm-und-Drang" he had opposed all power and authority, and had taken the part of the defeated in religion, history, society and morals. Had the French Revolution broken out fifteen years earlier, he would no doubt have been in the front rank of its admirers. As a minister, besides, he had many times pleaded the cause of the common people and the workers before his prince. But Weimar and the Italian journey had taught him respect for legitimate power, and for political and social organization. At the moment when he had finally overcome his own revolutionary tendencies, and, returning to the Werther problem, condemned Tasso in favor of Antonio; at the moment when he was reorganizing his life in terms of a new ideal of ethics and aesthetics, when he was himself becoming a

---

[1] See J. Droz, *L'Allemagne et la Révolution française*. (Presses universitaires de France, 1940, 500 pages).

bourgeois by the side of Christiane; this was the moment
the outside world chose to threaten his peace, to destroy his
balance by offering him the spectacle of a revolution in
accordance with the desires and principles of his youth.

His first reaction was to ignore this event which he later
considered " the most terrible of all." In his letters of 1789
it is not mentioned; yet from 1790 onwards, references
to events in France do appear. In 1792, he was unwillingly
swept up in the suite of Karl-August in the army invading
France, and in 1793 he was present, for the same reason,
at the siege of Mayence. He was thus an involuntary witness and will give his account thirty years later in the
Campagne in Frankreich and *Belagerung von Mainz*. He
was in no sense a frantic patriot or an ardent warrior.
The letters of this period are full of regrets and a desire to return to his home and normal life as soon as possible. There
remain two famous sayings from these campaigns: that of
Valmy, perhaps pronounced only afterwards, " From this
place and from this day dates a new era in the history of
the world, and you will be able to say: ' I was there,' "
and that of Mayence, often misinterpreted, " What would
you have me say? I am made that way. I would rather
commit an injustice than put up with disorder." But these
revolutionary events, in which he found himself involved
against his will, were too distant from his inner being and
too close to his surface ego to inspire important works.
Reise der Söhne Magaprazons (1792), *Der Burgergeneral*
(1793), *Die Aufgeregten* (1794), *Das Mädchen von Ober-
kirch* (1794) and even the *Unterhaltungen deutscher Ausgewanderten* (1794-1795) are weak, although the last work
at least gives us a foretaste of *Hermann and Dorothea*. In
fact, he continued to struggle for many years against the
" revolutionary nightmare," as he called it to Zelter four
years before his death, and we shall have to return to the
question to define the position finally adopted by Goethe
about the year 1800.

The Revolution not only failed to inspire Goethe to great works, but it actually prevented his working. This five-year period was unproductive. If one oxcepts the *Römische Elegien, Torquato Tasso* and *Meister,* to which Goethe returned in 1790 and completed only in 1796, we are left with little beyond *Reineke Fuchs,* an animal epic in hexa-meters, which is a satire on society and an exercise in ver-sification. But for those who are studying the poet's evo-lution towards classicism, the essay *The Simple Imitation of Nature, Manner and Style,* published in 1786 in Wie-land's *German Mercury* is of particular interest.

At the period of " Sturm-und-Drang " Goethe had taken his stand on a " characteristic " naturalism. He wanted to depict reality in its most individualized aspects and to make it seem real. Yet he opposed the theorists who did not recognize the fundamental difference between nature and art. In the *Learned Annals of Frankfurt* of December 18, 1772, he attacked Sulzer, who, in a recent volume on *The Fine Arts considered in their Origins, their True Na-ture and their Best Application,* had declared that the prin-ciple of the imitation of nature should be replaced by the embellishment of nature. The young Goethe disputed this, and thus continued his argument:

> What we see in nature is power; power devors; nothing present, nothing past, a thousand seeds trodden underfoot, a thousand seeds germinating every moment, grandeur and importance, infinite va-riety, beauty and ugliness, good and evil, all exist side by side with equal rights. And art is precisely the opposite; it springs from the efforts of the individual to maintain himself against the destructive force of the mass.

Thus in 1772 he assigned to art a mission of salvation which raises it above nature. We can discover in such an attitude one of the sources of his future classicism.

Numerous factors determine his evolution: Weimar, the Italian journey, the discovery of the archetypal plant and the anatomical study of the human body, his introduction

9. *Goethe, ca. 1792 (Watercolor by J. H. Meyer)*

to perspective and his efforts in art, the society of K. Ph. Moritz, H. Meyer, H. G. von Humboldt, Körner and Schiller, books on aesthetics. His essay of 1789 is the first landmark in this evolution. The artist begins by simple imitation of nature, then, tired of complete description, " he invents a manner (*Weise*), he creates his own idiom " sacrificing detail to the general impression; if the first process would suffice for a still life, this second one would be suitable for a landscape. The artist will finally be able to rise to stylized representation, provided he has a precise and profound knowledge of things, can encompass the progression of phenomena (*Gestalten*) with a sure eye, and place side by side the various characteristic forms he wishes to imitate. Goethe had discovered, as Otto Harnack points out, that all the forms of organic nature are progressions: each stems from an archetype, whose fundamental characteristics are revealed in each of its individual manifestations. By collecting together what they have in common, by separating the ways in which they differ, the artist will be able to arrange particular objects under general concepts, and will be worthy to cross the threshold of the sanctuary of art. In 1789, therefore, Goethe was close to French classicism, which studied " the general," but he had also discovered the " *Urpflanze* " and, as a scientist even in his conceptions of aesthetics, he sought the typical. We noted in *Torquato Tasso* that at least two of the characters can be considered as " types "; we shall see this " essential " character accentuated in *Hermann and Dorothea* and particularly in *Die natürliche Tochter*.

Scientific studies took on a new importance for him. First his botanical studies in 1790 inspired that extraordinary poem *Metamorphose der Pflanzen* and the *Versuch, die Metamorphose der Pflanzen zu erklaren* (1790) intended to show how the " *Urpflanze* " fulfills itself according to its own laws in innumberable different plants. Applying this concept to the animal kingdom, he discovered during a journey to Venice in 1790 that the cranium of the vertebrates is itself composed of vertebrae, a discovery which he published the same year in his *Versuch über die Gestalt der Tiere*. In 1791, he reported in *Beiträge zur Optik I*, the first results of the researches which were to lead to his theory of colors. Faithful to his great principle, he presented light and darkness as original opposites, whose conflict and union produced the progression of colors, they too being symbolic manifestations. Already he demonstrated the importance of the polarity of light and darkness, and asserted in conclusion that with these few experiments he had laid the foundation of all future research. G. Müller rightly emphasizes the interest of this scientific work and concludes that to the question asked by Faust, " Where shall I seize thee, infinite nature? " the poet found the answer in the fundamental forms of life's evolution revealed by symbolic cases. Goethe found these same forms in himself and made them the measure of his activity. Despite outside events, Goethe still published his *Beiträge zur Optik II* in 1792, as well as the *Essay on a general Method of Comparison*. In 1793 he wrote *Experience as the Mediator between Object and Subject* and in 1794 the *Considerations on Morphology*. Finally, in 1795, he published a *Sketch for a General Introduction to Anatomy based on Osteology* and his *Lectures on the First Three Chapters of a General Introduction to Anatomy*.

In the course of this period from 1775 to 1794, apart from his activity as a minister, which added to his practical acumen, Goethe gained valuable experience in three ways. First, he experienced love in all its aspects. It is surprising that he succeeded in depicting Gretchen and Lotte so naturally at a time when his personal experience with women was still very limited. But he had not then emerged from the German " petite bourgeoisie," and one has only to compare these heroines with Iphigenie or the princess in *Torquato Tasso* to realize that their creator was no longer the

same man. In the meantime he had met Baroness von
Stein, and knew what the love of two superior souls could
mean. Again, his Italian mistresses and Christiane Vulpius taught him to know and desire sensual love. Experience in love was to become a part of his past. Eros had
played a fruitful role in his life. It would undoubtedly
intervene again, but those destined to take their place in
the gallery of women loved by Goethe would be no more
than variants of types known already.

In the second place, Italy, which had haunted him since
childhood, was also behind him now, and with it the dream
of ancient Greece, which he no longer studied in Homer,
Aeschylus or Pindar, but saw in its Italian manifestation
as a poet who set direct contemplation above reflection.
It cannot be too often repeated that the best of the Germans
have a higher ambition than the imitation of Greek antiquity; they dream of grafting the German genius onto
the Greek. They have done it, to employ Neitzsche's convenient and eloquent expression, both in the Apollonian
and the Dionysian fields. In the latter the greatest name
is Hölderlin, in the former it is Goethe, whose categorical
imperative, " Let each be a Grecian in his own way, but
let him be one! " became a dogma for many poets.

Finally, the poet continued to be a scientist, not in a
dilettante sense, but as a savant, a seeker after truth. In
no writer can we observe so close a link between poetry
and science, because for him there were no strict divisions
of knowledge but rather a fundamental cosmic unity. He
now sought truth in a reality which was no longer the manifestation of an omnipresent God, but a diversity of phenomena with a common foundation, whose origin lay in
the idea of which they were the incarnation. It fell to the
savant to formulate this conception, and remained for the
poet to celebrate it.

He who aspired to raise ever higher " the pyramid of
his existence " had reached a summit where man, poet and

savant converged under three different but equally valuable aspects, inseparable from the monadic Goethe, or, to use his own terms, from the entelechy which bears this name. And yet, in the year 1794 was he not in danger? Was there no risk that he would allow himself to become submerged in the voluptuousness of an exclusively sensual love? Did he not experience difficulty in persevering to the end with works like *Faust*, begun twenty years before, while continuing to hope for the sudden flowering of a greater *Werther*? These scientific studies, which seem to have absorbed him completely and which formed the bulk of his current publications, threatened to turn him from his vocation as an artist and a poet. The fact that Goethe was isolated at Weimar magnified the danger. The complete edition of his works found few buyers, and he had no one of his stature to stimulate, guide or elevate him. Neither Herder, with whom his relations were becoming more and more strained, nor Baroness von Stein, now no more than a friend, could fill the void. At this moment, fate sent him Schiller.

Part III

Liberty within the law
1794-1709

Chapter 1

The friendship and alliance
of Goethe and Schiller

What would Goethe have been without Weimar? What
would Weimar have been without Goethe and the friendship
which bound him to Schiller? Let us try to imagine that
the meeting of these two great personalities had never oc-
curred! German literature, which benefited from so many
creative friendships, would lose its crown if despoiled of
its finest bloom, this Castor and Pollux of the literary fir-
mament. Schiller, for the last ten years completely absorbed in his " philosophy shop " and in history, would
perhaps never have found the road which led to *Wallenstein*
and to his third creative period. And Goethe? The general
public, too long misled by the epithets " Olympian " and
" The Sage of Weimar," was quite ready to accept him as
a poet crowned with laurels who dictates the tables of
the literary and artistic law to a docile court. The truth
was very different. There was no question of a natural and
welcome sovereignty, but rather of a " struggle for classical Weimar," and indeed, such is the justified title of a
clear and well-documented work by Albert Bettex.[1]

[1] A. Bettex, *Der Kampf um das klassische Weimar* (Niehans, Zurich,
1935).

When Goethe returned from Italy, he had changed to such a degree that his friends found him a stranger. His liaison with Christiane Vulpius estranged not only Baroness von Stein, but also Herder, and many other scandalized acquaintances. Even his friend Schiller, a rigid moralist, considered her a base-born concubine and hardly mentions her in his letters except to speak of " a woman of his household." Orthodox Christians, notably Fr. L. von Stolberg and Klopstock, could not submit to the authority of a man whom they considered a pagan. The rationalists, led by the famous Nicolai, whom Goethe had abused and conquered, were waiting for an opportunity for revenge. The irrationalists and the romantics, who were beginning to publish their works in the 1790's, although they took every advantage of his reflected glory were quick to reject and attack him. Finally, the Herder family, after a succession of incidents, cut themselves off from him completely, and even Karl-August began more and more to play the duke, and to withdraw his intimacy from the poet. Without Schiller, the Olympian would have been all but isolated on Olympus.

This solitude was dangerous. The poet had now entered a stable period of his life, which was not to be altered by any event of great importance. The period of his travels was over, and the researches which had led to so many discoveries were reduced to mere sorties into the world of science or bursts of introspection. The former threatened to distract him from literary creation, while the latter inclined him toward a retrospection which was to lead him, fifteen or twenty years later, to compile his memoirs. We have seen that each of his metamorphoses was provoked either by the influence of a human being, a Herder or a Baroness von Stein, or by an important event like his stay at Strassburg, his acclimatization to Weimar or his Italian journey. Each case represented an action of the outside world which gave his " daimôn " the necessary chance. By

installing himself permanently in Weimar, where he found
no new attractions and where he settled into an essentially
material and sensual family life, he would no longer have
felt any external impulsion to fulfill and express himself,
and Baroness von Stein. Therefore we must carefully examine the antecedents of their alliance, their meeting, their
common struggles, the effects of their friendship on their
work, and their efforts to elaborate a classical doctrine.

What a flash of lucidity we find in these words of Goethe
to Eckermann on March 24, 1829:

> The higher man rises, the more he is subject to the influence of
> demons; therefore let him not relax his watchfulness, lest his guiding
> will should go astray. It is thus that something of the demonic pre-
> sided over my meeting with Schiller; we might have been brought
> together (zusammengefürhrt) earlier or later; but that it should have
> come precisely at that period when I had my Italian journey behind
> me, and when Schiller was beginning to grow weary of his philoso-
> phical speculations, that is what was so important, and had the happiest
> consequences for both of us.

The poet fully realized that his " daimôn " had made a
timely use of " chance," choosing the moment when both
men had entered a decisive stage. It was also at the moment when both of them, admired for revolutionary work
which they had outgrown, found themselves isolated by
their very success, and were in danger of regarding each
other from a distance with sterile jealousy, and even of
abandoning their literary vocations. Lucien Herr [1] rightly
regards this extraordinary friendship as a drama, opening
in 1794, reaching its climax between 1798 and 1799 and
then gradually losing its passionate intensity, moving towards the sad dénouement at Schiller's death in 1805. This
drama, like *Iphigenie*, had a prehistory.

---

[1] *Correspondance entre Schiller et Goethe.* Plon, 1923, 4 vol. Fore-
word, p. vii.

Goethe's feelings for Schiller were simple; he felt like Corneille witnessing the triumph of Racine and sensing his own dethronement. At a time when he had already begun to move towards classicism, he found the whole of Germany inflamed by a play as revolutionary, and in his view as dangerous, as the *Brigands* (1781), then, after the succès d'estime of *Fisque's Plot*, by the even finer *Intrigue and Love* (1784). *Don Carlos*, itself, already classical in composition, still recalled the dramas of liberty for which he had set the example with *Götz*, but to which, with *Egmont*, he had bidden a final farewell. He was shocked and disturbed by the revolution which made the poet of the brigands a " French citizen " [1] and separates him even further from Goethe the minister and councillor. Thus, when begged by Dalberg to extend his friendship to Schiller he replied categorically: " Antipodal spirits cannot be set further apart from one another than a diameter of the terrestrial globe." [2] It is true that Goethe intervened in 1788 to secure him the chair of history at Jena University, but he was not enough of a philosopher to guess that Schiller's studies of Kant would lead him progressively towards an ideal of aesthetics very close to his own. In 1793 the treatise *On Grace and Dignity* astonished him again with sentences like this: " Animal formations themselves speak, their exterior revealing their interior. But here it is simply nature speaking, not liberty." Liberty was opposed to nature once again, whereas Goethe resolutely took nature's side.

Schiller's feelings up to 1794 were much more complex. As a young pupil at the *Karlsschule*, he had once witnessed the arrival there of the famous author of *Werther*; later, the fortunes of his errant life had led him from his native

---

[1] M. Baldensperger has shown that this news became known in Germany several years later.

[2] Quoted by Bielschowsky, *Goethe*, 11, 1. 110.

Swabia into Saxony, to Thuringia and even, on July 21, 1787, to Weimar, where everything reminded him of the traveller who was then in Italy. He was loved and admired, Schiller tells us, even more for his human qualities than for his literary works. He was the universal man, who put his whole being into each of his aspects. The following year, Schiller devoted himself to studies which aroused a deep admiration for Goethe. He compared his *Iphigenie* to Euripides', proclaimed Goethe's work superior, and said he considered it a model for the future. " Here the genius of a poet who needs fear comparison with none of the ancient tragedians, sustained by the progress of ethics and culture, and the less grim background of our times, has succeeded in wedding the noblest and the most delicate flowering of moral refinement to the finest bloom of poetry." To the beauty of the ancient form Schiller triumphantly opposed the finer humanity (*humanität*) of the new morality; above the " noble Greek " he set the superior humanity (*Menschheit*) " of the modern era." He already glimpsed that ideal of humanity which was to be the essential dogma of classicism.

The fact is that Schiller was no longer the man of his first plays, the representative of the Germany of " Sturm-und-Drang." When Goethe returned from Italy, having actually seen the art of Greek antiquity, Schiller, who knew only casts, had just begun to study it through books. In March, 1788, he composed his poem *The Gods of Greece*, which Goethe liked, although he rightly criticized its length. A letter to Kornerg, dated August 20, 1788, includes this significant passage: " I now read scarcely anything but Homer. In the two coming years I shall read no modern author. Each of them seems to run counter to my own feelings, while the ancients now give me true enjoyment. Besides, I have the greatest need of them in order to purify my own taste." He saw in Goethe the genius who had " written ancient poetry expressing new thoughts," the man who had achieved in himself the synthesis of Greek and German, the reincarnation of ancient perfection in a modern soul.

On September 6, 1788 (some say a day later), he at last met the great man at Rudolstadt. The Lengefeld family, (whose daughter Charlotte he was to marry on February 22, 1796), had ties of friendship with Baroness von Stein, and had high hopes of this meeting. Schiller found himself confirmed in his " great idea " of Goethe, but the latter, still full of Italian visions and preoccupied with the difficultes of re-adapting himself, did not make the slightest effort to meet him. In December, 1788, Goethe intervened to have him nominated at the University of Jena and encouraged him personally, as il foreseeing the need to install him and keep him in the vicinity of Weimar for a common task. Yet he continued to ignore him, to such an extent that Schiller, who was both under his sway and jealous of him, came to hate him for it. He dreamed of imitating him and winning his friendship, much as Goethe had formerly felt about Herder, but he could not bear to be so neglected. Thus he wrote on February 2, 1789, " I hate him... though I admire his spirit wholeheartedly, and have a great opinion of him... He has aroused in me a strange mixture of hatred and love," [1] and, on February 25, 1789, after acknowledging Goethe's pre-eminence in genius, in wealth of knowledge, in sureness of sensibility (*sichere Sinnlichkeit*), in artistic sense, he continued: " This man, this Goethe, stands in my way."

For another five years, though many circumstances brought them together, the two poets had no close relationship; yet, without knowing it, they were moving towards each other. In the decisive year, 1794, they corresponded with a view to collaboration on *Horen*, then they met personally at a scientific conference. That year, Schil-

[1] Quoted by Witkop, *Goethe*, pp. 244 et seq.

ler was preparing a great review, for which he could count on the help of Körner, Fichte and Humboldt. He could not afford to neglect the possibility of Goethe's collaboration, and appealed to him in a letter of June 15th in the name of a company (Gesellschaft) which had great esteem for him. Goethe doubtless took time to think it over, since he did not reply until the 24th, after several times rewriting his letter. But he was too isolated to refuse to enter into close relations with the best minds of his period. He felt the need for an exchange of ideas which would allow him to get on with some of his works which had reached a deadlock. He could not but approve the idea of such a review. He agreed " joyfully and wholeheartedly to become one of the company," and even expressed his desire for an early discussion to propose principles for the substance and form of the review. This conversation took place at Jena on July 20th and 21st; it was decisive.

The two poets met at a session of the " Society for the Study of Nature," founded in 1793, of which they were both honorary members. By chance they left the room together, and Schiller expressed his regret that so fragmentary a presentation of nature should make it uninteresting to the layman. Agreeably surprised by this remark, Goethe replied that the same was true for the man of science, and that another manner of presentation was possible, " not in its isolated elements, but active and alive in its impulse from the whole to the parts." He let himself be taken to Schiller's house, explained to him his ideas on the metamorphosis of plants, and himself drew a " symbolic plant." Schiller listened with the deepest interest, but objected that this was an idea not an " experience." [1] Goethe was astonished, and defended his " stubborn realism " against the philosophical arguments of his partner, without either of them scoring a decided advantage. When the conversation

---

[1] On this point consult Goethe, *Erste Bekannschaft mit Schiller.*

turned upon questions of aesthetics, however, they found themselves in complete agreement. This was an extraordinary meeting of two men, one of whom, so to speak, stepped down from the ideal, while the other raised himself from the real. It was a meeting on the plane of the Kantian idea, which one of them had thought out, the other seen. The conversation continued by letter, for it had set in motion a whole " mass of ideas " which had preoccupied Schiller for several years. He was inspired to write that extraordinary letter of August 23, 1794, in which, with true critical divination, he explained to Goethe his conception of his genius. Goethe, happy to find himself so well understood, did not hesitate to suggest, on August 27th, that they should work together as soon as they had defined their respective points of view.

Thus began a collaboration unique in literature. The evidence of it remains in a correspondence which Goethe made a particular point of publishing himself (1828-1829) to offer to the Germans and indeed to the world the gift of this " strange work " in which two friends—and what friends!—inspire one another by confiding to each other their ideas, their plans, their work. It is essential to the understanding of their mutual influence, and also to the understanding of German classicism and of the greatest literary period Germany has ever experienced.

One may be astonished at a friendship so intimate and fruitful between two such different minds, but it was precisely these differences which made it fruitful. It was an exceptional stroke of fortune for Schiller to have the friendship of a man who had so many advantages over him, and who could play for him the role that Herder played for Goethe a quarter of a century earlier. Goethe was also fortunate to meet at this particular time a man capable of helping him to keep moving forward. No doubt he could not, at the age of forty-five, receive from Schiller as much as he had absorbed from Herder; but he was to think and create in communion with a poet of the highest rank, whose philosophical development was much superior to his own, and whose still youthful activity was to give him new life, to lead him to produce more, and to take up again, and sometimes to modify, works which he had abandoned. Goethe expressed himself upon this common effort, sometimes contradicting himself. On December 3, 1824, he told Eckermann of his regret at having uselessly wasted precious time for the benefit of *Horen* and the *Musenalmanach*; the reason was that he wished to prevent his secretary from becoming the correspondent of an English newspaper. He contradicted his own assertion in his letter to Chr. L. Fr. Schultz on January 10, 1729. He recalled that period when " the spirit of Schiller was about to be revealed ": the public ignored the complete edition of his works, *Tasso*, and especially *Wilhelm Meister*. He thought only of Italy, and wished to return there in 1787. He concluded:

I really do not know what would become of me without Schiller's pressure... The friendship I had for him, the part I played in his poetic work, in his efforts and enterprises, held me back... Had he not been short of copy for *Horen* and the *Musenalmanach*, I would not have written the *Unterhaltungen der Ausgewanderten*, nor translated *Cellina*, I would not have composed the collection of *Ballads* and *Lieder* as they are found in the *Musenalmanach*, the *Elegien* would not have been printed, at least not then, *Xenien* would never have seen the light, and altogether many things would have been different.

This friendship signalled the end of Goethe's isolation. As his solitude became greater, he became ever more closely bound to Schiller, and they became fellow-warriors in *Xenien* (1796). Furthermore, beside the world of Weimar, in which Goethe had up to then lived and created, emerged a new and younger world, of Jena, which became the spiritual capital of Germany for several years. The two great men received visits from romantics like the two brothers Schlegel, Brentano and Tieck; from philosophers and thinkers like Fichte, Schelling, Hegel and the Humboldt brothers; from remarkable women such as Dorothea Veit, Karoline Schlegel, Karoline Wolzogen or Sophie Mereau, as well as from scientists, lawyers and theologians. Karl-August's ex-minister, the councillor who had broken with the court, was received with the greatest respect. He rediscovered the exuberance of his youth and renewed his creative powers. Schiller harried and pestered him to finish *Meister* and *Faust*; he forced ballads and poems from him. Then again, the aesthetical theorist, continuing the *Critique of Judgment* was dogged by theoretical problems. Fruitful discussion began—not the least of the riches of their correspondence—upon the various forms of poetry, on the relationship of the novel to the play, etc... Finally, what joy for both of them to be able to communicate plans and manuscripts to a friend whose criticism was enlightened and constructive! As a poetical work progressed it was submitted to a reader who was in a sense the contemporary of posterity, for like posterity he had the benefit of that " distance " which permits that objectivity denied to the creator.

Behrisch at Leipzig, Herder at Strassburg and Schiller at Weimar were three men who effectively intervened in Goethe's development: the first with his severe and caustic irony, the second with his immense knowledge and his flashes of intuition, the third with his philosophical views and his aesthetic conceptions. If the philosopher sometimes put Goethe on his guard, the poet contributed without any doubt to the rekindling of his creative fire. His influence can already be felt in *Wilhelm Meisters Lehrjahre*.

10. *Letter from Goethe to Schiller (December, 1804)*

Chapter 2

Wilhelm Meisters Lehrjahre

When he took the *Meister* manuscript with him to Italy and when he announced, in his letter of August 11, 1787, his intention of finishing the works of the second period of his life by his fortieth year, Goethe no doubt intended to take leave of his past and turn towards the future, but he did not succeed in doing so. The new creative period unfolded under the sign of Schiller, to whom part of *Meister*, like *Faust*, owes its completion. That is what we shall learn from a study of the composition of the new novel. It also resulted that the substance of the book itself was modified, and this will be the principal object of our study in the present chapter. Moreover, the poet was led to provide a link for a sequel, the *Wanderjahre*, the child of his productive old age, which we shall consider together with the second *Faust*.

After several false starts, especially at the beginning of 1791, Goethe finally got his novel back on its course, but it was only in 1794 that he actively set to work on it, less from taste, as he wrote to Herder in April or May, than to free himself by a sort of " pseudo-confession." In order to force himself to finish it, he even signed a contract in May with the publisher Unger. He regretted this very much, for he could not give his novel to *Horen*, for which Schiller begged his collaboration. The work progressed quickly enough for the first volume to appear in 1794 and the second at Easter, 1795. These two contain the six books of the *Sendung*, condensed into four. Schiller was one of the first to read them, and wrote a lengthy commentary. On February 1, 1795, Goethe told him that he had worked out the plan for the fifth and sixth parts, and on March 18, 1795, he announced that " impelled by a surprising instinct " he had begun the sixth part first (*The Confessions of a Beautiful Soul*). The fifth book was also finished in July, and the third volume appeared in the autumn of 1795. Then the work slowed down, for there remained only the dénouement. Yet the seventh book was finished in January, 1796, and the eighth at the end of June. When consulted, Schiller produced an abundant commentary on the work in his letters of early July. Goethe took note of his advice and revised the fourth volume, which appeared in October 1796.

It was, in fact, a new *Wilhelm Meister*, or rather, as Goethe wrote to Schiller on December 6, 1794, playing on the words " *Meister* " (master) and " *Schüler* " (pupil), it was a " *Wilhelm Schüler*." The author of *Götz*, like all the " *Stürmer*," had been smitten by a passion for the stage. There he had seen the perfect platform from which to preach justice and rebellion. He had hoped that Germany might one day have a national theatre, and his *Theatralische Sendung* had depicted the development of a great actor-author destined to create it. Since then Goethe had turned away from the theatre, and was hardly to return to it. He had cut himself off from his own youth, and his " dramatic double " had to become his human double; he had learned to recognize the necessity of law and submission to society. What mattered to the Weimar ex-minister was not the development of a theatrical innovator, but of a man and a social being. Besides, he was encouraged by a fundamental trend of Freemasonry. Max Wundt, the great expert on *Meister*, minimizes the masonic influence unduly; without this factor, it would be hard to understand a work in which the education of the hero is directed and controlled by the " Society of the Tower," a secret society with educational aims, as is found in so many novels of the period.

From then on the " Theaterroman " became a " Bildungsroman," and, together with *Iphigenie* and *Tasso,* a manual of human education. *Education in Humanity* might well be the title of a collection of the poet's classical works, all of which focus on the problem of the individual in the human community. The works of his youth, on the other hand, show us Titans in revolt against the community and against social obligations. *Iphigenie* already provided an example of a mediate, who, by the purity of her soul and by her faith in the gods, not only brings salvation to her family, but raises mankind towards a pure humanity. Next, *Tasso* put forward an ideal of renunciation and decorum, taught by women of noble heart; the individual, even though a genius, must bow before the laws of refined society, in which, not in himself nor even in God, he will find salvation. With *Meister*, Goethe went even further; Wilhelm is brought up by a secret society and trained for the part he is called upon to play in the community; his hero is merely an instrument in the service of a society which needs an elite. He travels, as in the *Sendung*, but the limits of his journey are no longer the troupe of strolling players and the established theatre, but life itself as it appears to the members of the " aristocracy of merit." He is thus brought into contact with a certain number of representative persons whom Goethe parades before him.

The first of these figures is the " beatiful soul," who appears only in the novel's sixth book, which Goethe began

as soon as he had condensed the *Theatralische Sendung.*
As he wrote to Schiller on March 18, 1795, he was at first
surprised to find that his book appeared to have been advanced by it, for this " religious book directs us towards
the future and towards the past, and, through the very
limitations it imposes, guides and leads us." In fact, the
fifth book prolongs the *Theatralische Sendung* in order
to show us Wilhelm Meister's failure. The " beautiful
soul " is the very antithesis of the players, of Philine, for
example; she lives only for " whatever is the highest." In
order to successfully detach his hero from the players
Goethe first had to immerse himself in a humanity of pure
religiosity, to prepare himself by a spiritual retreat to
enter into relations with the family of his " beautiful soul,"
all of whom represent an ideal of life. Besides, after his
Leipzig experience, Goethe had lived in the intimate circle
of Fraulein von Klettenberg, whose confessions he no doubt
used, before he met others who offered him an example
of the life of the mind, like Herder, or of the soul, like
Baroness von Stein.

In *Concerning Dignity and Grace* (1793) Schiller explains that one speaks of a " beautiful soul " when the
moral sense has made itself master of all man's feelings
(*Empfindungen*), to the point where one can without fear
entrust the direction of his will to his emotion (*Affect*),
without risk of finding oneself in conflict with its decisions.
Thus, in a " beautiful soul " it is the entire character which
is moral, not just certain of its actions. Here the " beautiful
soul " whose story constitutes a didactic novel within a
novel, is the Uncle's elder daughter. Physically frail but
spiritually superior, she has withdrawn from life in order
to turn to God. She lives entirely in the spirit, in a world
of peace and harmony and in tune with the universal
order: " I hardly remember order; nothing appears to me
in the form of a law; it is an inner force (*Trieb*) which
guides me, and always keeps me in the straight road;

I freely follow my disposition (*Gesinnungen*), and I know almost as little of constraint (*Einschränkung*) as of repentance." Is this ideal of the contemplative life, springing from pietist religiosity, what Goethe recommends to his hero? No. He admires it, but he invites Meister to turn away from the " beautiful soul," whom he makes a woman and an invalid. He permits Meister to know her only after her death, through confessions. The Uncle, though he respcted her sanctity, kept her apart from his nephews, for they were to be prepared for a life of action, not for contemplation. In the *Paralipomena* of 1793, where Goethe set down his list of characters, we find:

Wilhelm: an aesthetically ethical dream;
Lothario: an heroically active dream;
Emilie, Nathalie?: feminine reality, aesthetic, ethical, practical;
Julie, Therese?: pure domestic reality.

The " beautiful soul " does not appear there; her state is only an ideal, which may be capable of transfiguring the real, but is not itself a living reality.

One might suppose that beauty would offer Wilhelm Meister the ideal he sought, for the eighteenth century, preoccupied with aesthetics, made a cult of beauty. Even Schiller believed that beauty can elevate man to goodness. Goethe depicted an aesthetic humanity, represented by the Uncle, whom he made almost the same age as his niece, the " beautiful soul." A rich man, he left the service of the court, which did not suit him, and, having lost his wife and his son, he lives alone and for himself. He feels that his duty lies in " building up something which may serve as a model." He thus creates a marvellous setting for himself: he lives in a magnificent Italian villa, adorned with pictures and works of art, where he entertains to suit his pleasure. He feels that, while the " beautiful soul " has perhaps chosen the better part in seeking harmony with the Supreme Being (*das hochste Wesen*), we, the rest of humanity, have a duty to use the creative power in the depths of our being to achieve a coherent harmony with the different elements of the world around us. Furthermore, Goethe is in full agreement with Schiller when he makes the Uncle say that the man who aims at moral culture must at the same time develop the most delicate sensibility, " not to run the risk of falling from his high moral plane by giving way to the appeals of an unruly imagination, thus putting himself in peril of degrading his nobler nature by taking pleasure in tasteless trifles, if not worse." Wilhelm Meister understood the lesson well, and the Abbé, his adviser, gives his approval when he finds in art the true golden rule, the measure " by which and according to which our intimate selves are formed." Aesthetic education is thus a profound necessity, the means of raising man towards humanity. But it is not quite an ideal of an active life. It supposes great riches, employed for selfish ends, and, like the ideal of the " beautiful soul," implies renunciation of the responsibilities of family and communal life. Like the Helen episode in the second *Faust* it represents a transition, a stage on the road which leads to the good.

The " beautiful soul " and the Uncle represented the older generation and the end of the 18th century, with their disposition to build human life either on pietist mysticism or on educational aesthetics. Wilhelm Meister must now be brought in contact with the younger generation, turned towards active life, and set on the path towards his future ideal. The catalyst is Nathalie, the representative of moral humanity.

The Uncle has brought up this niece in an atmosphere of beauty, but he has kept her away from the influence of the " beautiful soul." She requires a pure activity, corresponding to her deep predisposition. She dedicates herself to others, she is all love, yet she knows nothing of love. When Meister asks: " Have you never loved? " she answers, " Never, or always." Like all her generation, she is passionately enthusiastic about education, and attaches the greatest value to rule: " There always remains in men's nature, or so it seems to me, a lacuna, which can only be filled by a clearly stated law." The Uncle says that she is happy, for " her nature demands nothing but what the world wishes and admires." Schiller, in his letter of July 3, 1796, insists that she should not be deprived of the description " fine soul " which is applied to her at the end of the novel, " for in fact Nathalie alone has a purely aesthetic nature." Does she then represent the ideal? For women perhaps, and Goethe intends her for Wilhelm Meister, who has mistakenly fallen in love with Therese; but not for men. She is one of those heroines of Goethe's who delight mankind; she is the lineal successor of the princess in Tasso; she is a manifestation of the Eternal Feminine, the incarnation of that ideal of femininity whose union with the masculine element creates, or re-creates, the complete being.

With these three characters, who represent partial prefigurations of the ideal being, Goethe prepares us for his conception of a valid life. A deeply and genuinely religious pagan, he does not accept the contemplative life, at least not for a man. But he considers it a necessary element and he would no doubt have agreed with Schleiermacher, who was to say a few years later: " Do nothing *through* religion but everything *with* religion." He would also certainly have said, " Do everything with beauty, in the light of beauty," for beauty is the visible and pleasing form of moral value. He could not imagine a disharmony between the beautiful and the good. Finally, the ex-" Stürmer," disciplined by Weimar and by Baroness von Stein and more and more distressed by the French Revolution, now proclaimed the necessity of law. He submitted to law as a value in the world of ethics and aesthetics, and perhaps also in the world of religion in the form of " reverence." Goethe thus advocated this triple preparation for the active world reserved for the human being, represented by Lothario and Therese.

Goethe did not place them upon as high a plane as Nathalie. He leads Meister to her only after introducing him to Lothario and Therese, who appear immediately after the " beautiful soul." He thus contrasts the religious calm of the *Confessions* with human activity, which is more tormented and less pure. The characters who now appear on the stage, particularly Jarno and the Abbé, the enlightened conscience of modern times, reflect Goethe's own evolution. While the characters of the first four books of the *Theatralische Sendung* were alive, real and concrete, these remain imaginative, typical, abstract; the first *were*, the second *signify*.[1]

Lothario is the " accomplished type of the superior man of action, in whom organizing ability and dominating power are allied to an exceptional gift for seduction and an ardent faculty of loving." [2] Passionate in love and in action, his mind broadened by travel, he is a liberal devoted to the cause of social justice, a patriot and a citizen of the world. He is no Utopian, and all acclaim him as leader. Therese, who is to become his wife, also owes her worth to an active disposition, but, conforming to the ideas expressed by Goethe and especially by Schiller in the *Lied von der Glocke*, while Lothario dreams of carrying out vast plans, she takes a narrower approach. She works in detail and finds pleasure in the ordered atmosphere of a proper household. She lacks culture, and offers no " problematical " characteristics. She is opposed to the demonic and romantic world of Mignon, the chimerical world of Wilhelm Meister, and even Nathalie's ethical world, for she regards morality simply as a necessary rule of life. She does not represent the " Eternal Feminine," only the feminine at its most human.

[1] Lichtenberger, *Wilhelm Meister* (Renaissance du Livre, p. 70).
[2] *Ibid.*, pp. 70-71.

Although he is not a Titan, the Wilhelm Meister of the *Theatralische Sendung* is still close to the " Sturm-und-Drang," and dreams of becoming a German Shakespeare. In the *Lehrjahre*, a didactic novel of a man of idealistic action, he becomes an example of humanity, both in art and in practical life, as an individual and as a member of society. We must pause to consider these two opposing principles.

Schiller has described Wilhelm Meister's evolution in a well-known formulation: " He passes from an empty and vague ideal to an active and precise existence, but without losing his idealizing energy in the transition " (to Goethe, July 8, 1796). This was not the opinion of the young romantics, however, who had followed the appearance of the work with passionate interest. Frederich Schlegel believed it to be one of the three chief events ol the century along with the French Revolution and the *Doctrine of Science*, published in 1794. But they were so disappointed by the hero's lapse into the reality of bourgeois life that Novalis described it as a " Candide aimed at poetry," and undertook to create the romantic sequel of the *Lehrjahre*. This was his *Heinrich von Ofterdingen*, unfortunately unfinished, in which he hoped to present in contrast a hero who rises from the shoemaker's shop to the sublime. In fact, *Meister* represents the synthesis of bourgeois reality and the artistic ideal; he does not become bourgeois, but returns to a practical life transfigured by beauty. Far from being a mistake, his time spent in the world of theatre was the occasion of an inner enrichment and the first stage in his ascent. To emphasize his progress, Goethe reintroduces Werner who has remained " petit bourgeois " and whom he contrasts with Meister, whose " realism " is " transfigured and ennobled " (Schiller to Goethe, July 3, 1796). Art, which is no longer the hero's exclusive aim, has ceased to be a world outside reality: it becomes a part of him and is incorporated into life, and especially into

the life of an elite society that is organized like a work of
art and permeated with beauty. As Korff remarks,[1] far
from separating man from life, art brings him back in
touch with it and acquires a social function. But we must
recognize that the world governed by the laws of religion,
of aesthetics and of ethics, as portrayed in the last four
books, is paler and less attractive than the demonic world
of Mignon and the harpist or the sensual world of Philine.
This is already the superior and insipid world of Stifter's
Nachsommer. Yet by allowing the intervention of demonic
powers, or of sensual love, Goethe has preserved in the
Lehrjahre the mysterious background of the *Theatralische
Sendung*. Even in the classical world where law is sovereign,
he has preserved the role of irregularity and even of ab-
normality.

With this novel we reach the end of evolution which led
Goethe to place the community above the individual, and
to turn away from the theatre towards practical activity.
Now " man is happy only when his spontaneous efforts
set their own limitations "; when he finds his true vocation, implicitly renounces everything else, thus accepting
the limitation without which there can be no growth or
mastery (" in der Beschränkung zeigt sich erst der Meister "). Goethe expressed this idea in his Journal for 1778:
" A clearer sense of limitation, and, through this, of true
expansion." He recognized that:

> Man can recognize himself only in man
> And life alone can teach him what he is.
>
> *(Tasso).*

and that the human being is formed in society *(Tasso).*
Though the renunciation may be painful, the society which
imposes it on us for our own good will recompense us by
allowing us to share in its unity. Thus society becomes

[1] Korff, *Geist der Goethezeit*, II.

the measure of a man, giving him his sense of direction and his position. Jarno expresses this in an important passage:

> It is good that at his entry into the world a man should think much of himself, so that he should wish to acquire many advantages, that he should strive to make all things possible; but when his development has reached a certain stage, then it is well that he should learn to lose himself in a larger body, to live for others, and to forget himself in action in accordance with his duty. Then only will he learn to know himself, for it is action which brings us in contact with others.

When the *Lehrjahre* appeared, some readers, considering only their ideological content, considered them finished; was not Wilhelm Meister entrusted with his son's education? Was he not awarded a " certificate of apprenticeship " and told that the years of his education were ended? This was the opinion of Wilhelm von Humboldt, who admitted, however, that Wilhelm Meister was still inconsistent and had not yet attained his full development (to Goethe, November 24, 1796). Other readers clamored for the sequel, among them Goethe's mother, his circle of friends at Frankfurt, and also Schiller, who awaited the " *Meisterjahre* " (to Goethe, July 8, 1796). No doubt Goethe had this project in mind, for on July 12th he answered Schiller that he would gladly talk to him about it, that he already had " the idea and the will " and that he would leave " Verzahnungen " (which Lichtenberger translates " *pierres d'attente* "—stones of expectation) to suggest the sequel... A quarter of a century later this sequel appeared in the *Wanderjahre*.

Chapter 3

Goethe and the French Revolution

Goethe watched the French Revolution with anxiety. We must now examine how the poet, who prided himself on writing only " poems of circumstance," sought to free himself from the " revolutionary nightmare." For several years, from 1789 to 1802, he tried to do so, first with the power of his innate sense of balance which was to lead him to reject the romanticism of Beethoven, then with all the resources of his intellect, which sought to weigh all the evidence before rejecting it. Neglecting those works which remained unfinished or which are of minor interest, we will consider only *Hermann und Dorothea* and *Die natürliche Tochter*.[1]

Hermann und Dorothea magnificently illustrates the affirmation that Goethe, when he attains perfection, succeeds in combining experience, learning and imagination in a

---

[1] On the question of " Goethe and the French Revolution " a bibliography may be found in Droz's work, already cited. Consult also two articles by Mm. Leroux and Goldmann in *Études germaniques*, Nos. 14-15.

harmonious whole. In this case he himself invites us to seek the inspiration of the work in his life, for he wrote to his Zürich friend Frau Bäbe Schulthess, " I have, as always, used in it all the current coin (*laufenden Ertrag*) of my existence." His " campaigns," in France and Mainz had already shown him the horrors of war, and the pitiful exodus of the refugees. Yet such events affect the invader less than the invaded. On the other hand, from 1794 to 1796, it was the people of the Rhineland, Goethe's compatriots. who fled before the French armies. He wrote the *Unterhaltungen* and the famous *Märchen*, in which the giant may well represent the French Revolution. He learned only later that among the refugees were his mother and his former fiancée, Lili Schönemann, since become Baroness von Turkheim. Threatened with arrest by the revolutionaries, Lili's husband had fled into Germany in July, 1794, where he invited his wife to join him. She set off. disguised as a peasant with her five children, resisted the insolent advances of some soldiers near Saarbrücken, and succeeded in reaching the frontier, then Heidelberg, Frankfurt and finally Erlangen, where she remained with her whole family for a year. From there, through Countess Henrietta von Egloffstein, and in September, 1795, from Zürich, through Frau Bäbe Schulthess, she once again got in touch with Goethe, whom she regarded as the inspiration of her spiritual life. She sent the message that nothing could ever detract from the " pure imprint " which his attitude had left on her soul. Thus the poet learned that the rich Frankfurt banker's daughter had been forced to flee by the Revolution, and that her courage in adversity was as great as the affection she still felt for him. He recalled those months in 1775 when he had lived between his father's house and the girl's drawing room. The story supplied him with models: his father for the innkeeper, his mother for the " Frau Wirtin," and for Dorothea, Lili Schönemann with her first fiancé, Goethe himself.

Although these events were too personal to form the actual subject matter of the future work, they could enliven an anecdote which Goethe had certainly read in Jocking's *Vollkommene Emigrationsgeschichte*, concerning the protestant emigrants of Salzburg, who were driven from their town in 1732. The son of a rich citizen of Altmühl falls in love with a Salzburg girl, obtains his father's permission to marry her, but presents her to him in the guise of a servant. The result is an imbroglio which terminates in marriage. At the end of 1794, having just received the first news of Lili's flight, he undertook the dramatization of this Salzburg tale, then decided to treat it in an epic which would be more suitable to the subject, to his age and to his current aesthetic leanings. He quickly dropped it to finish *Meister*, and because of his diffidence before this Homeric enterprise. He had hardly finished his didactic novel when he returned to *Hermann and Dorothea*. He was impelled by two literary events which he emphasizes in the *Elegie*. The year 1795 witnessed the appearance of a second edition of Voss's *Louise*, a bourgeois epic which Goethe had admired since its publication in 1784, and also of the *Prolegomena ad Homerum*, in which Friedrich August Wolf showed that the Homeric epics were not the work of a single genius, but rather of a line of poets whom he called the Homerides. Goethe wrote to the Wolf on December 26, 1796:

Perhaps I shall soon be sending you... the advance notice of an epic poem (he is referring to the *Elegie*) in which I do not conceal all I owe to that conviction you have so deeply planted in me (festeingepragt). For a long time I had wanted to try my hand in this field, and I had always been daunted by the great idea of the unity and individuality of the Homeric poems; now that you attribute these magnificent works to a family there is less temerity in adventuring into a greater society, and following the trail which Voss has so well blazed with his *Louise*.

Relying on his knowledge to create a literary work out of the resources of his own experiences, Goethe undertook to write a bourgeois epic, in which he aimed " to separate from its dross in the epic crucible whatever is contained of pure humanity in a small German town, and at the same time to reflect in a little mirror the great movements and transformations being enacted on the world's vast stage " (to J. H. Meyer, December 5, 1796). He casts the living reality of a Rhineland town, troubled by revolutionary agitation, into a Homeric mold. From September 11-19, 1796, he composed two-thirds of the work at the rate of some hundred and fifty lines per day, as if, wrote the astonished Schiller, " he had only to shake the tree for the finest, heaviest, ripest fruits to fall " (to Körner, October 28, 1796). After a long interruption, he returned to the work in March 1797, and completed it on June 7th. It appeared in October of that year.

Hettner has delivered the following judgment on *Hermann und Dorothea*: " In the most striking manner the proof was given that, on the one hand, subjects borrowed from modern everyday life, sentimental in Schiller's sense of the word, and simple in their conception and treatment; and on the other, German life and a classical form, full of style, were not irreconcilable antagonists." [1] Hettner has taken a point of view which is not quite Goethe's, but his judgment shows that the poet succeeded in reconciling the simple and the sentimental, the idyllic and the dramatic, the individual and the typical, the German and the cosmopolitan, the modern ideal and the ancient form.

This work contains the simplicity of an idyll, or, according to Schiller, the peaceful atmosphere " of a nature purified and carried to its highest moral dignity," of an ideal of beauty applied to real life. It is the evocation of a patriarchal atmosphere and the natural life of which Werther had dreamed. Simple people, unconcerned with great

---

[1] Hettner, *Literaturgeschichte des achtzehnten Jahrhunderts III, 3, 2. Das Ideal der Humanität*, 1879, p. 231.

11. Goethe's country home, outside of Weimar

problems, live in an established order, work in the fields, the kitchen garden, and the stable. The model is the mother, attached to her house and her simple responsibilities, or Hermann, before his transformation by love. On November 14, 1823, Goethe said to Eckermann, with a touch of irony, that Schiller had worn himself out trying to free sentimental from naïve poetry, as if the former could exist without the naïve foundation from which it springs. Instead of being content with a naïve idyll in the manner of Voss, he also wanted to " parade before us the sad reflections of the period." He became a " sentimental " poet by " referring the object to an idea " (Schiller), by introducing a drama into the idyll, where the " *Urphänomen*," which is the Revolution, plays a part analogous to that of destiny in Greek tragedy. War interrupts the idyll, bringing to the little town a group of refugees, the last wave of a disturbance whose origin is Paris. It is chiefly due to this background that Goethe's work attains that epic grandeur which *Louise* lacks. This " sentimental " atmosphere is represented by Dorothea's first fiancé, whose enthusiasm for the Revolution leads him to Paris and death; by the girl herself, suited for the joys of domestic life and motherhood, who yet is forced to kill; and finally, to a certain extent, by Hermann, who is transformed by love.

In order to introduce the reader into the peace of the German home, Goethe has chosen the countryside of his childhood for the setting, in a welcoming inn not far from the protective barrier of the Rhine. There his heroes grow up into clearly characterized and differentiated individuals. At the same time, they represent human types: " the chemist," " the innkeeper," " the pastor," " the judge."

The poet, now at the height of his classicism—and we may say, of his hellenism—has, as it is so finely expressed in his *Zueignung*, decked truth in the veil of beauty, of Greek beauty. The division into nine cantos dedicated to the nine muses, and the invocation at the beginning of the

13.

ninth, the use of Greek meters, Homeric epithets and classical turns of phrase, and especially the serene objectivity and plastic value of the work bring it close to that ideal defined by Winckelmann as " noble simplicity and calm grandeur." Goethe was aware of this, for he told Eckermann on January 18, 1825, that it was almost the only one of his major works which he reread with pleasure and emotion, particularly in the Latin translation.

In *Hermann und Dorothea* Goethe had examined the problem of the Revolution indirectly, from the point of view of its consequences, in order to provide his village idyll with an historical setting. But he wished to treat it more thoroughly with a work that was to be a " receptacle " (*Gefäss*), into which he " would hope to put, with all becoming (*gazimend*) seriousness, all he had thought for so many years about the French Revolution." He had prepared himself by outlining the work, for at this period he was acquiring the habit of arranging the result of his reflections in the form of a scheme. In the *Tag-und Jahreshefte* of 1799 (edited in 1823) he indicates four " Gen," which K. Gaiser [1] interprets as an abbreviation of " Genus " or " General " and explains in terms of the remarks of Goethe's to Riemer on April 4, 1814. Youth alone, he declared, knows variety and specification, while age, on the contrary, knows only genus and family. Thus Titian finished by painting velvet only symbolically. As for himself, in *Meister* he was still depicting variety, but in *Die natürliche Tochter* (and in *Pandora*) " he has passed on to the general."

---

[1] *Goethes Übersichtsthema über die franz - Rev. in Aus Unterricht und Forschung*, I. Jg. 1929. Part 3 and pp. 97-103. By the same author consult also the article *Goethe und die Revolution* in the *Neue Jahrbucher für Wissenschaft und Jugendbildung*, February 1930, pp. 90 et seq.

These are the four " Gen " he had in mind:

— I Gen - Absolute despotism with no real leader. In the ramifications at the top. Fear of nothing. Intrigue and violence. Mania for enjoyment. Becomes degraded.

> To live according to one's will is common,
> The noble being tends towards the law.

— II Gen - Subordinate despotism. Fear of superiors. Multiplication of Lieutenancies. Rule of families. Mania for possession.
— III Gen - Realism of ownership. Landed property. Resultant pressure. Dawn of obscure situation. Fermentation from below. Blast of whistle from the lawyers. Ambitious soldiers. Exercise of brutality by the whole. Conflict.
— IV Gen - Dissolution of ties. Towards the last form. Masses exercise absolute power. Harry the hesitant. Crush resistance. Strike down what is great. Raise up what is base. To strike it down again.
— V Gen - Missing.

This scheme was no doubt conceived shortly after Bonaparte's nomination as First Consul on November 9, 1799, which led Goethe to think that the truly revolutionary phase of the French Revolution was past, and that the time had come to conclude a problem which had been torturing him for ten years. A few days later the *Mémoires de la princesse Stéphanie-Louise de Bourbon-Conti* came into his hands. There he read the account of a natural daughter of the Duchesse de Mazarin who was legitimized and made a princess by the king. On June 6, 1773, however, just before she was to have been presented at court, she was kidnapped by her governess and taken to Lons-le-Saunier, where, on January 18, 1774, she was married to a nonentity. Later she obtained her divorce. She never left France, and was prominent for her loyalty to the king during the revolutionary period. Yet despite her *Mémoires* she never achieved recognition. Let us add that she died in 1825, and that Goethe never met her. He at once made up his mind to use the story, but the work made no progress, doubtless because the element of personal experience and

feeling was lacking. On December 6-7 he laid the foundations of the work. Then he put it aside, took it up
again in 1801 and 1802 and then, inspired by *Wallenstein*,
conceived the plan of a trilogy. He wrote only the first part,
which was finished in the spring of 1803, and staged on
the second of April.

Eugenie, natural daughter of a duke who is uncle to
the king, is to be elevated to the rank of princess. Her
step-brother, inspired by jealousy orders his secretary,
whose fiancée is Eugenie's governess, to arrange her disap-
pearance, by murder if necessary. She is kidnapped, and
it is planned to transport her to a tropical island, where
heat and fever will cause her death. At the port of em-
barkation she is told that she can save herself on condition
that she marries a commoner and lives her life in obscurity.
At first she refuses, but it is in vain that she begs the
support of the mob, the governor or the abbess. A monk
then appears, who tells her of serious disturbances threatening the state. In order to be able to participate later
to help her king and her country, she accepts the hand
of the local judge. She lives in her rural home, awaiting
the day for action.

Goethe conceived this play as an introduction, leading
up to the threshold of the Revolution and providing its
"Prolegomena." It must be admitted that we do not find
the vast scope we might have expected, that it lacks the
necessary political and dramatic conflicts, that it fails to
present the masses with the same conviction that Schiller
did in most of his plays, for example in *Wallenstein's Camp*.
Nor would we find it substantially different even if Goethe
had completed his trilogy, for which he left some notes.
In the course of the second part Eugenie was to have left
her husband and become the leader of the revolutionaries
in order to get to the capital: there, she would have found
the aristocrats in prison, and succeeded in delaying their
execution. About the third part we have little information,

but it is characteristic, and hardly revolutionary, that an essential episode should have been provided by the discovery of a sonnet on the glory of the king, which Eugenie had written long before and hidden in a secret cupboard.

Goethe could not write a play about the Revolution because, though he had had some slight personal contacts with it, he had not intimately experienced it. His " conciliatory " nature led him to seek a compromise in every situation, which was impossible in this case because he was by temperment disposed towards a position opposed to the Revolution. But it would be a mistake to represent him as an aristocrat, an enemy of the people, or a reactionary clinging to established institutions; he protested with great vigor against such accusations in his conversation with Eckermann on January 4, 1824, in which he spoke of his *die Aufgeregten* as a " profession of political faith." Goethe, who had pitied the distress of the Apolda weavers, and, as a minister, proposed social reforms, could not but be sensitive to the sufferings of the oppressed classes. He created the character of the countess who returns from Paris convinced " that there is certainly need to exercise pressure on the people, but not oppression," and that revolutionary uprisings by the lower order are a result of the injustices of the great; she was determined to act in accordance with these views, even at the risk of being treated as a democrat. He thought at the time, and he certainly still thought in 1824, that " a great revolution is never the fault of the people, but of the government " which has failed to be just and vigilant, and to improve the lot of the unfortunate. Goethe likewise refused to be considered a reactionary; he had too strong a sense of evolution not to realize that everything must move forward, that an institution perfect now may in fifty years time have become odious. It thus follows that without imitating events abroad, where the conditions of life and the same stage of development will not be the same, a country should reform according to its needs, and evolve in conformity with its laws.

The idea of law guided Goethe in politics as well as in art and life. " It is true," he declared to Eckermann, " that I could be no friend to the French Revolution, for its horrors were too near at hand, provoking my indignation every day and every hour, whereas its beneficient consequences could not then be foreseen." He was opposed to all sudden, arbitrary change, which does not spring from the gradual and necessary transformation of a living organism; he did not, however, fail to recognize, for instance in the episode of the fire, in *Hermann und Dorothea*, that destruction and annihilation, revolution and chaos may give birth to a better humanity. Just as he forswore Vulcanism in favor of Plutonism in considering the problem of life, in the realm of politics he preferred evolution to revolution. The metamorphosis of the political and social order should be, like any other, a slow progression, a continuous ascent. Thus we find a unity of thought, pronouncing itself in favor of enlightened authority which alone is capable of securing the good of the people.

From the aesthetic point of view *Die natürliche Tochter* holds enough interest to make us regret that it was treated with disdain! It cannot compare with *Iphigenie* or *Torquato Tasso*, and yet it is related to these two plays in construction, especially in the use of iambic pentameters. It aroused both praise and criticism; if one recalls that it was produced within a fortnight of *Messina's Fiancée*, one may consider Herder's remark, contrasting this " silverpoint sketch " with Schiller's powerful painting, as estimable praise. Particularly interesting is the evolution which it reveals in Goethe's work from the typical to the symbolic. If we compare productions as various as *Wilhelm Meister, Hermann und Dorothea* and *Die natürliche Tochter* we find that in the novel, whose first version dates from 1777, the characters are all clearly defined individuals, except the

Uncle, the "beautiful soul" and the abbé, who all three date from the rewriting in 1790-1795. Conversely, in the Homeric epic, the two heroes have only a name; they are already human types, though still full of individual reality. The others, however, the inn-keeper and his wife, the chemist, the pastor, the judge, represent social categories or functions, genera, and are hardly characterized beyond descriptive epithets. Finally, in the play, only the heroine has a name, and she might equally well be called "the Well-Born," since etymology suggests it, and since she is the daughter of a duke and of a great lady. We do not know the names of any of the other characters; they are simply the king, the duke, the secretary, the governess, etc. They have a symbolic value, and represent human types deprived of their transitory, material aspects, We can say of them all, more, even, than of certain characters in *Meister*, that they do not exist, but represent something. In the course of a decade, Goethe's evolution accelerated. The years 1796-1797 reveal the equilibrium attained with *Hermann und Dorothea*, and we can understand that Goethe retained a marked preference for this work. It already contains a tendency to symbolism which, as it developed, upset this equilibrium, and marked the first sign of the weakening of his creative faculty. Would Goethe recover his youthfulness?

The French Revolution, which was almost the last eruption of the outside world into Goethe's life, led us beyond itself. Now we must return to that year 1797 which witnessed not only the appearance of *Hermann und Dorothea*, but also the development of Goethe's friendly collaboration with Schiller.

Chapter 4

From maturity to old age
(1797-1810)

It may seem arbitrary to select the period, in Goethe's life from 1797 to 1810, for it is more usual to make a break in 1805 at Schiller's death. In fact, the latter event had direct consequences in the life and work of the poet, who continued, for example, to work on *Faust* as if still following the advice of his departed friend. Similarly, he went on with his scientific work, and published his *Zu Farbenlehre* in 1810. He began *Helena* and *Achilleis* in about 1800; it was after 1805 when he undertook his last Greek work, *Pandora*. Finally, he proposed to write, as a sequel to the *Wanderjahre* those *Meisterjahre* for which Schiller had asked him, and within the framework of the *Wanderjahre* he was to write *Die Wahlverwantschaften*. After 1788 and his return to Weimar, a few years were needed to liquidate the past; similarly, after 1805 the acquired momentum carried Goethe on to 1810. The parallel between these two periods of transition is underlined by the fact that in 1806, as in 1787, he undertook the publication of his complete works in twelve volumes, just as in 1828, at the age of eighty, he was to undertake the definitive edition. Thus he felt that with his sixtieth, as with his fortieth year, his work was about to change direction. In fact, his old age did not begin until 1811; the years from 1797 to 1810 saw a continuation of his productive maturity.

In the course of these dozen years the poet's life was uneventful. At first he thought of a new Italian journey with his friend Meyer, who went on in advance. Delayed for various reasons, he finally set off on July 30th for Frankfurt, after burning most of the letters he had received since 1772 and making his will in favor of his son August and of Christiane (1797). But meanwhile, illness had forced Meyer to leave Italy and return home to the town of Staefa on the shores of Lake Zürich. Goethe stayed at Frankfurt from August 3rd-5th, where he made careful preparations for his journey. He reached Staefa by way of Heidelberg, Tübingen and Schaffhausen, and from there the two friends made long tours in Switzerland. He was tempted to await the spring of 1798 before going on to Italy, or perhaps to France, but Meyer wanted to return to Germany and Schiller urged him to bring Goethe back with him, hoping that he would attend to the completion of his work. Goethe was back in Weimar on November 20th, and he did not leave again except for short journeys, particularly to Jena, where the highly intellectual atmosphere attracted him. These journeys also allowed him to escape from Christiane and from her family, who invaded his house, disturbed his peace and interrupted his work.

Many people came to see him, and two French visitors deserve special mention.[1] The stormy Mme. de Staël, who stayed at Weimar from December 13, 1803 to March 1, 1804, brought him the homage of the French literary world. A few years later she published her book *De l'Allemagne*

---

[1] The story of these two visits is told in detail by J. M. Carré in his *Goethe* (pp. 200-205 and 220-228).

and informed France of a previously little known literature. On a different plane, the French armies occupied the whole area after the battle of Jena. Christiane intervened with courage and success, as did the Duchess Louise, who succeeded in saving the duchy. Goethe expressed his gratitude to Christiane by marrying her on October 19, 1806. Napoleon came himself, and sent for the author of *Werther*, which he had read seven times. It was the memorable meeting of two men born to understand and admire each other. As a result Goethe, like Wieland, received the Legion of Honor in 1808; he was appointed an officer in 1818.

The chief event was the death of Schiller in 1805, for with him the poet lost his noblest friend and most reliable counsellor of the period. He himself was ill, and his solitude became even more painful in the following years with the death of the Duchess Anna Amalia (1807) and of his mother (1808). If we recall that Klopstock and Herder had died in 1803 and Kant in 1804, it is natural that he began to feel that he was entering old age.

During this period of calm and almost sedentary life, Goethe's mind showed considerable activity. Freed now of administrative responsibilities and stimulated by Schiller, he devoted himself to the University of Jena of which he was in charge, to the organization of exhibitions (September 1799, to 1805) and of prizes intended to encourage the arts, and, especially, to the development of dramatic art. In 1798 he rebuilt the Weimar theatre; in 1803 he opened a school for the training of young actors of which he was the director and only professor; he strove to bring his artistic conceptions to the stage, even in the scenery; he took counsel with G. von Humboldt, who had seen the Parisian productions, and adapted Voltaire, Terence, Italian and Spanish authors.

It is with these efforts that we must link Goethe's endeavor to elaborate a " classical " doctrine, and to found, with Meyer's help, the review *Propyläen*, which lasted only from 1798 to 1800 when it ended in financial failure. The attempt was characteristic, and shows the extent to which Goethe had an educational vocation. Romanticism had been born, and during these same years, 1798-1800, *Athenäum*, the manifesto of the new school, was appearing. The public was not yet completely divorced from the naturalism of the " Sturm-und-Drang," but under the influence of the romantics it sought out the religious and nationalist elements, and became passionately interested in medieval Germany rather than in Ancient Greece. On all these points Goethe, who called the healthy classical, and the sickly romantic, found himself at odds with contemporary trends. He entered into battle against them, and sought to take the public with him. From this period date most of the works in which he elaborated his classical conceptions: the introduction to the *Propyläen*; his essays *On Laokoon* and *On the Truth and Probability of Works of Art* (the first volume of *Propyläen*; *Der Sammler und die Seinen* (volume two); *Winckelmann und sein Jahrhundert* (1804); *Philipp Hackert* (1811). The moment has come to define, with the help of these writings and Eckermann, the nature of Goethe's classicism and—we might say—of German classicism.

Almost at the end of his life, on December 25, 1825, Goethe expounded his aesthetic conceptions to Eckermann, who has transmitted this passage of capital importance:

> There are few people who possess the imagination (*Phantasie*) necessary to grasp the truth of reality; they prefer to lose themselves in strange lands, of which they have no clear idea, and which their fantasy (*Phantasie*) can paint for them in strange enough colors. But there are others who adhere severely to reality, and as they are entirely lacking in poetry, they hold to it too strictly.

It would be impossible to characterize the three contemporary schools more exactly: the romantic school, now in its decline, the realist school, in process of birth, and the classical school, of which Goethe was the last exponent. The poets of the first, endowed with sensibility and an untrammeled imagination, fled from reality and set off in quest of the little blue flower, the symbol of the Absolute. To Wilhelm Meister, who fell from the ideal to the real, Novalis opposed, in his *Heinrich von Ofterdingen*, a humble cobbler's son who wished to rise, after passing through many " strange lands and states," to heights where the laws of gravity no longer apply. In opposition to these dreamers who longed for the Absolute, the realists were men at grips with hard reality; they placed themselves at its service, in order to present it to the public as it is, without embroidering it with the metaphysical poetry of *Werther*, or even seeking to make it " characteristic." The romantics were in danger of losing themselves in the world of fantasy, and at the other extreme, the realists were in danger of becoming absorbed in the humdrum. Between these two tendencies there was room for the classicists, who were able to make nature and art collaborate on a basis of equality, and to create archetypes. Goethe explained his position to Eckermann on April 18, 1827.

" Beauty," he said, " is an original phenomenon, which is never manifested itself, but whose reflection can be seen in the thousand different expressions of the creative mind, as varied and diverse as nature herself." The latter cannot, indeed, want to create anything other than the beautiful. " Her intentions are always good, but the conditions are not " in which she is led to create. Thus the oak can be very beautiful, but let it grow in a thicket, in marshy ground, or on a windswept hilltop, and it will lack either proportion, or strength or height. This is where the artist intervenes. He has " a double relationship with nature; he is at once her master and her slave. He is her slave in the sense that, to be understood, he must work with terrestrial means; but also her master in so far as he submits these terrestrial means to his highest intentions, and makes them serve him." Thus he will borrow from the different oaks the elements of beauty they possess, and paint them faithfully as they are; of them he will compose an oak which is perfectly beautiful, which is not *real* but *true*; he will reconstruct the original oak as nature wished to create it, as his mind sees it. The result is that " a completed masterpiece is the work of the human mind, and in this sense, a work of nature also " [*Propyläen*, I, 1. *On the Truth and Probability of Works of Art* (1798)].

He must therefore distinguish natural truth, which is gradually degraded, from artistic truth, which is reality regenerated and restored to its original purity. After thus defining the problem in this article in *Propyläen*, Goethe added that the artist should by no means aim at a work of art which has the appearance of a work of nature. In the introduction to his review he contrasted them even more clearly: " The true artist, who is a legislator, aims at artistic truth, the lawless artist aims at natural reality; the former takes art to its highest plane, the latter to its lowest."

Here we see the ideas of polarity and enhancement (*Steigerung*) which play a vital part in Goethe's thought. The artist finds himself confronted with nature as a " treasure house of materials " (Scharzkammer der Stoffe). In choosing any subject, he removes it from nature; in fact, he creates it, by " implanting in it the highest values." Then he treats it in a threefold manner: intellectually, for he seeks out its internal laws and discovers the underlying motives; sensually, to make it accessible and agreeable to the senses; then mechanically, to give his work life and reality. Thus the artist improves it, and raises it above nature, which supplied it. He must " by competing with nature produce something spiritual and organic, and give to his work both a content and a form such that it appears at the same time natural and superior to nature." It will improve on nature just as truth will improve on reality, by raising it to a higher power. Bode writes: " Goethe, the opponent of reality, is, at the same time, the high priest of reality."

Similarly, Schiller wrote that art gives back to the Creator a nature more beautiful than it receives. And on September 14, 1797, he wrote to Goethe:

> Two things are needed to make a poet, an artist: that he should rise above reality and that he should remain within the limits of sense. Where these two conditions are fulfilled, we have art of aesthetic value. But with an unfriendly nature, the artist is only too prone to leave reality and sense as well to become idealist and even, if his reason lacks power, fantastic; or again, if, limited by his nature, he wishes and has to remain within the bounds of sense, he will at the same time willingly cling to reality, and will become, in the narrowest sense of the word, a realist or even, when totally devoid of imagination, servile and vulgar. In neither case have we aesthetics.

This passage is all the more remarkable in that Schiller, as we have seen, was descending from the ideal to the real, whereas Goethe was mounting from reality to the ideal. They met halfway in the domain of truth, which is also the sphere of beauty; it was there that their collaboration was to bear its fruit.

Goethe's theoretical activity undoubtedly hindered his artistic creativity. It is a striking fact that his artistic productions were most prolific particularly at the beginning and the end of the period we are studying. At the beginning he wrote *Wilhelm Meister, Hermann und Dorothea* and the Ballads of 1797—*Die Braut von Korinth, Der Gott und die Bajadere, Der Zauberlehrling*—while under the influence of Schiller, in which he developed the epic element at the expense of the dramatic, and the ideal at the expense of the lyrical. At the end of this period he finished the first *Faust*, planned the return of *Pandora*, began *Wilhelm Meisters Wanderjahre* and wrote *Die Wahlverwandtschaften*.

Goethe set *Faust* aside after his arrival at Weimar. There was nothing in common between the scientist, metaphysician of the *Urfaust* and the duke's minister, between Gretchen's lover and Baroness von Stein's. The poet was therefore reduced to publishing the *Fragment 1790* in Volume VII of his work, finishing it with a dash and the note " for this time," which gave grounds for hope of a sequel. In February 1788, Goethe drew up a new plan, and thought he had recovered the thread of his work; yet he did not return to it. He would perhaps never have done so had Schiller not asked him, on November 29, 1794, to send him the unpublished parts of this " Herculean Torso," and obtained from him, in the course of the year 1795, first the plan, then a promise of publication in *Horen*. Only in 1797 did Goethe get down to his work, printed or in manuscript. He divided the " disjecta membra " into a numbered scenario, and planned on June 23rd, and perhaps composed on the 24th, the famous *Zueignung*. His Swiss journey interrupted the work, which he took up again in April 1798, and continued, irregularly enough, until 1801. He already had a second part in mind, and wrote the *Helene* episode, which he had conceived as early as 1797. Schiller, who had never ceased to urge him on, was in despair. Goethe could be stimulated only by the necessity to produce a complete *Faust* for the projected edition. He finished it in 1805 and published it in 1808.

If Schiller could have seen the completion even of the first part, he would certainly have rejoiced, not only at having made a contribution by his friendly pressure, but even more at having led Goethe to develop its ideological content. In his conversation with Eckermann on May 6, 1827, the poet denied having intended to develop an idea, and the most he would admit was that he had led his hero " from heaven to hell by way of the earth." Yet he did take a definite attitude, and in a work reminiscent of Dante, fixed the destiny of man between God and the

12. Goethe at the age of fifty (Portrait by Frederich Bury)

Devil. The *Urfaust* gave us the confession of a young man
who questioned science but had no doubts about love, of
a Titanic " Stürmer," athirst for knowledge and delight.
The hero now is no longer an individual representing his
period, but the typical representative and sorrowful witness
of a humanity which gropes through the darkness towards
its destiny. He has become the stake in a battle between
God and the Devil; the mouthpiece of the one, he bears
the sufferings of the other, who does not believe that any
man alone can resist him, and who finds refined pleasure
in destroying the best " servant " of the omnipotent Father.
Thus Goethe has raised his work to the metaphysical plane,
where the struggle unfolds between good and evil, between
divine light and the darkness of hell. On the human plane,
the debate and wager between Mephistopheles and Faust
corresponds to this conflict, presented in the " prologue to
heaven." Faust, while superior to all other men, has yet
not understood the aim of human life, but wishes to acquire
the highest human stature, and is already assuming a
symbolic character. Science and love, in terms of Christianity, are merely temptations; the first leads to magic, the
second to the death of the guilty woman. Both are dangerous to the soul, but is there no redemption? Goethe has
not given the solution, he has not let his hero into the
" great world," but leaves him instead in the situation of
a criminal who has sacrificed a human life, as he himself
had sacrificed Friederike. However, he knows that though
" a man goes astray as long as he strives," this effort is
his law and his glory, and that God will lead the good
man out of the darkness and into the light.[1]

Despite Schiller's efforts, *Faust*, an essentially Germanic
work, made progress only by fits and starts, probably be-

[1] See Bianquis, *Faust, poème de la lumière*, in *Études germaniques*,
Nos. 14-15.

cause Goethe was distracted by the ancient world. Around 1800 his Hellenic cult became more and more imperious, reaching its climax with *Pandora* (1808). This, then, is the moment to examine the poet's Hellenism, which gave rise to his famous dictum: " Let every man be a Greek in his own way, but let him be one."

It would be wrong to think of Goethe as the prototype of the Hellenized German. In fact, before achieving the synthesis in *Faust*, he oscillated between the Nordic world, where nature is heavy and misty, where life is lonely and contemplative, where man yearns for the absolute, and where art is essentially musical; and the Mediterranean world of Nietzsche's dreams, where a sunny and luminous atmosphere favors a more extrovert existence, where men are under the spell of a smiling reality and the plastic beauty of shapes and objects. In his first letter, Schiller had written to Goethe these remarkably perceptive lines:

> Had you been born Greek, or even Italian, if from the cradle you had been surrounded by a smiling nature and idealized art, your way would have been much shorter, perhaps you might even have had no need to set out on it. You would have needed only to observe objects to perceive the necessary form, and your first efforts would have developed great style in you. But, as you were born a German, as your Grecian spirit was projected into this nordic world, there remained for you only this choice: either to become a Nordic artist yourself, of by the power of thought to supply to your imagination what reality withheld from it, so to speak, give birth to a Greece conceived in yourself (*von innen heraus*) by reason (August 23, 1794).

The very terms of this appraisal invite us to see in the poet's oscillations the spiritual progress of a German animated in turn by Germanic imagination and Greek reason.

Goethe grew up in an atmosphere impregnated with French influences, in a house decorated with Italian prints, in a town into which the occupation had brought a breath of seventeenth and eighteenth century France. At Leipzig he had learned from Oeser and Winckelmann. In the autumn

of 1769, and again on his return from Alsace, he visited
the collection of antiquities at Mannheim, and we know
that in the course of the same year, 1771, he read Riedesel's
Travels through Sicily and Greater Greece. The result of
this pre-classical training was the poem, *Der Wanderer*,
written at the latest in April, 1772, anda published in 1774.[1]
At Niederbronn, in the course of a ride from Strassburg to
Saarbrücken, Goethe felt himself " bathed in the spirit
of Antiquity, whose venerable ruins, remains of bas-reliefs
and inscriptions, capitals and shafts of columns, shone beneath my eyes in the farmyards, amid the mass of agricul-
tural implements." At Mannheim in 1771, he was in a
" forest of statues," which gave him a foretaste of the monu-
ments of antiquity, so that his faith in Nordic architecture
came, little by little, to be shaken. Thus in *Der Wanderer*,
he contrasts the art of a defunct civilization with nature
which is at once simple, fruitful and devouring; he conjures
up, among the ruins of ancient temples, a simple peasant
girl, with a child at her breast. He finishes with this prayer:

Guide now the course, O Nature
Of my foreigner's stumbling footsteps,
Which o'er the tombs
Of a sacred past
Are wandering.
Lead me to shelter, shield me from the north wind,
There where a grove of poplars catches the noonday sun!
And when, at evening, I seek out my home,
There, in my cabin lit
By its last rays,
Grant me, I pray thee, such a woman's welcome,
A child upon her arm.

Is there not, in this renunciation of the North, an ideal
of Winckelmann's transposed into practical life, the dream
of an existence of noble simplicity in the peaceful grandeur
of a Homeric countryside?

---

[1] See Wolff, *Goethes Gedichte*, pp. 120-127 (Text) and 491-503
(Commentary) and also E. Trunz, *Hamburger Ausgabe*, I, 434-435.

Goethe had already undertaken those Greek studies
which would lead from Homer to Pindar, from the bucolic
Wanderer to the outburst of *Wanderers Sturmlied*. His
knowledge of Greek was equal to his Latin, but we have
seen that, on Herder's advice, he had applied himself to a
study of the Greeks. He did not abandon Homer, and yet,
in the second part of *Werther* he relegates him to the background in favour of Ossian, and in favor of Aeschylus and
Pindar in his reading. From now on, two antique landscapes
live side by side in him and in his work: one is inspired
by Homer and Theocrites, the other is a Titanic landscape,
in which a Promethean race learns to love and defy the
Gods. Goethe, who derided Wieland's Alexandrian Hellenism in *Götter, Helden und Wieland* invents a genius strong
enough to seize the sacred fire of the gods or to create a
humanity that disdains it. The two conceptions are already
opposed according to the idea of polarity so dear to the
poet, and it is important to emphasize that they express
the Eternal Feminine and the Eternal Masculine. It is the
man, the " Wanderer," who journeys in quest of a goal
and finds either a " naïve " woman, capable of revealing
it to him, or a Titan, a projection of his inner impetus who
encourages him to revolt.

But how could Goethe persist in this conception of Hellenism, when he was so little inclined to tragedy that he
later proposed to continue Aeschylus's *Prometheus Bound*
in order to reconcile the Titan with the Gods? Had he not
already set Minerva, goddess of wisdom, at the rebel's side?
As he advanced towards the ideals of Weimar he inevitably approached a new conception, and his *Prosperine* was,
by the very choice of a female as heroine, the first milestone
on the road which led him from Prometheus to Iphigenie.

In 1780 Goethe wrote to Baroness von Stein that he was
reading the Greeks in order to cleanse and purify himself.
At that period he was veritably obsessed with the idea of
purity; he had just written *Iphigenie*, whose heroine re-

presents purity, truth and piety. He placed her in a landscape of sky and water, the temple and the sacred grove,
where she reigned supreme, an Appolonian landscape, dominated not so much by the statue of Diana as by the living
image of the priestess. No longer does a rebellious Titan
occupy the center of the stage, but the descendant of Tantalus whom the Gods condemned to eternal hell. This
woman was chosen to redeem the family of the Tantalides.
With her, Appolonian Hellenism, compounded of measure,
mastery and, already, renunciation, replaces Promethean
Hellenism, guilty of " Hubris " and immoderation. Goethe
envisioned her as the original type of the human being,
the " *Urmensch*," ideal and true, to which we should aspire.
He was now far from the heroes he had formerly dreamed
of, and he turned to Prosperine, Iphigenie, Nausicaa, and
then to Helen and Pandora, thus coming nearer to Racine.
He saw these characters across seventeen centuries of Christianity, across Raphael's St. Cecilia and St. Agatha, who
dictated his desire to give Iphigenie only speeches they too
might have spoken. He gave his Greek characters a modern
soul, imbued with the ideal of humanity which belongs to
German classicism.

The cult of Ancient Greece and his admiration for Winckelmann were still partially theoretical. His travels in
Italy and Sicily finally allowed Goethe to *see* with his own
eyes, if not Greece itself, at least a Mediterranean countryside which resembled it. The yearning which filled Mignon's song was at last appeased. The first result appears
in *Hermann und Dorothea* in which his Germanic heroes
are seen with Homeric simplicity. He then turned away
once more from his compatriots to depict purely Greek characters. Three works, all unfinished, date from 1797 to
1808: *Achilleis*, *Helene* and *Pandora*.

Achilleis was born of Goethe's ambition to be " the last
of the Homerides," but one would be tempted to call this
work the death of a tradition. Among the works to which

he was inspired by antiquity, this is the only one in which he was almost entirely objective. He was preoccupied, not with expressing himself, but with depicting the ancient world in the manner of Homer, trying to fill the gap between the *Iliad* and the *Odyssey*. Stimulated once again by Schiller, he completed the first canto on April 2, 1799; it was never continued and remains an academic exercise, sometimes brillant, sometimes mad, heavy-handed by sententious reflection. Taken all in all, it is the sterile product of a " stubborn Homerism."

Helene, an episode of 265 lines, was conceived in 1797 and composed in September, 1800. It answered a deep need of the poet and constituted what Charles Du Bos would have called a " *glaise d'attente*." Later resumed at the beginning of the third act, it became the keystone of the second *Faust*, where it represents the revelation of beauty. At the end of the Trojan War, Helen returns to her husband's home, not knowing whether she will be queen or prisoner, but desiring to purify it. She encounters one of the Phorkyades, who symbolize total ugliness in Act III, and hears him declare that " beauty and modesty never go hand in hand together." This episode seems to form the link between *Iphigenie* and *Pandora* and shows how much importance Goethe attached to the theme of the return, and to what extent the poet shared the tendency of German thinkers to imagine an evolution of the world in three stages. To the unity of the golden ages has succeeded the duality from which we suffer, and we must struggle to recapture a superior unity, of which our sufferings and our efforts will have made us worthy. Apollo sends Orestes to Tauris to " bring back the image of *the sister*," not the goddess Diana, but Iphigenie, the priestess; she is to have the privilege of purifying the ancestral home, and reigning in it as a Vestal. Menelaus orders Helen, who is guilty of failing to resist her Phrygian ravisher, to precede him to the royal palace, there to prepare tripods and receptacles, dry wood and clear spring water for a sacrifice. She wonders if she will be the victim. Will her beauty once more reign triumphant, or must she expiate her lack of modesty? Finally Pandora, the mediatrix between heaven and earth, also returns. As her name implies, she brings every gift to men, for she is at the same time beauty, like Helen, piety, like Iphigenie, and peace and security. In a scheme which he has left us, Goethe gives the following indications about her: beauty, piety, calm, sabbath, Moria (for this last expression, Lichtenberger adopts the interpretation of the majority of commentators: the New Jerusalem). For Goethe, " beauty is a manifestation of nature's secret laws, which without it would remain forever hidden from us " (*Sprüche* No. 197). It is thus alloyed with truth and goodness. He was also to discover the supreme natural laws, necessity and God, in great works of art. Pandora, the bearer of all gifts, appears as a synthesis of Iphigenie and Helen, even of all Greek heroines, in whom Goethe saw the original type of the Eternal Feminine. Ever since 1793 when he had launched the cry of rebellion with his *Prometheus*, he had awaited the return of Pandora; she came back to him in 1806.

At that date he evoked his heroine once more, assimilating Ulrich's mother, Baroness von Levetzow. In 1807 he planned the new work, destined for a review entitled *Prometheus* which Leo von Seekendorf and Stoll hoped to publish in Vienna. Finally on June 20, 1808, he sent Stoll *Pandora*, two fragments of which appeared in the review. The whole was not published until 1850.

In a countryside " in Poussin's grand manner " are confronted, on the one hand, the domain of Prometheus: caves, rocks and forest; on the other, that of his brother, Epimetheus: chalets, orchards and waters. The former is no longer the rebellious Titan, but the Laborious who reigns over the Useful, the blacksmiths and warriors, shepherds or ploughmen. He devotes his energy to the service of life and of power. Realistic and insensitive, he admires only action, and R. M. Meyer describes him as " a Philistine on a colossal and heroic scale." [1] Epimetheus is his living antithesis; meditative, in love with beauty, he is a useless dreamer who dreams away his life and suffers from the disharmony which exists between his visions of love and the harshness of reality. They both equally represent Goethe, who says " yes " to the active as to the contemplative life. In the words of Litchenberger, " The conversation between the two brothers is in fact a dialogue between the lobes of his brain." Pandora has already come down to the earth, but whereas, in the *Prometheus* of 1773, she had been the Titan's daughter, here she has become the wife of Epimetheus, and represents the appearance of the ideal to the first men, their first step towards that humanity which Goethe celebrated in *Iphigenie*. This union could not last, although we do not quite know why; perhaps because the spiritual ascent of man does not belong to the world of continuity. Pandora one day left Epimetheus, leaving him with *Epimeleia* (care), and taking *Elpore* (Hope) away with her. From this time onwards, Prometheus reigned alone, and, under his guidance, mankind turned its back on useless beauty to enter a period of labor and conquest. But Goethe continued to long for the day when Art and Science, Beauty and Power would be reunited, when the real would be tranfigured by the ideal: he awaited Pandora's return. This he foreshadowed in the love of Epimeleia and Phileros, Prometheus's son, who inherited his dynamic vigor but who is also linked to Epimetheus by his taste for beauty and desire for love. The two young people deserve happiness, for they are capable of renunciation and accept death. Is this not already Homunculus breaking himself on Galatea's chariot? Death does not want their sacrifice, for times have changed, and, with

[1] *Goethe*, p. 359.

the dawning of the new day, Eros announces the return of Pandora, who is to consecrate the young couple as the founders of a new era.

Pandora is not a drama but a great spectacle, where, in a series of living pictures of high artistic merit, Goethe has enshrined his master ideas as in a richly decorated vase. Gundolf, paying homage to this magnificent fragment but underestimating its poetic value, has no hesitation in recognizing it as a decorative poem of circumstance. It is, in fact, an opera libretto, the text of one of those future masterpieces of which Wagner dreamed, and we cannot imagine it without the accompaniment of choirs, music and dancing.

This device of scenic mythology permitted Goethe to use the ancient fable to express his hope for the future of mankind and of Germany. " Former centuries," he explained to Riemer on May 10, 1805, " sited their ideas in the intuitions of the imagination; ours sites them in concepts. In the old days the great visions of life were incarnated, given the features of Gods; today we make concepts of them." He made *Pandora* a symbolic work. whose characters are personified human types, bearers of eternal truths. Goethe himself in this sense bracketed it with *Die natürliche Tochter*, contrasting it with *Meister*. Gundolf sees it as the first poem in which Goethe represented " the human forces which determine his image of the world," and as the allegorical synthesis of *Faust* and of *Wilhelm Meister* considered as symbolic works. This is playing with words; *Pandora* is a synthetic work, but in the sense in which Schubarth conceived it when he asserted that it concentrates all the elements which the poet has dispersed in *Werther, Wilhelm Meister, Faust*, and even *Die Wahlverwandtschaften*. Goethe told Eckermann that Schubarth sometimes went a little too " deep," but that he was always " robust," and that with him everything was " weighty " (October 21, 1823). It is an esoteric work in which the smiths celebrate the four

elements, and a Grecian work by virtue of its cloak of
mythology. But the myth has been re-thought by a modern poet; it will always remain a favorite piece for the
" happy few."

With *Pandora* Goethe bids farewell to the Greek world,
which he was to evoke again only at the end of his life,
identifying it with the Germanic world in his second *Faust*.
He took leave of his maturity, renouncing all expansion to
turn to his inner resources. He returned to a theme of his
youth, the powerful personality in rebellion against the
Gods, and superimposed a theme which already belonged
to his old age: renunciation crowned with hope. Epimetheus was not to know the joy of holding the perfect beauty
of Pandora in his arms, but he saw his dreams realized in
the union of Phileros and Epimeleia. Thus we can understand the contemporaneity of *Pandora* and *Die Wahlverwandschaften.*

Chapter 5

Die Wahlverwandtschaften

While *Pandora* represents a synthesis of works and ideas dating back to the poet's youth, *Die Wahlverwandtschaften* [1] appears at the end of this third period as a manifestation of that " renewed puberty " which Goethe mentioned to Eckermann on March 11, 1828, and, from another angle, as the prelude to an old age of renunciation and meditation. A transitional work, it may be considered either as a product already bearing the marks of age, or as the love novel of a man whose heart is yet young and who is still reflecting on the problem of the relations between the sexes.

Die Wahlverwandtschaften is one of the " confessions " in which Goethe revealed himself most fully, not, indeed, in terms of his life, but of his intimate thoughts. Truth appears at the same time at its richest and at its most veiled. He himself preferred this work, to the point of considering it his best, if we are to believe Laube; and Odile, its heroine, always remained one of his favorite daughters. Yet he was

[1] Consult: A. Francois-Poncet, *Les affinités électives de Goethe*, 1910 and P. Stocklein, *Wege zum spaten Goethe*.

at the same time conscious that he had expressed himself enigmatically, for on August 16, 1809, he wrote to Zelter: "I am sure that the transparent yet opaque veil will not prevent your eye seeing within, to the form which in fact I intended to create." In order to make this veil even more opaque, he destroyed all the preliminary work, manuscripts, plans, rough drafts and copies which belong to *Die Wahlverwandtschaften*. This makes a study bearing on the origins, matter, structure, moral and style of the work even more necessary and more difficult.[1]

No doubt the first idea for this work dates from the spring of 1807, when Goethe was collecting "motifs," sketching out plots and planning the stories destined for *Wilhelm Meister Wanderjahre*. *Die Wahlverwandtschaften*, "conceived in the form of a short story" and intended, like *Pandora*, to express the sorrow of renunciation, naturally found its place in a work which was to bear the subtitle: *Die Entsangenden*. By May 1st he told whole passages of it to councillor Mayer as if he were reading from a book. He stated that the subject was too important, and too deeply rooted in him, for him to be able to bring it out easily, and also that, in spite of himself, the short story was growing into a novel. On May 29th he began to "schematize," and on the June 1st, to dictate. On July 30th he finished the work, or at least, as far as one can conjecture, all that concerns the action properly speaking: that is to say, the first part and the last seven chapters of the second. Then, starting in September, having allowed for sufficient distance, he "studied" his work, but he was not able to go on with it until April, 1809. He soon pressed on vigorously with the final revision, which was completed in July, and the novel appeared at the end of that year.

[1] Here we follow the introduction to our own translation of *Affinités électives* (Édit. Aubier).

Goethe was able to finish his novel—while *Pandora* and *Die natürliche Tochter* remained unfinished—and to write it rather quickly, because he had been carrying it within him for several years, nourishing and enriching it from his own substance, from his studies and his life. But this time, if one tries to classify or even to date the strate which compose the work, one discovers that the intellectual theme preceded the living experience, and that it was the latter which provoked the crystallization of the whole.

The original germ of *Die Wahlverwandtschaften*, as it was explained in a notice which appeared in August, 1809, in the *Morgenblatt für gebildete Stände*, was a chemical principle. Goethe told Riemer that he had discovered the idea, and even the title, in the work of the Swedish chemist Bergmann, *De attractionibus electivis*, translated in 1785 by Taber under the title *Die Wahlverwandtschaften*. He had probably read it in about 1798. He must also have read a similar work by Gehler, and at this time he was much occupied by scientific questions, particularly by electricity and magnetism. Furthermore, Schelling had taught him that chemical affinities are also subject to the fundamental law of universal attraction. On October 23, 1799, he wrote to Schiller that there is between the passions " a tender chemical affinity (*Verwandtschaft*), by virtue of which they attract and repel each other, combine and counteract each other, separate again and become reconstituted." From then on he was in possession of the idea of this chemical law, stated by Bergmann, upon which he grafted a Schellingian philosophy: if one puts with a body composed of the elements A and B two more elements, C and D, of which the first has affinities with B and the second with A, then the body AB will disintegrate, producing the two new combinations BC and AD. By putting human beings in the place of these bodies and elements, Goethe had the plot of his novel.

But Goethe could only create from experience, not, like

Schiller, from an idea. He was too used to living his work to be able to write without the support of the exterior world and of his own life. The world offered him numerous cases of romantic divorce, and many literary works, for instance Fr. Schlegel's *Lucinda* or Wieland's *Love and Friendship at the Test.* In his personal life, his recent union with Christiane (1806) provided the necessary climate for an apology for marriage, and in his repressed passion for young Minna Herzlieb, he found both the amorous atmosphere necessary for the creation of Odile and the wish to exalt renunciation once again. He now wanted to present a voluntary death, not a suicide such as Werther's, but an act of expiation and redemption. Yet we do not feel that this blaze of love aroused by the bookseller Fromann's adopted daughter. who inspired the *Sonette,* can explain the enigmatic sentence: "One cannot fail to recognize in this novel a deep sentimental wound, which, while healing, doubts if it will ever close a heart afraid to heal." But even without Minna Herzlieb, love and the "Eternal Feminine," incarnate in Odile, represent a superior world which Goethe contrasted with the social world, with Charlotte von Stein's world, thus creating a moral conflict between passion and duty, a tragic drama of conflict between the individual and society.

This is really a play, as Hofmannsthal points out in his *Conversations on Tasso.* More exactly, the work is composed of a love drama and a novel of the girl's education, which fills the first eleven chapters of the second part and was undoubtedly written in 1809. All the rest can easily be seen as a play in five acts or five episodes, to adopt the Greek terminology, whose composition is typical of the German theatre. The very numerous dialogues correspond to those of all plays, and scenic indications are not lacking. The first act gradually presents the limited number of characters who are to evolve within the framework of the castle: first Edward and Charlotte, then the Captain, who is destined to become element C. They decide to invite Odile, element D. At the end of the fifth chapter, as at the end of the exposition in *Andromaque*, we know the protagonists of the drama; the problem has been posed, and we have the presentiment that destiny must run its course. In fact, as soon as the girl arrives, the affinities begin to play their part. The two new pairs are constituted, the action being precipitated by a fête and the arrival of an unmarried couple. At the end of what we call the second act, in chapter eleven, we reach the first dramatic climax: Edward and Charlotte are united in love, the one thinking of Odile, the other of the Captain, and a child is conceived, who will be the fruit of a real " moral adultery." The dramatist is on his guard, rejects the simple solution of divorce followed by a double marriage, and devotes the third act to a " return." Charlotte, mistress of herself once more, struggles to stave off events, but Edward's exalted passion gives the action new life, and leads to a second climax. It seems impossible to delay the solution. Then, just as he once fled from Charlotte Buff, and for a time separated Werther from Lotte, the author sends both men away. First the Captain, and then Edward go off to the wars, thus postponing any decision. Calm seems to have returned to the castle, where the women remain by themselves. After some months, Edward returns and surprises Odile, out for a walk with Charlotte's son who was born in his absence, and he cries out his love for her. Delayed by him, she decides to cross the lake, and on her way accidentally drops the child who drowns. Charlotte agrees to a divorce, but Odile adamantly refuses and decides to return to her school. The play would end with this fourth act did not Edward impulsively go to the girl in the inn where she was to spend the night, and bring her back to the castle. There she lives among her friends, awaiting death which will come and deliver first her and then Edward. Is not death the tragic end of all great passions?

Here, as in *Iphigenie* or in *Tasso* or in classical French theatre, we find a "drama of the soul," where the action depends on the characters. We also find a "*Bildungsroman*," whose heroine is Odile. Commentators have criticized the "intermission" or "huge parenthesis" formed by the first eleven chapters of the second part, or they have tried to justify it from the point of view of aesthetics. After such serious vicissitudes it was necessary to relax the tension in order to emphasize the tragic dénouement; it was to be the dramatic author's "*retardierendes Moment*." It was also necessary to allow time for Charlotte's child to be born, and for Edward to return from the war, during which time Goethe did not want to leave the stage empty. In our view, these chapters hold more than an aesthetic interest.

First, they have a romantic value. We have discovered in *Die Wahlverwandtschaften* a drama, and we could do the same in many stories, for instance in G. Keller's famous *Romeo and Juliet in the Country*. But when the short story unintentionally became a novel, Goethe had to pad it out and reduce the speed of action proper to any short piece. He succeeded by introducing a whole world, that of his heroes, into a closed society. In this way he also highlighted the human worth of Odile, examining her prodigious growth and development.

Of the four characters, two, Charlotte and the Captain, do not evolve. Edward hardly changes; he is simply raised by love to a higher power. Thus it is necessary that the fourth, the pivot of the action, should be transformed. Let us try to imagine Odile, an innocent girl just arrived from boarding school, or tenderly in love and just deserted by her lover, faced with the dilemma forced upon her at the end of the novel! Powerless to solve it, carried away by a feeling at once too sudden and too strong, she could only submit to events instead of guiding them towards the necessary dénouement. She must ripen in order to become conscious of her nature and her duty. There may be yet

13. Goethe's wife (Portrait by Frederich Bury)

another reason. Goethe had provided the model for a " *Bildungsroman* " which most of the German novelists have followed. But it was always a man's education; a woman's had not been written and is still lacking, whether because authors have generally been men, or because feminine authors find it repugnant to detail their most intimate experience, particularly in the realm of love. Goethe, with his cult of the " Eternal Feminine," was bound to attempt to write, or at least to sketch, a girl's " *Bildungsroman.*"

He is full of tenderness for Odile, whom he has known from childhood; he follows her to her boarding school; he introduces her with affectionate care, seen from without by the headmistress, from within by a master enlightened by tender sensibility. She appears, already radiant but still innocent, at the moment when she is to enter the world of men. He confronts her with the domestic occupations to which she seems destined. Above all, he reveals love to her through this fascinating man, whom he has deliberately toned down, for it is a portrait of himself. Edward once gone, he makes himself her spiritual guide and he introduces other characters who initiate her in art and pedagogy, travellers who tell her of mysterious lands or explain her affinities with nature. He intervenes directly in her daily journal, which then only is she capable of keeping, and the " red thread " of passion seems to symbolize Goethe watching over his heroine, whom he dreamed of educating so that she should be both his spiritual daughter and the ideal mistress.

Die Wahlverwandtschaften thus seems to be a double work, which combines a classical drama and an educational novel. In each the same problem is posed, that of love and marriage.

It is the work of a " moralist " and is closely related to French works such as *La Princesse de Clèves* or *Strait is the Gate.* If Goethe chose marriage, it was as a microcosm, reflecting all the antagonisms which exist in the world, and

as a field of experience accessible to all. In 1821 he wrote
to Zuper that the subject of his book was furnished by
Christ's words about the man who covets another's wife.
It is certainly true that by refusing happiness bought at the
price of Edward's and Charlotte's divorce, Odile recognizes
the rights of the latter. Dare we deduce that Goethe was
proclaiming the sanctity of marriage, the foundation and
crown of all civilization? This is what Mittler, who is
thought to be Goethe's mouthpiece, proclaims. We think
not. The union of Edward and Charlotte was a youthful
folly committed at a time when they should have known
better. In fact, nature wished to create the two couples
bound by electric affinities: too impatient to wait, Edward
thwarted nature's will, and had to atone. In his younger
days, Goethe might have proposed the triangular household
of *Stella*, but in 1805 he had just rewritten the end. Now,
preferring injustice to disorder, redemptory suffering and
death to forbidden happiness, he bows before human law.
And that is where the tragedy of the work resides: having
come into conflict with the conjugal order established by
society, Odile, Goethe's beloved daughter, must give way
and renounce. But though her voluntary death can redeem
her soul, it does not solve the problem, for Edward dies,
the captain goes away, leaving Charlotte condemned to
grow old alone and unhappy. If traditional morals are
satisfied, Goethe is perhaps less so. He introduces an unmarried couple, the baroness and the count, whom he de-
picts as attractive as well as scandalous; the countess dies,
making way for a suitable marriage, bound as much by
true affinities as by the law.

Above the law, which is a prime necessity in our earthly
life but which is imperfect, Goethe splendidly proclaims
the sanctity of a union which fulfils nature's intentions.
He never blames Edward's and Odile's love, and certainly
he does not condemn the sentiments of his beloved heroine.
He multiplies the evidence—for instance their simultaneous

headaches—and flushes to show the necessity of their mutual love. And even when Odile lets herself slip towards death in obedience to her conscience, she cannot long remain parted from Edward; the two lovers are but one. " Then they were no longer two human beings, but a single being, absolutely and unconsciously contented, satisfied with itself and with the world." Finally, the novel closes with a radiant prospect: Charlotte herself gives Edward " his place " beside Odile; they rest side by side, like Tristan and Iseult. On the day when the dead awake to a better life, they will enjoy happiness together. Goethe explained his attachment to Baroness von Stein on the grounds that she must have been his sister or his wife in an earlier incarnation. Similarly, in a new life the Divinity would unite Edward and Odile, Charlotte and the Captain, bringing about what human error had prevented, and undoing the link proclaimed indissoluble by social tradition. The only earthly marriage which can be sacred is one consecrated by nature's intention; the master-mason uses lime to cement the stone to the ground, just as the law cements the union of those whom nature inclines towards each other, but he knows well that its weight is enough to anchor it (I, 9, p. 88).

The conflict in the novel is the less capable of reaching a decisive solution because Goethe has also posed the problem of Odile. She is one of those beings summoned by Goethe from another world; she is a Mignon, more developed and less strange, but still partly veiled. She possesses the magic charm of a " celestial child " who passes through the earth to fulfill herself and be transformed by love.

This work, so rich in matter and heavy with meaning, is also valuable for its style, for it is " the purest and most perfect narrative prose that Goethe wrote " (Gundolf). In *Werther*, the luxuriance of phrase reflected the torrential nature of the story, whereas here, the essential principle is a classical economy of means. No character, no gesture, no event, no detail is superfluous, and no scene is added for effect, to introduce a picturesque motive, to please the reader. All is thoughtful and measured in the true sense of the word, and only perhaps in the chapters of " the great parenthesis," can we find a certain lengthiness to criticize. Just as the structure of the work expresses its substance, so does the style exactly fit the thought. It expresses it with vigor and weight, without masking it under too great a richness, and simply, without descending to banality or platitude; it is clear and picturesque, yet there is no conscious effort to choose the rarest work; it is firm and powerful without stiffness, of a high tone without overemphasis; imagery is rare, yet the whole is visual and imaginative. To present the movement of tragedy, Goethe prefers the use of verbs and nouns; he uses adjectives only sparingly, and without seeking out those which characterize too clearly. As he wishes to present action in a logical sequence he dedicates his main clauses to them, reserving subordinate clauses for secondary matters and for detail. He avoids long periods except when developing a general idea, as is the case in the fifteenth chapter of part two. Finally, to render the story more vivid, he makes frequent use of the historic present tense. Such a style is difficult to define because of its lack of adornment, to which it owes its beauty.

Goethe produced *Die Wahlverwandtschaften*, one of the gems of German literature, when he was in his sixties. It is a complex work, in which Goethe reveals himself in all his richness as a man, a savant, a dramatist, a moralist, a stylist. It is a classical work, the radiant creature of a clear mind which dominates imagination and sensibility without stifling them. This deliberate and conscious complexity, the chastened and controlled form, might have rendered it cold or even a little boring, whereas in fact it pulsates with life and passion. Goethe, who dreamed of allying Greek beauty to modern German thought, has here achieved a masterpiece, whose formal beauty, worthy of antiquity, clothes a new spirituality. It is a Greek statue with the inner life of a medieval figure, and was possible only after a long Christian and moral evolution.

Studying the work of André Gide—whose Alissa in *Strait is the Gate* recalls Odile—Charles Du Bos made use of an astute comparison: he evokes rock-crystal which, while limpid in appearance, is unfathomable. This perfectly fits *Die Wahlverwandtschaften*, where the apparent simplicity is a translucent veil through which the informed reader may discover by slow degrees, at various depths and on different levels, the riches not revealed at first reading. His contemporaries were misled, many were disappointed, shocked or indignant, and their coldness recalled the reception of *Iphigenie auf Tauris* after its revision in Italy. Goethe was less surprised than hurt.

At the time of its publication, he had just reached the age of sixty. Having seen forty as a turning point, how could he contemplate sixty, the gateway to old age, otherwise than with tortured distress? It remained for him to grant us, as Carossa so well puts it, a new image of old age. It is, indeed, this Goethe whom our age finds most interesting, as if we had needed another century of experience to understand the author of the *Divan*, of the *Wanderjahre* and of the second *Faust*, to appreciate the importance of his oriental and religious message, of his political and social ideas and his visions of the future. " The Young Goethe," the " Classical Goethe," " the Olympian of Weimar " have in turn aroused enthusiasm, while the universality of his " Symbolist " period was despised. To the present age has been reserved the merit of discovering and enjoying the " Goethe of Old Age."

Part IV

Towards wisdom
1810-1832

Chapter 1

The autobiographical works

It would be possible to question the date at which we begin this last part, and to object that *Pandora* and *Die Wahlverwandschaften* are already works of old age. We feel that they are both creations of a genius which has not yet begun to fade, poetic products born of a profound need for self-expression, and that they are linked to the works of maturity. From 1810 onwards, however, Goethe seems to have renounced creation; he devoted himself to his memoirs, and returned to poetry only when influenced by chance events and to complete *Faust*. *Pandora* is still an expression of his cult of Greek antiquity; but in 1810 he came to know Sulpiz Boisserée, whose influence replaced Meyer's, and who guided him back to medieval German art, which he had admired in the days of " Sturm-und-Drang." He was shortly to turn to oriental poetry and advance towards a universal literature, After the classical and Hellenic period, there followed a period of universality. At the age of sixty, despite the *Wahlverwandtschaften*, Goethe knew that he must prepare for old age. The time had come to write his memoirs.

At the beginning of *Dichtung und Wahrheit*, Goethe puts words into the mouth of an imaginary friend who, having read the twelve volumes of his complete works, asserts that they do not make a coherent whole. He suggests that the author should set them in chronological order and indicate the events of his life which provided the subjects, the examples which influenced him, and the theoretical principles that he followed. In fact, he had been thinking of an autobiography for two or three years. His secretary, Riemer, recalls that he had often urged him to write it, and that in 1808, on the eve of his fifty-ninth birthday, Goethe had promised to begin it in the following year. This information is probably accurate and confirms our opinion that at the age of sixty, as at forty, the poet wished to renew himself again. A letter to Zelter of August 22, 1808, shows that he already knew how he would record the story of his life. The death of his mother on September 13, 1808, certainly encouraged him to fix in writing a period which now lived in his memory alone. On October 25, 1808, he announced to Bettina that he was writing his " confessions," and begged her to write down anything his mother may have said " about me and mine."

For a year Goethe collected material for his work, and on October 11, 1809, he arrived at a first outline, beginning in the year 1742 (" Charles VII, crowned on January 24th, resides at Frankfurt; my father nominated Imperial Councillor, May 16th) and goes up to 1809. It is noteworthy that in 1775 and the following years we seek in vain the name of Charlotte von Stein, but it is the same with his other loves, for Goethe did not lack a sense of propriety. This chronological survey was followed by information about the period, and a query on the direction of his life:

> My life, a unique adventure.
> No adventures to make me strive to develop
> What nature had put in me.
> Effort to acquire what nature had not put in me.
> As many true as false inclination.
> Therefore: eternal martyrdom without real enjoyment.
> Obituaries despicable.

In May, 1810, in the course of a journey with Riemer, he conversed at length about " Biographica et Aestetica," which seemed already to foreshadow " Truth and Poetry." He was concerned less with human life and its adventures than with man himself, considered as an element of nature, whose existence is metamorphosis. On May 18th he added a most important page to his journal, suggesting the plan of his autobiography. After indicating his intention to consider his life from the " ironic " point of view in order to raise the biography above it, and to satisfy both understanding and reason, sensibility and imagination and achieve " a satisfying whole," he wrote:

METAMORPHOSIS

The basis of everything is physiological. There is physiology-pathology, in, for instance, organic nature's changes of state, passing from one stage (*Stufe*) of metamorphosis to another. This is readily distinguished from the truly morbid (*morbos*) state.

The action of the outside world produces hindrances, which are often pathological in the first sense of the word. But they may also provoke a morbid state, and, by a series of inverted metamorphoses, destroy the being.

Whoever writes a confession runs the risk of becoming pitiable, for one confesses only weakness and sin, and one must not proclaim one's virtues.

This important passage deserves the attention of all authors writing their own biographies, and E. Beutler has written an intelligent commentary upon it. First, we must carefully distinguish the pathological from the morbid. We must undestand the former, as Burckhardt does later for historical evolution, as that which must be suffered. Now, man is an element of nature, and just as the caterpillar must be transformed to become first a chrysalis, then a butterfly, so must man submit to painful mutation in order to reach, by stages, the goal assigned him by his " demon." Each of these metamorphoses means suffering, is " physiological-pathological," is a trial undertaken with a happy result in view. Here we see Goethe's optimistic, anti-

tragic temperament, which, for example, obliges Faust to
to live through several tragedies before eventually attaining
the sphere of conciliation. Similarly, Hegel believed that
when all tragedies are past, history will be the realization
of the Ideal. The morbid, on the other hand, bears the
danger of retarding or clogging the development of the
human personality; it springs from the outside world, and
this is where the " hazards " of life come into play. In
the second place, and as a result, Goethe is led to point
out two of the dangers which threaten the biographer:
either he will make an exhibition of his weaknesses and
vices, or he will exalt his virtues. Was he thinking of the
Confessions of St. Augustine and of Rousseau? It was probably the latter's example that led him to reject the title
" Confessions " which he had used in his letter to Bettina.

On May 31, 1810, Goethe drew up a new outline, which
we possess for the years 1770-1771 and 1774-1797. Yet the
whole year was given over to preliminary studies, and it
was only on January 29, 1811, that he began to write. The
first part appeared in October of the same year, the second
a year later, the third in May, 1814. The work was then
interrupted by the composition of the *Divan*. Goethe only
finished the last five books, which are concerned with the
year 1775, at the end of his life. Appearing in 1833, they
formed the last volume of his posthumous works.

Dichtung und Wahrheit has more than once been compared to the similiar works of St. Augustine, Rousseau, K.
Ph. Moritz, Cardano, and even to Saint-Simon's *Mémoires*.
However, Goethe needed no such models and examples; he
had before him the finest subject he could dream of, for
this " Bildungsroman " originated in his own experience.
He had always expressed his deepest ego, in his works,
as well as thinking and creating objectively, or, as he says
in *Bedeutende Fördernis durch ein gestreichtes Wort*, " ge-
genständlich." The ego, both subject and creator, was thus
confronted at a sufficient " distance " with the work which

was its own emanation and expression. The creative ego was re-creating its own childhood and youth, lived half a century before in totally different cities and environments. No longer was the model in danger of distortion by the prism of creative imagination or the vibrations of recently aroused emotion. Elevated above himself and his own life, Goethe was in the situation of a romantic, ironically playing with his creation.

It is true that other dangers threatened the poet; the first was error, caused by lapses of memory or the desire to make his life appear poetic. The title of the autobiography has been too often adduced to prove that Goethe placed " Poetry " before " Truth " deliberately as an invitation to the reader to regard his confessions as only poetical. The argument is valueless, for the original title was *Wahrheit und Dichtung*, and the poet changed the order simply for reasons of euphony, the *d* of *und* clashing unharmoniously with the *d* of *Dichtung*. The work contains some errors of detail, for example about *Werther*. This does not prevent the whole being " true "; the poetry itself gives it truth. Goethe introduced the word poetry into the title of this book, " treated," he writes, " with great care as to accuracy," so as to avoid a second danger, that of dryness; he wished to use a " half poetical, half historical " treatment, as he tells us at the end of his introduction. As his own biographer, there was a risk of producing a dry and boring chronicle. On March 30, 1831, he said to Eckermann: " These are exclusively the results of my own life, and particular facts serve one purpose only, they confirm a general observation, a higher truth. I called the book *Wahrheit und Dichtung* because its high aspirations raise it above the realm of base reality." Thus Goethe succeeded in creating a new kind of autobiography in which one finds personal confession, which must be truth, the lyrical novel, which may be poetry, and the history of a period, which is reality.

In 1717 he condensed the essence of human destiny into five radiant but mysterious Orphic strophes, which formulate the progression of a poet's existence. This progression stretched before him like a mountainous panorama dominated by five peaks: demon, chance, love, necessity, hope.

He places *Dichtung und Wahrheit* beneath the sign of demonic determinism, for he begins with his horoscope, which forecasts a unique existence, and devotes the last book largely to demonism, the source of the dynamic which animated Egmont, Napoleon and Goethe himself. Gundolf [1] is wrong when he sees this as a " poetical device " like the miracle which concludes *Die Wahlverwandtschaften*. Nowhere, perhaps, has Goethe described more clearly the direction of his life which was, not only in the formative years, but right up to his death, a quest for the " Supersensible," an effort to establish contact with the world of the spirit whose sphere is between the human and the Divine. That " something " which he vainly tried to define in *Dichtung und Wahrheit*, which he described to Eckermann on March 2, 1831, as " what can be analyzed neither by the understanding, nor by reason," seems close to the Dionysian as depicted by Nietzsche. This demonism affects musicians more than painters; its action is positive, not negative like Mephisto's though it sometimes acts as a brake to a too rapid development (to Eckermann, October 23, 1828). Goethe knew that he was in its power, but tried to protect himself against it, for he mistrusted its excess while admitting its usefulness and even its necessity. " The greater a man is," he told Eckermann on March 24, 1829, " the more he is influenced by demons, and can only remain on his guard, to see that his directing will does not leave the straight road." *Dichtung und Wahrheit* is fundamentally the story of an exceptional being who must

[1] *Goethe*, p. 69.

fulfill himself according to his own law, and seek to remain himself despite the " chances " of existence.

These " chances " fill *Dichtung und Wahrheit*, where Goethe describes, on different levels, the various environments in which he found himself. He does this with so keen a sense of their influence on the development of his personality that he has been the model to later biographers. He is, in fact, the founder of the scientific biography. First it is the family circle and the events of his childhood; then around the house stretches Frankfurt, town of the coronation and of the fairs, which provide some famous passages; next the French occupation introduces a foreign element, and forms a link with Leipzig and Strassburg, the centers of two new worlds. Beyond these circles, which enclose the existence of the child and the young man, there is the cultural atmosphere of the period, and Goethe takes pains to indicate the literature of the time; beyond this we find the remote worlds of ancient Greece and the Bible. To these many influences, and spiritual ferments, the biographer adds Shakespeare, Ossian, Spinoza and Rousseau. It seems as if, by a series of providential " chances," the whole of Europe collaborated to enrich Goethe, and to be reflected in *Dichtung und Wahrheit*.

E. Beutler points out three surprising omissions: his mother, the music of J. S. Bach and *Faust*. Goethe was conscious of the first gap, and wished to fill it; he dictated a few pages, based on the information provided by Bettina, under the title *Aristeia der Mutter*.[1] These were to have been included in *Dichtung und Wahrheit*, but when Bettina published her *Goethes Briefwechsel mit einem Kind*, Eckermann gave up the idea. As for Bach, whose name does not appear in *Dichtung und Wahrheit*, his absence may be explained by the fact that at the time of Goethe's arrival at Leipzig, nobody performed his music any longer;

---

[1] Gedenkausgabe, X, pp. 855-862.

baroque music, like baroque architecture, remained beyond the poet's understanding. A remark of Goethe's seems singularly revealing. In 1814, Schutz and, later, Mendelssohn played him Bach fugues: he thought he was "looking into God's heart before the creation." The fact is that he was a man of the cosmos, not of chaos, the disciple of Apollo, not of Dionysus. Lastly, as to *Faust*, E. Beutler explains this absence in terms of Goethe's desire for conciliation and appeasement. He could not evoke *Faust* without recalling its origin in the trial of the Frankfurt infanticide of Susanne Margarete Brandt, who was executed on January 14, 1772.

When one is in love, as Goethe wrote, chance attracts the wandering being into new labyrinths; there is no limit to his straying, for the path itself is a wrong turning. He thus invites us to consider his childish love for Gretchen, his liaison with Kätchen, the Sesenheim idyll, and finally his passion for Lili Schönemann as diversions from the true path. *Dichtung und Wahrheit* gives us very little information about what might be called Goethe's amorous development, for he did not carry his autobiography beyond 1775; it was difficult for him to evoke his love for Baroness von Stein, who died only in January, 1827. Thus in this field *Dichtung und Wahrheit* does not give the same completeness as in the others, where one feels that the old man has sometimes enriched his youth by superimposing the impressions of maturity.

The fourth Orphic strophe is devoted to necessity. Its tone is one of sorrow and disillusionment which is foreign to Goethe: "We must pluck from our hearts all that we hold dearest." Far from fulfilling his dreams, man must learn renunciation. We find the essential passage on renunciation in the sixteenth book of *Dichtung und Wahrheit*: "Even our physical and social life, customs, habits, experience of the world, philosophy, religion, to say nothing of innumerable chance events, all cry: we must renounce."

En osant mettre mes tres respectueux
homages au pied du Throne , Votre
Excellence voudra bien suppléer a tout
ce que je ne pourrois exprimer que
tres faiblement

Flatté d'avoir recu ce Gage precieux
des mains de Votre Excellence je
La prie d'agréer et mes treshumbles
remercimens et l'assurance de la —
haute consideration avec la quelle
j'ai l'honneur d'être

de Votre Excellence

le treshumble et tresobeissant
Serviteur
de Goethe

Weimar
e 12 Novembre
1808.

14. *Letter from Goethe, thanking Napoleon for the Legion of Honor*

Since this passage is found in the middle of his eulogy of Spinoza, a philosopher whom he studied chiefly in his Weimar days, we may suppose that this is an error of memory. When, in 1773-1774, the young Stürmer first discovered Spinozan pantheism, he accepted that the whole world was divine without drawing the usual conclusion that its laws, particularly that of renunciation, are necessary. The same passage evokes the superman who is capable of recognizing " what is eternal, necessary, in accordance with the law," and thus provides grounds for hope.

The Orphic poet himself wishes to escape from the determination that enchains and thwarts him. He hastens on to the strophe where Elpis (hope) reveals eternity. This strophe seems to be the bridge connecting Faust's cry of hope on receiving the revelation of the human law, and the young poet straining towards the future. Everything in *Dichtung und Wahrheit* is development, like the growth of a fine tree, which, given favorable conditions, reaches skyward, rounding out its trunk each year. The whole is a river of hope, from the horoscope which promises an exceptional life, to the last pages where Goethe speaks of his faith in the future.

Such richness of material might perhaps have left a certain impression of monotony, had the poet not been a master of the art of presentation and variety. In *Dichtung und Wahrheit* we find in turn fragments from memory, like the story of the French occupation, or that of the Emperor's coronation, true chronicles of a Frankfurt bourgeois, love stories, short tales, like that of the dancing master's daughters, and even fairy tales (the new Paris), literary essays, artistic considerations, reflections on religion, etc. The author arranged these diverse elements thoughtfully, enhancing them by skillful juxtaposition. Sometimes he related them harmoniously, as when Gretchen is associated with the Emperor's coronation. Poetic truth tempers the austerity of the story and beautifies its majesty.

16.

The artistry of the biographer is equally evident in the composition of the chapters, each organized around a central theme, and in the transitions, which are often reflections. Gundolf emphasizes Goethe's love of transitions, and contrasts it with the effects of antithesis so dear to St. Augustine and to Rousseau. He cites one of the numerous cases of transition by association: the story of *The Vicar of Wakefield* allows him to pass from Herder to Friederike, because Goldsmith's work is linked to the former (Herder read it to his Strassburg friends) and the evocation of an idyllic environment associates it with the girl. Goethe also knew how to interrupt, to avoid boredom, or to excite curiosity by introducing a subject which is to be developed only later. In fact, these are the memoirs of a great artist.

Goethe did not continue *Dichtung und Wahrheit*, but he wrote other autobiographical works, of which the most revealing is the *Italianische Reise*. In 1787, with the aid of his friends and his journal, he had written an account of his journey for Wieland's *Mercury*. On various occasions in 1795, 1798, 1811 and 1813, he intended to revise and rewrite it, but he only set to work in 1814, publishing the first book in 1817. The second was written in 1820, and appeared in the definitive edition of his complete works. Other works in this category include his *Campagne in Frankreich* and the *Belagerung von Mainz*.

Thus, from his sixtieth year onward, Goethe felt the desire to recall and describe his past life. The pleasure in telling, which he had inherited from his mother, the need to create great figures which he could *see*, and to obtain release in poetical works seem to have disappeared. One might expect age to bring a drying up of the creative imagination, but at this moment a new love came into his life and turned the memorialist of *Dichtung und Wahrheit* into the poet of the *Divan*.

Chapter 2

Der Westöstliche Divan

The years 1811-1814 were the years which decided Napoleon's fate. Goethe continued to admire him and found no cause for rejoicing at Germany's regained freedom, which substituted for the French occupation "Cossacks, Baskirs, Croats, Magyars, Cassoubs, Samoyedes and hussars both brown and otherwise." [1] Nevertheless, he agreed to compose *Des Epimenides Erwachen*, which was played at Berka in honor of the return of Frederick-William III. In this poem of resistance he allegorically celebrated the victory of peace and freedom over the demons of war, and hailed the awakening of a new Germany.

These years were a time of withdrawal and hard work for the poet, filled with the preparation of his Memoirs and interrupted by visits to the waters of Carlsbad and Teplitz. He went for his health, and met there the Austrian empress Marie-Louise, whose marked kindness delighted him. On August 13, 1812, he wrote from Teplitz to von Reinhardt that " to live in such a way at the end of one's days gives the agreeable feeling of dying at sunrise, and

[1] A. Luden. Quoted by Witkop, *Goethe*, p. 338.

convinces one through the evidence of the inner and outer senses, that nature is eternally productive, divine to the roots, living, faithful to its types, and that it is in no way subject to age." There is a certain bitterness in this happy statement, the bitterness of the man of sixty who knows that youth is over and who, when faced with beauty, feels the difficulty of renunciation, and a yearning for rebirth. Both the man and the poet were to experience a second youth; its fruit was the *Divan*, composed between 1814 and 1818, with later additions. It was Goethe's first and only great collection of lyric poetry, composed of twelve skilfully ordered " books " of unequal size. The oriental titles create an atmosphere which cannot be captured in translation: *Moganni Nameh* (Book of the Singer), *Hafis Nameh* (Book of Hafiz), *Uschk Nameh* (Book of Love), *Tefkir Nameh* (Book of Reflections), *Rendsch Nameh* (Book of Ill-Humour), *Hikmet Nameh* (Book of Maxims), *Timur Nameh* (Book of Timur), *Suleika Nameh* (Book of Zuleika), *Saki Nameh* (Book of the Cupbearer), *Mathal Nameh* (Book of Parables), Parsi Nameh (Book of the Parsees) and *Churd Nameh* (Book of Paradise).[1] He completed these twelve books with very long notes and dissertations to assist in the understanding of the *Westötliche Divan*. Their style was greatly admired by Heine, and their importance in the history of Orientalism is emphasized by such an expert as H. H. Schaeder in his essay appearing in Beutler's edition.[2]

The latter has no hesitation in naming the *Divan*, with *Faust*, as Goethe's most important and most subjective work,

[1] Translator's note: for the English titles of the books of the Divan, I have followed E. Dowden's translation, *West- Eastern Divan*, London, 1914.

[2] In 1938 he published a book on *Goethes Erlebnis des Ostens* which establishes him as the greatest expert on this matter. Beutler's edition was published in 1943 by Dieterich, now at Wiesbaden (XIV-858 pages). Consult also Taha Hussein's article on *Goethe et l'Orient* in *Hommage de l'Unesco a Goethe*.

although he admits that it is not popular. For many years it was hardly known, and at the beginning of our century the original edition was not yet exhausted. The work of Wurm and Düntzer, and particularly of Burdach, who edited and annotated it in the Weimar edition of 1888 and the Jubilee edition of 1905, were necessary before we could understand this dialogue [1] of East and West across the gap of distance and the centuries. At the time when the great German musicians were composing their symphonies, Goethe, composed this great lyric cycle which is at once a traveller's journal, a love song and a religious hymn, and shows his progress towards symbolism.

> North and West and South are shivered
> Thrones are tumbled, Empires tremble;
> Flee thou to the cleanly Eastland,
> Patriarchal air to breathe there.
> Where, with loving, drinking, singing
> Chiser's spring shall soon renew thee.
>
> (December 24, 1814).

It is very difficult to deny this will to flee which Goethe expresses with the imperative " *flüchte*," or to interpret the verb as a wish to turn inwards. In his *Tag-und Jahreshefte* of 1815,[2] Goethe described the deep impression made on him by the poems of Hafiz in von Hammer's translation, which acted as a stimulant to a new creative outpouring " with the greater violence because I felt, to the highest degree, the need to flee from the real world, which was manifestly endangering itself, and silently to take refuge in an ideal, pleasant world to which I was linked by desire, aptitudes and will." Soon after reading Hafiz's poems, he made his first escape, back to the land of his childhood which he had not seen for seventeen years.

---

[1] " Divan " means a gathering where there is conversation.
[2] Quoted in Beutler's edition by Schaeder, pp. 789-790.

Two successive journeys took him through the Rhineland; the first, from July 26 to October 27, 1814, led him by way of Eisenach and Hanau, to Frankfurt, then on to Wiesbaden, Biebrich, Bingen, Heidelberg, Mannheim etc...; the second, from May 24 to October 11, 1815, brought him back to Frankfurt, but he went down the valley of the Rhine as far as Cologne, and spent longer in the Heidelberg-Karlsruhe area.

These journeys proved vital and stimulating in a way which reminds us of his experience in Italy. He discovered his own native land, rich in natural resources and artistic treasures, and the Rhineland people, whose zest for life reminded him of the Italians. He described the festival of Saint Roch at Bingen on October 16, 1814, in one of the finest pieces of prose in German literature. His many conversations with Sulpiz Boisserée, and his stay at Heidelberg in September, 1814, where he saw his new friend's collection of Rhenish pictures, revealed medieval Germany to him, just as his Italian journey had introduced him to ancient Greece. The young Cologne Maecenas, whose collection later became the core of the Munich Pinakotheck, had tried, as early as May, 1811, to interest him in Dürer's period. At Heidelberg, where he stayed with the Boisserées from September 24 to October 9, 1814, he spent all his time studying the picture-gallery (which he revisited between September 21 and October 7, 1815). His enthusiasm was boundless! " They were different from us, those fellows, yes indeed! Let us set them in their rightful place, let us sing their praises, let us sing them again and again forever." [1] He registered his admiration in his article on *Art and Antiquity in the Regions of the Rhine and Main*, which he published in the *Morgenblatt für gebildete Stände* of March 9-12, 1816. " Here I had suddenly found a whole new and entirely unknown world of shapes and colors, which

---

[1] Quoted by Witkop. *Goethe*, p. 344.

forced me out of the rut of my old views and feelings — a new, eternal youth." [1] Thus, influenced by Sulpiz Bois-serée, Goethe turned his back on ancient Greece. Instead, he bathed himself in Flemish art, which he considered a national art, thus Rhineland moved towards the romantics. The *Divan* is, first of all, the product of an escape. E. Beut-ler, who calls it " a daily journal in verse," shows us, in his commentary on the first book, how the poet passes from a cosmic vision to the narrower field of the terrestrial world, then to an even more limited circle, the poet himself. In the poem *Art' ges Häuschen hab'ich Klein*, Goethe is com-fortably settled in his carriage, and he finds himself " as happy in solitude as in the company of pretty girls " and sees forests, field and mountains move towards him. This poem [2] was written at Eisenach castle on July 25, 1814. The word " Hejira " (from the Arab hidjra — emigration, expatriation) is thus significant; it announces the poet's de-parture westwards, towards the land of his birth. Many poems, true " traveler's songs," mark the stages in his jour-ney: *Phänomen* (July 25, 1814) was inspired by a rainbow seen in the morning on the way to Eisenach; *Liebliches* (July 25, 1814) by the Erfurt neighborhood; *Ziviespalt* (July 26, 1814) by the remembrance of hours spent at Eisenach; *Im Gegenwärtigen Vergangenes* is dated Fulda, July 26, 1814, 6 P. M.; *Derb und tüchtig* reproduces the poet's state of mind the same day; *Alleben*, written during the night of July 29-30, 1814, owes its inspiration to the dust which is the tiresome companion of a summer journey, and to a storm which Goethe met on the road from Frank-furt to Wiesbaden. Beutler, who provides this exact infor-mation recalls (p. 377) that other works were also inspired during his travels: *Wanderers Sturmlied* and *An Schwager*

---

[1] Quoted by Beutler, p. 368.
[2] It is included in full by Beutler in *Essays um Goethe*, I, pp. 299-300.

Kronos between Darmstadt and Frankfurt, *Die Geschwister* between Jena and Weimar, and, later, *Marienbader Elegie* in the coach bringing Goethe back from Carlsbad. Thus it is not surprising that the first book of the *Divan* is to a great extent the poet's travelogue.

It is also the link between West and East, between Goethe and Hafiz. As Goethe abandoned his ideal to seek greater universality, he took Hafiz as his guide. In childhood the poet had been introduced to the Biblical East; then, in 1772-1773, to the Mohammedan East; and a little later, to the Hindu East. He wrote in the second book of *Dichtung und Wahrheit*: " Those monstrous, shapeless and colossal figures could not, in fact, satisfy my poetic feeling; they were too far from truth, to which my mind continually aspired." The Italian journey, directing him towards the typical and the true, could not but turn him away from the East and its symbols. Yet by 1791 he was praising *Sakountala*, which gave him an example of a prologue for *Faust*. Herder introduced him to didactic and amorous Persian verse, and by the beginning of the century he was becoming more and more interested in the spiritual world of the East. Thus he was ready to receive the revelation of Hafiz. In *Hermann und Dorothea*, he had been happy to be the " last of the Homerides." Now he dreamed of equaling Hafiz, though he knew it was but an idle dream.

The Persian poet Shems eddin Mohammed was born in about 1320 and died in 1389 at Shiraz. He got the name " Hafiz " from the fact that he knew the Koran by heart; he declared that he owed all his achievements to the sacred book. He taught as dervish, sufi and sheik, occupied himself with theological works, and attracted numerous disciples. Despite his otherwise grave and austere attitude, he also sang the pleasures of love and wine, and was a great lyric poet. Goethe ends his note on Hafiz with this summary in which he himself seems to appear: " Satisfied with mediocrity, joyful and wise, taking his share of the good things of this world, casting a distant eye upon the mysteries of the divinity, but, on the other hand, equally rejecting religious practice and the pleasures of the senses, so that the sum of his poetry, while appearing to educate and teach, must in fact keep at all costs a sceptical mobility." This note, probably dating from 1817 or 1818, shows that the poet's enthusiasm waned rapidly, and explains why the poem *Hafis, dir sich gleich zu stellen* does not appear in the *Divan* itself, but after it.

Goethe turned to the Persian poet, not only because he recognized in his life, in his profession as an educator and in his sensual poetry features which were his own, but also because Hafiz represented the mystery of the distant East and the hope of a renaissance. *Hejira*, the first poem, was written on December 24, 1814 in the midst of the festival atmosphere with which the Germans surround the glorification of the Savicur. It expresses modern man's desire to rejuvenate himself at the spring of Chiser,[1] to " trace the first origins of the human races " who remained in direct communication with God, and for whom the Word was still an oral message. The Weimar poet tried to imagine himself among the shepherd's caravans, consoling himself along the trail with the poems of Hafiz. This man of sixty dreamed of love and houris, the supreme earthly happiness, without fearing for his heavenly bliss, for this poetry assured him of eternal life. An extraordinary departure for a pilgrimage to the East! The wish for renewal is marvelously expressed in the famous poem *Selige Sehnsucht*, the pearl of the *Divan*, which, more than any other, is " *Westöstliche*." Goethe borrowed it from a work by, or at least attributed to, Hafiz.[2] At the end of July, 1814,

---

[1] Through Hammer Goethe knew of Chiser, who keeps the spring of life.

[2] Beutler's edition, pp. 380 et seq. Read also Rang, *Goethes " Selige Sehnsucht "* (Herder, Fribourg, 1949, 80 p.).

he put the *Divan* in order, having already written some thirty poems. On July 31st he wrote these five famous verses:

> To the sages only tell it,
> Crowds are quickly moved to mocking;
> I aspire to praise the Living
> Who in flame must seek his dying.
>
> In the coolness of the love-nights,
> When life you received, and gave it,
> Then a strange emotion grips you
> When you see the candle flaming.
>
> You remain enclosed no longer,
> In the dusky shadows hiding;
> And a new desire now calls you
> To a higher matrimony.
>
> There's no distance can discourage,
> You come flying, fascinated,
> And at last, in love with brightness,
> There you are, poor moth, consumed.
>
> And until you've understanding
> Of this dying and becoming,
> You are but a guest in shadow
> Upon this dark world benighted.

With a true intoxication, which Beutler describes as more Dionysian that Apollonian, Goethe aspires to a metamorphosis in the form of annihilation and regeneration. He aspires to—but he does he really hope for?—death in the flame of love.

When Goethe declared that he was as happy as in the company of pretty girls, he did not suspect that he was on his way to a charming girl, Marianne von Willemer, who was destined to play a part in his life and in his work. She was then Maria-Anna Jung. A talented dancer, she was born in 1784 and adopted by the banker von Willemer, a widower, with three children. On September 27, 1814, she became Frau von Willemer, and it is possible that the banker hastened the marriage because he had guessed that she and Goethe already had a tenderness for each other.

The poet had met her at Wiesbaden on August 4th and soon conquered her whole family. Yet love was not born until 1815, when for several weeks Goethe was the Willemers' guest; or to be exact, on September 8th when he left the famous *Gerbermühle* to flee to their house in Frankfurt. It was there, on September 12th, that he wrote his first poem to Marianne, the fourth in the " Book of Zuleika." He gives her the name borne in the Koran by Potiphar's wife who was in love with Joseph, and he calls himself " Hatem " (the generous). He intended generosity in the sense of he who gives himself, and to whom is given; under this title he blesses the occasion which robs him of what love remains in his heart; now impoverished, he enjoys a " renewed destiny " in her arms. Marianne responds with a very beautiful love lyric, which later appears under the title *Suleika* (September 10, 1815): " overflowing with happiness," she does not blame the " occasion," but joyfully offers Hatem her life and declares herself happy in his arms. From this time on, the loving couple are worthy to be numbered among the immortal lovers, and the leaf of Gingo Biloba is the symbol of this miraculous love. None can tell whether it is a " living entity, divided in itself " or " two beings fused together and mistaken for one." The lover feels himself both single and double. The amorous dialogue continued, on September 17th, with *Als ich auf dem Euphrat Schiffte* and *Dies zu deuten, bin erbötig*, in which Goethe interprets a dream of Marianne's. But on the evening of the 18th, Goethe departed; he decided to renounce. He had to choose between Marianne and life, between conjugal happiness and adventure, between the fulfilment and degradation of love consummated, and, on the other hand, the pure and happy exaltation of a dawning love. Like Werther, like Edward in *Die Wahlverwandtschaften*, Goethe fled while there was still time. On October 6th he was able to write Willemer a letter addressed to both of them, " united in an enviable happiness." He stated that he was hurrying home by way of Würzburg, consoled only by the fact that, without compelling need yet unresisting, he is following the path marked out for him, so that his yearning may be addressed the more purely to those he leaves. He never saw Marianne again.

This amorous adventure of Goethe's [1] has not had the attention it deserves, for it was one of the finest of the poet's life, and the last to lead to the creation of a great heroine, Zuleika. The young woman had given him the transcending joy of knowing himself loved at the age of sixty-five, and she had made him feel love again. This was no longer the juvenile passion of Leipzig or Strassburg, the " marriage of souls " of Weimar, the voluptuous revelations of Italy, nor the conjugal fire of his *Bettschatz*, but the union of two superior hearts, a confident and total interchange, an unshadowed and fruitless love. Werner Milch quotes the fine passage where Hoffmansthal contrasts the impetuous love of the young man, who wants all or nothing and loses sight of the world, with that of the mature man, who knows how to take and how to give, who must master life, who consciously stakes his all. What such a love meant to Goethe we find magnificently expressed in that great poem *Wiederfinden*, which he composed on September 24, 1815, a week after leaving Marianne. At the time of the Creation, the elements were separated. But God created Aurora, and ordered those who were made for one another to seek each other; thus these two met, " models of joy and sorrow " forever. Goethe had known love for the last time; by renouncing his beloved, he became himself again.

As for Marianne, she had gained the experience of an exceptional love and, spiritually enriched, she rose to the level of the poet. Werner Milch has good reason to admire

---

[1] Consult Werner Milch's well-documented and sensitive little book *Bettine und Marianne* (Artemis Verlag), 1947; also Hans Pyritz, *Goethe und Marianne von Willemer* (Metzler, Zürich, Stuttgart, 3rd edition, 1948) which is indispensable.

the sudden blossoming of this woman, several of whose poems Goethe included in his *Divan : Hochbeglückt in deiner Liebe ; Was bedeutet die Bewegung ? Ach ! um deine feuchten Schwinger ; Wie mit innigstem Behagen,* and especially that *Nimmer will ich dich Verlieren* whose last two lines express the lesson of the *Divan*:

> For in love life has its being,
> And the life of life is spirit.

The Book of the Singer, the traveler's journal, the Book of Hafiz, the western poet's hymn to the eastern poet, and the Book of Zuleika, a love duet in alternating strophes, are the three panels of this great triptych of escape, which leads ultimately to God. We must not seek in the *Divan* a profession of faith, or of Goethe's adhesion to any religious dogma. Yet here, more than in any other of his works, we feel the presence of God, who appears at the beginning as one of the five " talismans ":

> It is God who owns the Eastland!
> It is God who owns the Westland!
> And the Northland and the Southland
> Have in peace His hand's protection

Wilhelm Flitner has devoted a substantial study to Goethe's religion as it is revealed in the poems of the *Divan* and in the notes, particularly in *Mahmoud von Gasner*.

Goethe, who had previously written that as an artist he adopted polytheism, now moved towards monotheism; the pantheist in *Werther* never ceased to evoke a transcendant God. In the ascent of the human being towards God, he distinguishes three steps: " Pure natural religion," which adores the universal father in nature; polytheism. which has the drawback of dispersing and dissolving itself; " faith in the single God," which always elevates the spirit by restoring to the individual the unity of his own ego.[1] Mo-

---

[1] *Mahmoud von Gasner.*

notheism itself also contains three stages: the Jewish religion, which always " gives a certain impression of stubborn rigidity, but at the same time a free and shrewd spirit and a lively activity," the Mohammedan religion, which has the drawback of not " freeing its sectaries of a limited and confused mentality," and finally the Christian religion, with its mystical spirituality. Goethe's preference lay with Christianity. It " is worthy of the highest praise, for its pure and noble origin is ceaselessly strengthened in that, after the worst errors into which the blindness of man has led it, it always suddenly reappears, in the beauty of its brotherhoods for the appeasement of the moral exigencies of mankind." The poet rejects the Indian doctrine, whose " origins were worthless," and even the much purer polytheism of the Greeks and Romans which " was bound, after all, to lose itself in false paths, and mislead its followers." In his view, the great sacred book is the Old Testament, the " book of books " and sum of poetry, while the Koran, despite its beauties, is monotonous and lacks poetry, like Mohammed himself.

No religion can be conceived without a mediator, and at the beginning of the century the romantics had shown much concern with this problem. In *Blütenstaub*, Novalis devoted an important passage to it: anything, he says, may play this part, but " as man becomes more independent, so the number of mediators diminishes, while their quality improves, and his relations with them become more varied and reach a higher plane: fetishes, stars, animals, heroes, idols, Gods, God-in-Man. " Goethe's religious thought progressed from the multiple mediator to the mediator par excellence, Christ. Yet he drew no practical conclusion from this, for he used other mediators to reach God: beauty and love.

First there is the beauty of nature. Here, following Saadi, Goethe was astonished and delighted to see a peacock's feather in a copy of the Koran. In this small object he beheld the greatness of God, whose glance encompasses the world; since he was worthy to admire His glory in this humble splendour, he was worthy to approach the sanctuary. There is also the beauty of the soul which transcends that of the body:

> This lyre, what, does it sing? It sings, and strongly:
> The best fiancée need not be the fairest.
> But if we are to number thee among us,
> Aspire to what's most beautiful, the finest.

Goethe remained faithful to the conception of beauty which he expressed in *Pandora*: it comes from God and leads to God.

Beauty is naturally allied to love; it creates love, which is the great mediator between man and the Divinity. In this matter Goethe, who is close to Novalis and Dante, takes his place in that great line which goes back to Plotinus and to Plato.[1] Zuleika's name fills the *Divan*, but it becomes confused with Allah's; thus the Book of Zuleika ends with these lines:

> When I recite the hundred names of Allah,
> In each echo a name for thee's repeated.

To love women is to adore God and to deserve Paradise, where those will enter who have believed, who have seen the divine mystery, who have lived the battle of life:

> For I have been a man, I proudly claim it,
> By this I mean that I have faced life's battle;

and those who have loved the "marvels of youth," and above all, those who have sung the life and the battle of beauty and love — the poets:

> Whoever here has sung in praise of women
> Deserves, when he attains the home eternal,
> To walk in joy beside them there for ever.

[1] Consult Franz Koch, *Goethe und Plotin*.

Goethe's religion in the *Divan* may be considered " mystical " poetry. The Old Testament is the source of religion for him, because it is full of poetry. It is through poetry that God reveals himself to us; thus the poet is a prophet. In the note on Mohammed Goethe tried to define the distinction between them:

> Both are seized and inspired by *one* God, but the poet disperses in enjoyment the gift which has been confided to him to produce enjoyment, or at least a pleasing life... The prophet, on the other hand, goes straight for one clearly defined goal; he wants to proclaim a doctrine, and through it and about it to assemble the multitudes as if round a standard.

Just as the first must be varied and inexhaustible, so the second must remain single-minded and monotonous; that is exactly what Goethe condemned in the Koran. Now, it is not a question of teaching a doctrine valuable in time, but of uniting time to eternity; not of surrounding God with an " Ecclesia " but of establishing a link between God and men, of revealing to them the divine mystery.

Goethe did not believe in the possibility of mystic communion; but he was none the less open to mystery and to the mystic world. He sensed the presence of a celestial sphere to which man can gain access only through poetry, which by its symbolism is capable of attaining what is beyond scientific laws and aesthetic " types." He wrote that, " true symbolism exists where the particular represents that which is more general, not as a dream or shadow, but as the living and immediate revelation of the inaccessible." According to the closing lines of *Faust II*, what happens is but the symbol of what does not happen, its sign and cipher. Goethe has emphasized the importance of this latter term in the poem *Geheimschrift* (Book of Zuleika) and the note *Chiffer*. The poet prevails over the prophet by virtue of his superiority: he has variety and is inexhaustible, he can decipher God's signs and explain them to men. Even more than the prophet, the poet is the voice of God.

15. *Goethe in his study, 1831 (From a painting by J. Schmeller)*

Thus the *Divan* is, with *Faust II*, Goethe's great symbolic work. He was conscious of his withdrawal from the plastic world of the Greeks and from his own classical work, and in the Book of the Singer, he contrasted poetry and sculpture.

> Let the Grecian his clay model,
> Moulding it into a statue,
> And, by skill of his own fingers,
> Minister to his own rapture;
>
> It is our voluptuous pleasure,
> Having dived into Euphrates,
> In the element of water
> To disport ourselves in freedom.
>
> If I thus cool my soul's burning,
> It will ring out in my singing;
> Water drawn by hand of poet
> Shapes itself in balls of crystal.

The subject of this significant poem comes from a Hindu legend told by the Grimm brothers in their preface to *Der arme Heinrich*, 1815: " With their pure hands, they (poets) can, like the innocent souls of the Hindu legend, round into balls the water which others, if they wish to bear it away, must pour into earthenware vessels." Its content is dictated to Goethe by his discovery of medieval Germany, by his discovery of the East, and by a new and romantic conception of poetry. In the " Cabinet of Antiques " at Mannheim he had the impression of being in the midst of a forest of statues, and his Italian journey had inclined him towards Greek plastic art. In 1789 he wrote

> The Greeks' Academy
> Remained yet open, for years had failed to shut the door.

For twenty years he had preached to artists the gospel of classical Greece. Now he bade farewell to " earthly images," to static and limited Apollinism. He wanted to unite the fire of his soul and the waters of the Euphrates into a song that would rise toward God. He was never so close to romanticism, yet he did not flounder in romantic excesses.

17.

To measure his evolution at a single glance, it is enough to compare these two famous lines from Torquato Tasso:

> And if, in all his torments, man is silent,
> God granted me the gift to cry my pain.

with the two lines from the *Divan* expressing the same idea.

> If I thus cool my soul's burning,
> It will ring out in my singing.

Goethe in his maturity proclaimed the poet's mission with an Olympian calm; Goethe, the old man rejuvenated and renewed by walking the soil of his native country, by taking flight towards the East, by rediscovering love and thus giving life new meaning, cooled his burning soul in the waves of the Rhenish Euphrates, and celebrated Zuleika, earthly lover and celestial mediatrix.

The *Divan* represents a new peak of attainment in Goethe's career. As a young " Stürmer " he had expressed his personal feelings in his poems, and had conveyed his fundamental ideas through his heroes; he had given voice to the individual. In his classical period, he created characters made of his own flesh and blood, who were also generic types, governed by the same scientific laws that apply to phenomena. Now he could be limited neither by the individual nor by the general. He knew that laws do not explain all things or type all men; behind them both exists the unknowable and the mysterious. He was in the position of the thinker whose greatest happiness is " to have plumbed what may be plumbed, and to have a quiet reverence for the unfathomable (" *Maximen und Reflexionen* "). He chose recourse to symbols in order to reveal the inaccessible, to make the ephemeral eternal:

> All that happens
> Is but a symbol;
> What is imperfect
> Here becomes event.

In the *Divan* he still retains the fire of maturity; at the same time, he has already gained the wisdom of old age.

Let us try to imagine a reader in 1819 who discovers this work without knowing its author. How could he suppose that this abundant flow of love and poetry was the work of a poet of seventy? Yet this was Goethe's age; we now see him entering upon old age with a full heart.

Chapter 3

The Sage of Weimar

His love for Marianne von Willemer represented Goethe's last effort at expansion, the final manifestation of a desire for eternal youth, and at the same time it represented the poet's consent to renunciation. Can one agree with Günther Müller that he was entering the decade of " the great resignation? " We think not: the man who had planned to " raise ever higher the pyramid of his existence " could not surrender on the threshold of old age. Although no longer physically young, he still had a fiery heart and vigorous mind capable of continued development. He was yet to earn the appellation " the Sage of Weimar." His life was freed of outside events, and only one last love, his feeling for young Ulrike von Levetzow, was allowed to break through into his inner world. The man in him was slowly dying, but the thinker, the savant and the poet still flourished with a vital force which could be thwarted only by death. He himself considered it his greatest duty to " withdraw his activity ever inward."

Yet as he looked around he realized that to live long means to survive many of those one loves; his wife died

on June 6, 1816, creating in him and around him emptiness, and the silence of death; death also claimed others,
friends and men whom he admired, like Napoleon (1812),
Byron (1825), then, at closer and closer intervals, Charlotte
von Stein (1827), duke Karl-August (1828), the grand duchess Louise (1830), his own son August (1830), whose
death forced this saying from the octogenarian: " *Non igno-
ravi me mortalem genuisse.*" The death of this son, whose
conduct had been far from exemplary, affected him profoundly. On June 17, 1817, August had married Ottilie
von Pogwisch, who looked after the poet's house in place of
Christiane Vulpius; she gave him three grandchildren, Walther, Wolf and Alma, whose lives have been fully recorded
by Oskar Jellinek.[1]

By this time, Goethe had come to enjoy a fame which
now spread beyond the frontiers of the Germanic world
and brought him innumerable visitors. He had become the
center of a spiritual universe which knew no frontiers.
He was even forced to defend himself against intrusions
which threatened his time and his peace, displaying jealous
care and a sense of order inherited from his father. Strict
economy allowed him to keep a tight control on household
expenses. Perhaps this was the time when he most methodically practiced the " art of living," [2] for he knew that
his years were numbered and that he must now live
without haste, but without waste of time. We are reminded
of the maxim which his English friends caused to be en-
graved on the seal they gave him in 1831: " *Ohne Rast, doch
ohne Hast.*"

The companion of his last years was to be Johann Peter
Eckermann. who had come to visit him on June 10, 1823,
and remained with him, to become his secretary and con-

---

[1] *Die Geistes-und Lebenstragödie der Enkel Goethes* (Oprecht,
Zürich, 1938, 115 pages).
[2] See Robert d'Harcourt, *Goethe et l'art de vivre* (Payot, 1935,
201 pages).

fidant, much as Wagner was to Faust. The man has been the subject of varying judgments, as has also his principal work. In any case, Eckermann did not lack talent, and, to a certain degree at least, he sacrificed himself to Goethe's fame. As to his famous *Gespräche*, if they are not, perhaps, " the finest German book " as Nietzsche claimed, and even though they idealize the Olympian of Weimar, they none the less present a summary of Goethe's thought, an inexhaustible collection of ideas and suggestions, which Goethe probably did not formulate quite as we find them here, but which are, nevertheless, his. Eckermann had one more merit; just as Schiller had stimulated Goethe and urged him to finish *Faust I*, so Eckermann encouraged him to write *Faust II*.

There were other important personalities who lived in the Sage's orbit, assiduously frequented his house, and who also recorded their conversations with Goethe. First there was his friend and artistic adviser J. H. Meyer, whose influence we have already stressed; then Fr. G. Reimer, who was August's tutor from 1803 to 1812, and helped the poet in his literary and scientific work; Friedrich von Müller, chancellor since 1815, who visited him regularly and who, with Eckermann and Riemer, was to edit his posthumous works; finally, the Swiss naturalist Friedrich Jacob Sorel, called to Weimar as tutor to the heir apparent, whose recollections complete the others.

To these regular visitors we should add friends like Zelter, who came frequently from Berlin, and the numerous visitors attracted by the poet's fame to his house adorned with works of art and excellently classified collections. He received them with a monarch's arrogance, but if they succeeded in pleasing him, he treated them with friendly good nature. Among the best known of his many visitors we may cite, in 1817: Achim von Arnim, Bettina's husband, Brentano, Tieck and Varnhagen von Ense; in 1818: Hegel; in 1819: the English painter Dawe, who painted a portrait of him, and some American scientists; in 1820: Carus and Platen; in 1823: Baron von Stein and G. von Humboldt; in 1824: H. Heine; in 1825: Victor Cousin, Carl Maria Weber; in 1826: Wilhelm Muller, Grillparzer, Alexander von Humboldt and several representatives of the nobility, among them prince Pückler-Muskau; in 1827: Ampère, A. G. Schlegel and Ludwig I of Bavaria; in 1828: princes Wilhelm and Georg of Prussia; in 1829: Mickiewicz and David d'Angers, who made a bust of him; in 1830: Thackery. Goethe also carried on a voluminous correspondence, particularly with men of science. Almost up to his death he followed certain newspapers attentively, among them the *Globe*, and he made a practice of reading a book every day. It is astonishing that between his seventieth and eightieth years, he became the spiritual center and first citizen of such a diverse world.

Goethe hardly left Weimar again except for his regular cures, chiefly at Carlsbad and Marienbad. At the latter spa in 1821 he met Ulrike von Levetzow, who was seventeen and his last love.[1] In that and the following year, he stayed in the pension "At the City of Weimar" kept by Frau von Brösigke, whose daughter, Frau von Levetzow, he had already met and admired. In 1821 it was her granddaughter who attracted him. This young and radiant schoolgirl, brought up in Strassburg, probably evoked memories both of himself at the age of twenty at Sesenheim, and of his beloved Odile in *Die Wahlverwandtschaften*. He was very pleasant to her, and, a pedagogue to the last, strove to instruct her, by describing flowers, rocks, stars and literature in a lively and agreable way.[2] He remembered her in 1822, but if he had behaved like a grandfather the year

---

[1] For Goethe's love for Ulrike von Levetzow, consult Mlle. Bianquis, *L'élégie de Marienbad*, in the collection published by the University of Strassburg in 1832 (pp. 387-410) and Charles Du Bos, *Le dernier amour de Goethe*, in his *Goethe*, pp. 357-402.

[2] See Ulrike's letter quoted by Du Bos, pp. 367-368.

before, this year he become a fond father to her, calling
Ulrike his " dear little daughter," or his " favorite." On
July 24-25, he wrote the *Aeolshärfe*, a love duet. His love
burst out the following summer, during which the old man
made himself conspicuous with the girl. He begged the
duke to ask her hand in marriage for him; Ulrike refused the match.

The last days in Carlsbad were, to outward appearances,
gay enough, but in the coach taking Goethe back to Weimar he was stricken with grief, and dictated the famous
Marienbader Elegie.[1] Preceded by the poem *An Werther*,
(the beginning of March, 1829), a hymn to music inspired
by a Polish pianist, Mm. Szymanowska, it forms the center piece of the *Trilogie der Leidenschaft*, which is the swan-
song of the lyric poet.

During this long period of twenty-two years (1810-1832),
which one dare not call old age, Goethe was at work. He
composed the *Divan* and his autobiographical works; he
published the first edition of *Wilhelm Meisters Wanderjahre*, and in the course of his last few years he wrote the
second *Faust*; finally, he devoted himself more and more
to his scientific work, and decided to give the results of his
earlier researches to the scientific world. Thus the moment
has come to make a brief survey of that part of Goethe's
product. It was the subject of numerous works [2] to which
we would refer the interested reader for more detail, for
despite its importance, it only comes incidentally within
the scope of our studies.

As we have seen, Goethe became engrossed in the study
of botany and geology while he was at Weimar. His bo-

---

[1] It figures in *Pages immortelles de Goethe* and also, enthusiastically
commented, in Du Bos' *Goethe*.

[2] See particularly Michéa, *Les travaux scientifiques de Goethe*
(Éditions Aubier) and the same author's article: *Goethe savant méconnu*
in *Études germaniques*, Nos. 14-15, pp. 162-173. Vietor devotes an
important part of his big work to "Goethe the Savant."

tanical research, based on the work of Linnaeus, led to the great discovery which he announced in 1790 in his memorandum *Die Metamorphose der Pflanzen*, and which later became an accepted authority. August St. Hilaire wrote in the *Comptes rendus de l'Académie des Sciences de 1858*: " Goethe's work is one of those few which not only immortalize their authors, but themselves become immortal." At the same time he was studying the animal kingdom in an effort to establish the first archetype and to trace its metamorphoses. In 1784 he discovered the existence of the intermaxillary process in man, but he did not publish the account of his discovery until 1820. In 1790 he discovered the vertebral theory of the cranium; unfortunately he was preceded in the announcement of it by Oken in 1807. In 1795 he sketched out an *Entwurf einer allgemeinen Einleitung in die Vergleichende Anatomie*, but then abandoned the preparation of the great work planned on morphology. We have already had occasion to notice his studies, researches and observations in the geological field in Thuringia and in Italy. He followed them up in every country he visited, in France, in Switzerland, in Bohemia, compiling a mineralogical collection of over 18,000 specimens. He was called " the mother of ores " and gave one of them the name " Goethite." He was not an innovator in this field, however, as he was in botany and zoology.

He wished to make a contribution to optics, a field in which he violently opposed Newton's theories, and was himself opposed by the consensus of opinion of the physicists. His labors lasted for some twenty years, after his return from Italy, during the course of which he published, in 1792 and 1793, the two *Beiträge zur Optik* and in 1810 his *Zur Farbenlehre*, which he later completed. His theory was attacked, but without affecting his certainty that he was right, for in 1823 he proudly said to Soret: " This Newton, whom everyone admires, these unfailingly accurate mathematicians and wonderful calculators, these judicious observers, they are all wrong; I alone am right in spite of them all, I alone possess the secret, which they could so easily discover, which would be self-evident to them if only they would open their eyes and see straight."

What matters to us is not so much the scientific value of his work as its importance to him, and the influence it exerted on his poetic genius. No doubt we should not take too literally his declaration to Eckermann on February 18, 1829: "I am not vain about all I have produced as a poet. Other excellent poets were my contemporaries, before me there were some even better, and there will be others after me. But to have been, in the difficult science of colors, the only man of my own time to have seen clearly, that is what I find flattering, and what gives me a sense of superiority over many men." No one could contest that the poet turned man of science was no amateur, that he took his work most seriously, and that he wished and believed himself to be a scientist.

Goethe profited by his efforts to participate in scientific progress. On May 11, 1810, he wrote to Baroness von Stein that he did not regret having given up much time to his study of colors: "Thanks to them I have acquired a culture which I would have found difficult to attain in any other way. Besides, my work will have many consequences which may delight me later and which will doubtless be useful to others." In fact, the scientific study of nature served him as a school of art. It heightened his powers of observation, and altered his approach from particular phenomena to laws, and in the work of art, from the particular to the universal, from the characteristic to the typical. From that time on, science provided him with the subjects of many poems, particularly the *Metamorphose der Planzen* and *Metamorphose der Tiere* and those forming a collection with the Schellingian title *Soul of the World*. It was a chemical theory that gave him the central idea of *Die Wahlverwandtschaften*, and scientific themes were to enrich the two great works to which he dedicated his last years.

According to Pyritz [1] Goethe once compared his scientific work to the ballast of a balloon, without which it would be in danger of soaring too high; to come down it would be necessary to make a hole in the balloon's envelope. That is why, he continued, " besides poetry I make these serious scientific studies." This is a revealing remark: Goethe was afraid of getting his feet off the ground, of forgetting reality and becoming lost in the ethereal; he recognized his need for ballast. His administrative duties at Weimar had provided precisely this; his scientific studies had the same aim, or, at least, the same effect, and thus played an important part in Goethe's development. No doubt it was a similar reason which kept the poet from an active interest in music, although he continued to study and practise the plastic arts and to draw inspiration from them, particularly for the second *Faust*. He was more at home in the world of the eye than in that of the ear.

Following Eckermann's lead, critics have looked upon Goethe in his last fifteen years too much as the Olympian, ruling over men's minds. Certainly he was a sage who was sought after and revered. But he was isolated in his greatness, and criticized as well as admired. Though the duke celebrated the fiftieth anniversary of his arrival in Weimar as the jubilee of their friendship, yet in 1817 he relieved him of the directorship of the theatre, of which he had been in charge for a quarter of a century, because the poet did not allow a dog on the stage which had seen the production of classical masterpieces. The world visited him, but the scientists would not accept his discoveries; the romantics turned away from him more and more, and after the revolution of 1830, which interested him less than his

[1] *Goethe und Marianne von Willemer*, 3rd ed. Metzler, Stuttgart, 1948, p. 9.

discussions with Cuvier and with Geoffroy Saint-Hilaire, a new literary school arose which was interested in politics and which severely reproached him for his indifference.

If one looks past the splendid frame which surrounds him, one discovers a man alone at the end of his days, without a true friend, without love, with no deep joy, hastening to complete his development and his work before death strikes. It had threatened him several times since his twentieth year, and in 1823 a heart attack was nearly fatal. Yet he was to live long enough to revise *Wilhelm Meisters Wanderjahre* and to complete the second *Faust*, his final message to the world.

Chapter 4

Wilhelm Meisters Wanderjahre

The poet's last labors were devoted to the completion of *Faust*, which was conceived in 1773 to 1774, and the continuation of *Wilhelm Meister*, conceived, perhaps, at the same time as *Werther*. Both works represent summations of experience. They are both presented in the form of triptychs, the latter as the *Theatralische Sendung*, commonly called the *Urmeister*, the *Lehrjahre* and the *Wanderjahre*, and the former as the *Urfaust* and the first and second parts of *Faust*. Finally, the subtitle of the novel of old age, *Die Entsagenden*, could, in the singular, be applied to the play. Yet the novel has not achieved the fame of the play, nor tempted musicians, illustrators and translators in the same way. It is little known and much less admired. Inferior as to poetry, too didactic and less orderly, it cannot impress to the same degree. Yet the discovery of the *Urmeister* in 1810 as well as the growing importance of social questions have increased the value of this great fresco in which Goethe reveals himself, first as the belated "Stürmer," then as a Shakespearian, then as a classicist passionately interested in the development of the human being, and finally as the social thinker, haunted by the questions which were to dominate the modern world.

In tracing the genesis of the *Wanderjahre*, we shall find that this work was in the forefront of Goethe's thoughts almost as much as was *Faust*. As we watch the work itself unfold, we shall see that it is a semi-poetic, semi-didactic presentation of the great milestones of human society.

After the completion of the *Lehrjahre*. Goethe had continued to think about a " *Meisterjahre*." Writing humorously, he wondered how his " William the Pupil " could usurp the title " William the Master," but he could not but admit that his pupil, having served his apprenticeship, should prove his mastery or, more exactly, acquire it by travel. Besides, he had left him on the point of setting out for Italy, and in order to turn the Society of the Tower into a world-wide organization, he had sent Jarno to America and the Abbé to Russia. In the novel itself he had arranged " *pierres d'attente*," destined to serve as a bait and a support to the plans he had in mind. Yet in the course of the first few years he was too absorbed in other works and too preoccupied with the progress of the French Revolution to carry out his project. In 1798 he announced in *Propyläen*: " Letters of a Traveler and his Pupil, under romantic names, connected with *Wilhelm Meister*," which was to include considerations of ethics, geography, nature, etc. However, he gave up the idea. He next sketched out continuations of the *Unterhaltungen deutscher Ausgewanderten: Die neue Melusine, Der Mann von fünfzig Jahren, St. Joseph der Zweite*, the latter in the spring of 1799. But it was not until 1807 that he began a first " campaign of construction."

On May 17, 1807, at half past six in the morning, Goethe began to dictate the *Wanderjahre*. He began with *St. Joseph der Zweite*, then *neue Melusine, Die gefährliche Wette* and *Der Mann von fünfzig Jahren*. At about the same time he began *Das nussbraune Mädchen*, then translated a short

16. Marble bust of Goethe by David d'Angers (1828)

story by an unknown French author, *Die pilgernde Törin*. He now had the title, and an overall view of his work. The title appeared for the first time in the Journal on May 17, 1807. Gerhard Küntzel declares [1] that it is connected with the Christian idea of " peregrenation," of the earthly pilgrimage of human life. He suggests that the *Wanderjahre* are intended to present a pedagogic education, prolonging that of the *Lehrjahre* on a higher plane and vaster scale. But the story of Wilhelm Meister now became, if not a pretext, at least a framework for the short stories which point to the same conclusions as the novel itself. It is what the Germans call a " *Rahmenerzählung*," that is to say, a story within a framework. We may add that its is also a pedagogic and social story, whose prototypes were provided by Rousseau and Pestalozzi. Goethe himself declared that " it was not to be an integrated and composed picture, but a series, and a frieze of figures connected one to another by luxuriant didactic tendrils." He also spoke of the " romantic themes " which formed a part of the *Wanderjahre*; the other " themes " were didactic. In 1808 he began one of these " short stories," *Die Wahlverwandtschaften*, but it won its independence and absorbed the poet, who could not publish the first volume in 1810 as he had hoped.

From 1810 to 1819 Goethe worked only sporadically, for this was the period of *Dichtung und Wahrheit* and the *Divan*. But on July 29, 1810, he wrote to Cotta that his work had become dear to him, and that he now saw all it could accomplish. Then, probably stimulated by the developments in the world around him, he gave up the idea of a " story within a framework " in favor of a great fresco retracing the history of civilization. By the end of this period, he had published most of the short stories, yet with the novel itself he had made no progress.

[1] Introduction to the *Wanderjahre*, Gedenkausgabe.

18.

He returned to it in 1820. He worked without pause, finishing it in May, 1821, and *Wilhelm Meisters Wanderjahre* or *Die Entsagenden*, Part I, appeared in the month of July. It was clear that he intended to continue the novel; and many readers demanded the sequel. He worked at it in several bursts from 1821 to 1825, then, almost uninterruptedly, from January, 1826, to 1829. This new version appeared in volumes XXI, XXII and XXIII of the complete edition (1829). The romantic part had been reduced, for the author had cut out three of the short stories. The didactic part, however, is developed further than in the 1821 edition.

In this complex work, which brings together elements as disparate as a novel connected with the *Lehrjahre*, short stories, a pedagogic Utopia, maxims and even a few poems, a careful analysis allows us to discern a reasoned plan, especially if we do not lose sight of the master idea. The essential problem for Goethe concerned the relations of the individual, particularly of the superior individual, and the community, whether reduced to the scale of the married couple or enlarged to a group, a state, a race or a colony in the new world.

The division into three books corresponds to the three stages of social evolution. Bielschowsky [1] enumerates them as follows: at the first stage stands the patriarchal state, represented by the artisan St. Joseph II, and based on family love; at the second stage emerges an enlightened absolutism, in which the rich, moved by love for their fellow men, dedicate themselves to their subjects; the third stage witnesses the establishment of a democratic régime, in which a group entitled " *das Band*," a group of workers which has freely elected its own chief, prepares to colonize land in America. Flitner [2] connects these three stages with

---

[1] *Goethe*, II, p. 536.
[2] *Goethe im Spötwerk*, p. 219.

the *Époques de l'esprit* which Goethe published in 1817 in *Kunst und Altertum*, based on the works of Gottfried Hermann, and also on Herder's theories concerning language and history. Once emerged from primitive chaos, man passed through four successive ages: mythical-poetical, theological, philosophical and prosaic. The first three are marked by Homer, Hesiod and Socrates; the fourth by total confusion, by the absence of reasoned control and true authority. In order to go beyond this stage, it is necessary to rediscover the truths of the ancient periods, to " humanize " the values they have bequeathed to us and to vitalize them with a new inspiration from below. These ideas, which it would be interesting to compare with those of Auguste Comte, are brought on to the stage in *Die Wanderjahre*, where they are dominated, however, by the two great laws of renunciation and work.

The story opens on a note of renunciation. While the *Lehrjahre* had continually broadened Wilhelm's horizon, his travels must lead him to concentrate on a more limited field in which he can achieve mastery. The Association seizes him away from the happiness of love and obliges him to travel. He is not to remain for more than three days under the same roof, nor to move less than a league away, nor to return within a year to the place he has left, nor to build up new relationships anywhere, nor to mention the past nor the future to any member of the Association whom he may chance to meet.

He sets off with his son, Felix, and in the mountains he relives the flight to Egypt (the title of the first chapter), and encounters St. Joseph II (the title of the second). He thus makes contact with the biblical period and its simple faith, and at the same time with handicraft, the first stage of human work. Bielschowsky considers this biblical idyll as an " overture " to the work, where the different " themes " reverberate. While the *Lehrjahre* had led Wilhelm into inns or castles, to meet players or aristocrats, that is to say, people who feed on illusions or live on their heritage, the hero now discovers the happiness of a life of labor and renunciation. Goethe exalts the craftsman not because he wished to abase the intellectual, but because manual work is creative and brings happiness. The poet who had formerly exalted the theatre now praises labor, after making Prometheus, in *Pandora*, a " *homo faber*," a laborious and useful craftsman. He also meets Jarno, now a geologist, who bears the significant name " Montanus." The latter shows him the need to renounce " general culture " and to specialize:

> Now is the time for specialization... Practice to become a good violinist, and be assured that the conductor will eagerly show you your place among the performers... To limit oneself to one's trade is the wisest part. For the mediocre, it will always remain a trade, for the man of value it will be an art; as for the superior being, by doing one thing, he will do everything, or, to express myself less paradoxically, in the one thing he does well, he will see the symbol of all that is well done.[1]

The two travelers next enter a castle, the center of a broad domain ruled over by an enlightened aristocracy which owes its formation to Beccaria (1738-1793) and Filangieri (1784-1867). With St. Joseph II, all had been perfect, but within a small compass; the modern age must reach an equal perfection on a very much vaster scale. It is not a question of a household, but of the whole world. The *Lehrjahre* had proposed to us the aesthetic ideal of life represented by Lothario, the European who had gone to America; *Die Wanderjahre*, a far grander and much more modern attempt, presents the American " Uncle," who has settled in Euope. To create the modern social order, men are needed from the New World, unprejudiced, cultivated, practical and altruistic. The Uncle's grandfather, a German who had spent much of his life in England, emigrated to America and made a considerable fortune. The Uncle

[1] *Wanderjahre*, I, 4. Gedenkausgabe, VIII, p. 43.

himself came to visit Europe; entranced by the ancient civilization he found there, he remained, intending to play the part of a liberal nineteenth century " grand seigneur."

His spirit is reflected in the inscription which he has inscribed on the walls of his castle, especially in the following two: " From the useful to the beautiful through the true," and " Possession and common property." Whereas Lothario, a cultivated man of the eighteenth century, an egoistical hedonist, had provided his home with an atmosphere of beauty and luxury, the Uncle has banished all that is not useful: in his domain there is neither park nor flower, and in his castle the hall and the staircase are adorned with geographical maps, for he admits only portraits to be works of art. He believes that one must first create what is useful, and from there one may rise to the beautiful, the climax of human activity. Hersilie, the wit, finds amusement in twisting the maxim, which becomes, for women at least: " From the beautiful to the useful through the true," and one could propose, as far as *Faust* is concerned, yet a third arrangement: "From the true to the useful through the beautiful."

The second inscription, " Possession and common property," is more significant for it leads to the heart of the modern problem. The wise and gentle Juliette explains the apparent contradiction when she declares, " No one should attach capital; the world will be able in time to make its revenues the property of all." Let each add to his fortune, but so that others may benefit! Let him be an egoist, but for the sake of others! The Uncle genuinely considers his good as common property of which he is the caretaker. He has long adopted the liberal motto, " The greatest good for the greatest number," having transformed it into, " To many what they desire." The enlightened despotism of the eighteenth century sought authority to secure the happiness of the people, and one may speak here of enlightened capitalism. Chapter six of the first book, where these ideas are stated, appears only in the edition of 1829, and thus dates from the time when Goethe was following the Saint-Simon movement with great interest. One can see in the poet's social conception an echo of Saint-Simon's theories combined with eighteenth century liberalism.

In the castle of the Uncle, who is, in a sense, a superior Lothario, the two nieces, Juliette and Hersilie, spoke often of their " Aunt," another symbolic character, who bears the name Makarie, " the happy." This name, so Spranger [1] tells us, appears in the ancient gnostic's world of aeons. She is a Nathalie carried to the final power, and recalls the " beautiful soul " in many respects although she is distinguished by the active part she plays as counselor and spiritual directress. Wilhelm is ordered to go to her; he is received in her castle by her faithful Angela and by her astronomer, modeled on Francis Xavier von Zach (1754-1832) who in 1792 had built the observatory at Seeburg near Gotha.[2] Then he is received by Makarie herself, an " extraordinary old lady," carried in an armchair by two lovely girls. They speak of the family, and the Aunt shows an admirable sense of psychology and an ability to understand souls from within. The astronomer then reads an abstruse manuscript on mathematics, and that evening he invites Wilhelm to observe the stars with him. The hero, impressed and somewhat overcome, dreams that Makarie is transformed into the morning star. Deep intuition! for he learns that she has reached that stage of cosmic harmony to which men aspire. Angela tells him that the Aunt " not only bears within her the whole solar system, but she can move there in the spirit as an integral part of it." [3]

These details were necessary to the understanding of this

---

[1] *Goethes Weltanschauung*, Insel Verlag, p. 193.
[2] Spranger, *Goethes Weltanschauung*, p. 197.
[3] *Wanderjahre*, I, 10, Gedenkausgabe, VIII, p. 139.

strange character, who is the incarnation of the sidereal world, just as Montanus represents the terrestrial, or we might almost say, the mineral world. We have alluded many times to Goethe's effort to place men on a ladder which leads from the infinitely small to the infinitely great. We can now consider the cosmos in which he lives as a pyramid, which Spranger has schematized.[1] At the base is nature, with its three kingdoms, mineral, vegetable and animal. It is a common conception, banal even, at a time when " Nature " inspires the poets, when Novalis proclaims that the difference between these three kingdoms is less one of nature than of degree. In the center rises man, the crown of creation, who cries with Faust:

> Two souls, alas! are warring in my breast:
> And each of them desires to flee the other;
> The one, with brutal, elemental passion
> Clings to the earth with every claw it has;
> The other strives to rise from out the dust
> And soar towards the realm of the sublime.

Man's material aspect drags man downwards; his spiritual part, the source of the Faustian " *Streben*," lifts him towards the heights of the divine sphere, through, in spite of and by means of the demonic, whose powers rule him. We are bound, guided and elevated by the law of nature on the lowest plane, the moral law in the heart of a man and the divine law in the starry heavens, the deep meaning of the *Urworte Orphisch* now appears in its inexhaustible grandeur. Governed by his demon, man tries to escape it through chance. Eros, universal law, leads him to a necessary order, to a limit which he accepts. There remains the hope of drawing the bolts and passing through the dreadful portal, of passing through the " walls of brass " which enclose us in the little " canton " of the world. We must agree with Spranger, when, after quoting this last

---

[1] *Goethes Weltanschauung*, p. 21.

strophe, he writes: " It is the leap into the transcendent, the breach through which, across the demonic morld, organic nature can reach the divine sphere." [1] Makarie, woman and star, appears as the superior being who has achieved harmony between the terrestrial and the celestial spheres; she moves with equal ease among souls and among constellations, the enigma that Faust wished to resolve by passing the gates of death has ceased to exist for her, for she hands on to us a higher law, which must rule our lives as it does those of the stars. In Makarie, who is perhaps the most symbolic of Goethe's creations, all his heroines seem to attain their moral perfection.

Makarie, who in the 1821 edition remained in the background, now emerges at the center of the action, appearing near the end of the first part when father and son are both about to receive a pedagogic training. Similarly, Helen appears in the middle of the second *Faust*, to provide a vision of beauty for the hero before he takes action. Makarie is the revelation of the divine, who indicates to the world below the path it must follow.

Their road leads the pilgrims into the " pedagogic province," where Wilhelm leaves his son for a year. In according such importance to education, Goethe is fully representative of a period smitten with pedagogy. We know furthermore that he was inspired by the school founded by Ph. Emm. Von Fellenberg at Hofwyl, near Berne, in which certain of Pestalozzi's principles were applied. As Fichte had advocated in his *Speeches to the German Nation*, Goethe envisaged the establishment of an actual seminary, where new men could be trained with a view to a new society. It is indicative of the poet's development that instead of advocating an aesthetic education founded on the cult of beauty, he recommends an ethical training, the teaching of moral and religious laws, as befits one

[1] *Goethes Weltanschauung*, p. 47.

who comes from Makarie's world. One of the first lessons is on respect; the passage which is devoted to it is of vital importance to anyone interested in Goethe's religion:

"Respect!" the three repeated (these are the directors of the province of pedagogy). "Everybody lacks it, perhaps even you. You have seen three sorts of gesture, and we teach three kinds of respect, which only reach their perfect virtue and efficacy when they mingle to form a whole. The first is respect for what is above us. This gesture which you have seen, with the arms crossed upon the breast and a joyful skyward look, is what we prescribe for young children; by means of it we expect them to witness that there is a God above, whose presence is incarnate and manifested in parents, masters and superiors. Next comes respect for what is beneath us. Hands linked behind the back and the eyes lowered and smiling tell us that one should look upon the ground with happy serenity; it provides our food and disperses joys beyond the telling; but it also brings us sufferings out of all proportion. If someone has suffered some physical hurt, whether through his own fault or not; if others have wounded him, intentionally or otherwise; if any terrestrial element, though without volition, should harm him: let him reflect upon it, for these same dangers will remain with him throughout his life. But we release our pupil as soon as possible from this position, just as soon as we are sure that his lesson of the second degree has sufficiently acted upon him; we then exhort him to take courage, to assert himself manfully, to turn to his comrades and model himself upon them. Then he stands up straight, proud and bold, but not in egoistical isolation: only in the society of his equals can he face the world. There is nothing we can add to these precepts.

The three have no respect for any religion based on fear. Those based on reverence for what is above us, such as the pagan religions, are called *ethnic*; those based on reverence for what is our equal, *philosophical*, and finally, those based on reverence for what is beneath us are termed *Christian*. They do not profess any one of these religions but all three at once,

for it is in fact from their sum that true religion springs: from these three reverences the supreme reverence results, reverence for oneself, and from this in turn all the other flow; it follows that man thus raises himself to the highest point he may reach; he has the right to regard himself as God's and nature's masterpiece, vulgarity through presumption or through egoism.

This doctrine, they add, is contained in the *Credo*,

for the first article is ethnic, and common to all peoples, the second is Christian and applies to all who strive with suffering and are glorified through suffering; the third teaches us a sublime communion of saints, that is to say of those who attain the highest degree of goodness and wisdom.

The three stages of the first book, as Flitner observes, had prepared us for these revelations: Saint Joseph II derives from Christianity, the Uncle practices a philosophical religion, and Makarie represents ethnic religion as well as the possibility of a new humanity, which is precisely that exercised in the pedagogic sphere of moral life and action in the service of the community. The two great motives of renunciation and work reappear under the names of reverence and specialization.

As if to remind Wilhelm of the lesson of Montanus, a collector to whom he is directed at the end of the first book asserts: "All life, all action, all art should come after a profession, which can be acquired only by limitation" (which recalls "*in der Beschränkung zeigtsich erst der Meister*"). "To know and practice one thing thoroughly brings a higher culture than mediocrity in a hundred" Thus care is taken to continually examine the pupils' aptitudes in order to determine their true vocation. They are divided into "regions," where they may practice agriculture or the training of animals, where they may become miners or artists. Thus Felix, whose father had once dreamed of founding a great national theatre, specializes in the training of horses.

"Possession and common property" was one of the Uncle's maxims; "individual and community" might have been the motto of the pedagogic province, where the individual was educated and developed to be of service to society. In the mind of Montanus-Goethe, each is but an instrument in the orchestra. Thus in Chapter XI of Part Two Wilhelm tells Nathalie of his decision to become a surgeon. He explains how he arrived at this choice, how he was influenced by Jarno-Montanus who had shown him that general culture was but foolishness (*Narrenpossen*), and that one should specialize in order to achieve mastery of one's own profession for the benefit of the community. He receives permission to remain in the same place for several years in order to perfect his skill, while his son is to become a horse-trainer.

The third book, the most austere despite the romantic tales which are intended to brighten it, is the most important, for it presents the democratic community of the future. We find transformed those who have accepted the " fundamental law " of brotherly association: to be a specialist among other specialists. The charming Philine of the *Theatralische Sendung* has now become a dressmaker; Lenardo, who had thought only of enjoying himself, is now a craftsman, working in wood and iron. Friedrich, endowed with good handwriting and a remarkable memory which had formerly earned him the job of prompter at the theatre, has been appointed " chancellor," secretary and treasurer of the " Band." This group of specialist craftsmen is a pendant to the troupe of players of the *Sendung* of the *Lehrjahre*, and forms a striking contrast to them; the one is eighteenth century rococo, the other is nineteenth century technical. Let us add that instead of being led by more or less suspect characters, such as Melina, it has true leaders, " *Vorgesetzte*," who remind us of the overseers, " *die Oberen*," of the pedagogic province.

Emigration is the central problem of the third book. Goethe's views on this subject varied. Although hostile at first, by 1827 he was willing to praise America for being free of useless memories and vain quarrels. His conciliatory temperament led him to divide the " Band " into two: one part emigrates with Lenardo, the other turns to domestic colonization, led by Odoardo, a powerful personality who appears in Chapter IX. The two leaders put forward their arguments in great speeches, which are novel in Goethe's work. Lenardo transforms the " *ubi bene, ibi patria* " into " My country is where I am useful," [1] and he enumerates the duties of each member of the community: to honor all religions, each of which is contained in the *Credo*; to admit all forms of government, for they all demand and develop national activity; to practice and exact morality such as is dictated by self respect (Chapter IX). Chapter XII furnishes practical information about the future city.

Odoardo presents his plan for colonization. It is concerned less with principles than with trades, which he calls the " severe arts " to distinguish them from the " liberal arts." Although artists may be permitted to produce works which are not perfect, this is not true for stone-cutters, masons, carpenters, tilers, etc. These workmen, apprentices, craftsmen and masters are to be grouped into corporations which will demand faultless craftsmanship, for the slightest imperfection spoils the whole and every error has its consequences.

Goethe has not shown us these groups at work, for he never wrote the " *Meisterjahre* " as Schiller had urged. He limited himself to relating, at the end of the *Wanderjahre*, how Wilhelm, thanks to his medical skill, restored his drowned son to life. He also took care to marry his characters suitably, but his embarrassment is obvious.

We have neglected the " short stories " in order to simplify and explain a turgid work whose ideological interest

[1] Compare with this interpretation a line from the *Prolog* which Goethe wrote in 1802, when *Was wir bringen*, written for the Lauchstädt theatre, was produced at Weimar: " Our country is where we developed." At the beginning of the century, it was still the voice of the classical poet, of Baroness von Stein's lover, which spoke; twenty-five years later, Goethe could still regard Weimar as his country, but because he had been a minister, had been able to make himself useful there.

is greater than its romantic appeal. This is certainly no longer a " novel " revolving around the life of a character in action. In the *Theatralische Sendung* Wilhelm Meister was already undergoing events rather than shaping them, but at least he experienced them all. In *Die Lehrjahre* he was no longer the true center, for the Society of the Tower either directed his actions or left him to himself. In *Die Wanderjahre* he is outside the action, which is centered entirely in the problem of the community. Theatrical vocation, human vocation, social vocation—such might have been the subtitles of the three panels of this triptych, united only by the constant presence of Wilhelm Meister.

To measure *Meister's* importance in Goethe's development, we must compare it with *Werther*, for these two novels share a simple point of departure, that is, the impossibility of living a bourgeois life while carrying on a profession. We have on the one hand a character similar to Hamlet, who spends himself, disintegrates and falls back into nothingness; on the other, a man who is constantly surpassing himself and rising towards his fulfilment, and who achieves his full stature by becoming a part of the community. Werther is the incarnation of the sentimental subjectivism of his period. As an artist, he seeks the complete development of his personality, and thereby comes into conflict with society, which causes his ruin. Meister, a character in process of formation, appears first as an artist not unlike Werther in the *Theatralische Sendung*: at the end of the *Lehrjahre*, he is a cultivated man ready for action; finally, in the *Wanderjahre*, he becomes a useful citizen. Thus he progresses, as Kierkegaard later wished to do, from the aesthetic plane, where he feels, to the ethical plane, where he acts, and finally to a religious plane, where he serves. He is not, therefore, crushed as Werther was, but dominated, directed, and finally absorbed by a community, multiplying his strength by that of all the others.

Finally, it is not too far-fetched to see in Wilhelm Meisters's development the reflection of the evolution undergone by Germany, a land of thinkers and poets, which was to become a land of men of action, and later a land of technicians. Thus this vast work, begun as a poem and ending as a didactic recital, reflects the eighteenth century, and its enthusiasm for aesthetics, the nineteenth century and its preoccupation with pedagogic and social problems, and even the twentieth century, the period in which specialization and technology reign supreme. Born of a society in process of disintegration and ripe for revolution, it has a value for our own society, which is in process of reconstruction and in search of its own form.

Chapter 5

Faust II

Just as Goethe had extended his first *Meister* under the title of *Wanderjahre*, so he was tempted to continue his *Faust*, the work which the young Hegel considered an " absolute philosophical tragedy," that is to say, the drama of the man who strives with all his powers for reintegration with the Infinite.[1] Just as we owe *Meister* to Schiller's intervention, so we owe *Faust* to Eckermann's. In fact, the second part was long confined to the *Helena* episode, which dates from 1800. At this time Goethe realized, as he wrote to Schiller on September 23rd, that " only from this climax has one a true perspective view of the whole." But he could not succeed in transporting his heroine to the Rhineland, in integrating Greek beauty with medieval Germany. Determined not to turn her into a " caricature " (*Fratze*), he even had the idea of basing a serious tragedy on the episode already composed, entitling it " *Helen's Return*." He changed his mind, however. He certainly seems to have considered a satyrical drama, for

---

[1] Quoted by Beutler in the *Frankfurter Zeitung* of the 3rd of November, 1940.

the file which contained the fragment bore this note: " Helen in middle age—satyrical drama. Marginal episode for *Faust*." December 16, 1816, Goethe dictated a summary of the second part [1] for *Dichtung und Wahrheit* which is close to the realism of the first. Years passed without his achieving his project. In 1823 he even considered publishing the plan of *Faust* in the later part of *Dichtung und Wahrheit*. Eckermann advised against this, and encouraged him to complete it instead. Goethe set to work again on February 25, 1925. He began with the *Helena* episode in the center of the third act, which he completed in 1826 and published in 1827 with the title *Helena: klassische-romantische Phantasmagorie*, an interlude in *Faust*. Then between 1827 and 1830 he wrote the first two acts, the fifth in 1830 and 1831, and finally the fourth. In 1832 he finally revised the whole, at the end of which he wrote a solemn "Finis." On March 17, 1832, three days before his death, he wrote his last moving letter to G. von Humboldt, in which he took leave of a work conceived sixty years before.[2]

We may now examine this monumental work as a whole. Like a medieval mystery, it takes place on three planes: heaven, earth and hell. Indeed Goethe, who had projected a descent into hell, told Eckermann on May 6, 1827, that the action leads from "heaven to hell by way of the earth." To study *Faust* as a whole we must forget that it has two parts, and consider it in its unity of thought.

---

[1] It is reproduced in Witkowski's-masterly edition of *Faust* (9th edit., Brill, Leyden, 1936, vol. 1, pp. 533-535).

[2] At the end of his edition Witkowski provides an important bibliography (more than two hundred titles), to which we refer the reader. We will add *Faust I*, commented by Carl Endres (Benno Schwabe, Basle, 2 vols., 1949) and Erich Trunz's edition of *Faust*, which is to be the second volume of the "Hamburger Ausgabe," but is also to be published separately.

The problem of the man who is no longer guided and supported by Christianity is posed, developed and resolved. It is introduced in the " Prologue to Heaven " and in Faust's discussions with Mephisto, for the first 1,867 lines may be considered as a great " Prologue to Earth." The problem is posed from three points of view, divine, human and infernal. The Devil establishes a link between God and man, for he has the right to live both in heaven and on earth. It is developed in the remainder of the first part, where Faust experiences the " little world," and in the second, where he goes into the " great world " before embarking upon creative activity. The development takes place in three dramas which we may call the tragedy of Gretchen, the tragedy of Helen and the tragedy of action. It is resolved for God, for man and for Mephistopheles, who loses his wager but—as we shall see—remains necessary so that man should not cease to struggle.

It is God who knows; He knows that human nature is constantly straying, and also that the good man, in his confused aspirations, is aware that he is on the true path and will ultimately be led, according to divine will, " to the light." It is Mephistopheles who repudiates; he is the incarnation of the destructive spirit, and sees only the imperfections of Creation and the miseries of the Creature led on to destruction by his reason and appetite for knowledge. Faust, representing humanity, doubts, aspires, seeks; the *Streben*, the pathetic effort to extend his limits, is the finest possession of a human being. He is the godless man in search of the divine, for despite himself, he is the heir to Christianity. Rudolf Steiner rightly sees " the impulsion of Christ " at work in him. He doubts God, for reason does not reveal Him; he doubts science, which can indeed make him master of phenomena, but which does not allow him to seize what Kant called numina; he even doubts existence for, shut up in his laboratory, he has known only lifeless theory and has never discovered the

289

verdant tree of life. He is a Titan of thought, a pessimistic and sometimes nihilistic Titan and, despite very obvious differences, he prefigures Nietzsche's Superman.

This man is to become the stake in a wager between God and the Devil; the latter will triumph if he can turn the man whom God considers as his servant away from his course. Faust himself will make a wager with Mephisto, in which he stakes his soul, but there is a fundamental difference from the *Volksbuch* and the other works it inspired, for Faust is not the man to be satisfied with the Evil One's usual lures of gold, power or love. He can only be tempted after summoning the Spirit of the Earth and recognizing his own impotence, and after trying to pass the gates of death to discover life and drawing back on hearing the paschal message announcing a beyond in which he does not believe. Earth possesses him again, and he now wishes, as André Gide puts it, to " assume as much of humanity as possible," to live a total life, to live every life. But he must find an aim for his life, the direction assigned to man. He disdainfully rejects the pleasures recommended by Mephisto, the future companion of his pilgrimage through life, and longs only for the time when he will be able to say to the fleeting moment: " Stop, you are so beautiful." This will be the moment of his triumph and his fall. The pact once signed, the action begins with the first temptation: love.

A prelude introduces the tragedy of Gretchen. In the Auerbach tavern Mephisto offers Faust, though without real hope of tempting him, the basest of the pleasures he controls. In the den of the sorceress he transforms him into a handsome young man, and by revealing perfect beauty to him, the magic mirror excites an insatiable desire for the Eternal Female Body. Gretchen appears, but this humble and delightful girl, conceived as we know, in 1774, cannot represent the mirror's ideal of beauty. At the moment when Faust says " Yes " to life, she offers him a total and innocent love, made up of small and loving daily cares, as simple as the life of the peasants met in the curse of the paschal walk. This love blossoms on the plain of earthly reality and simple humanity; it is based on physical desire, in which a feeling of human compassion tempers the cynicism of a Don Juan. It cannot satisfy Faust, who does not have the right to become involved in a bourgeois existence at the cost of renouncing life. The liaison was one of those errors which God permits to man; the desertion of Gretchen represents the Devil's share. Like Goethe, Faust sacrifices the girl to the beauty of the magic mirror, to Helen.

Both ethically and aesthetically, the magnificent scene which opens the second part of *Faust* is a transition from Gretchen's tragedy to Helen's. In order to absorb further experience, Faust must forget Gretchen, for remorse would prevent him from pursuing his course. Ariel and the spirits of the air pour the waters of Lethe upon him, and the hero awakes stretched on a flowery lawn in a heavenly countryside. This rebirth through forgetting is accompanied by a new aesthetic intuition; the soliloquy in which he breathes his joy culminates in the famous line—" 'Tis through its mirrored colors we seize life."—which recalls that sentence from the *Essay on Meteorology*: " The truth... we can never know it directly, we can only contemplate it in reflections, examples or symbols, in isolated or related manifestations." [1] The professor of science, who had devoted his life to the study of phenomena, understood that he could only admire their beauty. This line is the key to the tragedy of Helen, and raises it infinitely above the Gretchen episode. We are no longer on the plane of nature and physical love, but of the spirt and of Eros.[2] We have left the domain of the real for that of illusion

[1] Quoted by Witkowski, vol. II, p. 291.
[2] Korff, *Faustischer Glaube*, p. 85.

which characterizes the " great world. " Helen will not be real, like Gretchen; she will be true, like the Apollonian Beauty of the classics, true to the original type of woman. If Goethe is, as Paul Valéry said. " the great apologist of Appearance," [1] it is here, perhaps, that he best deserves the title.

It is no longer a matter of a transient and purely physical love between two dissimilar beings, but of the union of a noble and beautiful woman and a polished gentleman. Faust leaves the modest ambient of Gretchen to live at the court of the emperor. There, Mephisto evokes the image of Helen, and descends to hell where he obtains from Persephone (in a scene which the poet never realized) permission to bring back to earth this woman, who had been the object of so much admiration and so much blame. Faust joins her in a medieval castle situated somewhere in Greece. He appears as a knight, like one of those German noblemen led to the Orient by the Crusades. He approaches her gallantly, and makes her his wife and his sovereign. In his behavior toward Gretchen, he had been insistent and cavalier; in the presence of Helen, he is zealous and courteous. To please her, he speaks in antique meters; conquered, she adopts Germanic rhyme. This marriage represents the symbolic union of Apollonian classicism and Germanic " Faustianism." The perfect creation will be one which combines the depth of Nordic thought with the beauty of Greek form. A son is to be born of this brief union in a magic castle filled with symbolism. While Gretchen's child perished at its mother's hands, Helen's is a handsome youth, Euphorion, and has been variously interpreted.[2] Goethe invited Eckermann to re-

---

[1] *Nouvelle Revue Française*, June 1932, p. 939.

[2] On this point consult F. Baldensperger's liberally documented article: *Pour une interprétation correcte de l'épisode d'Euphorion*, in the special number of the *Revue de littérature comparée*, January-March 1932, pp. 142-158.

gard him as the personification of poetry, " which is bound to no period, to no place, to no person " (December 20, 1829), and also suggested the most remarkable exponent of contemporary poetry, Byron, who " is not antique, nor yet romantic, but is the present day itself."

This union cannot last either. Disguised as the hideous Phorpkyad, Mephisto is ever present, unwilling to countenance the victory of Beauty and human genius. Moreover Goethe, who had given the subtitle *Die Entsagenden* to *Wilhelm Meisters Wanderjahre*, knew that even in Arcadia, renunciation is the law of man. Finally, he knew that the union of Hellenism and Germanism was a fragile thing, and that its fruit would be hard to rear. Led on by youthful mettle, Euphorion scales the cliffs, falls and is killed. Faust tries in vain to hold back Helen, who must accompany her son to Persephone's kingdom; he retains only her draperies and her veil, which are transformed into clouds which bear him upward.

Was this symbolic marriage, which Goethe's art transformed into a living reality, another temptation like the union with Gretchen? Not quite, for it was rather a necessary experience: the revelation of Beauty, without which human works would be imperfect and would lose what Schiller called " the power of idealization." Helen represents the ideally beautiful form reserved for those who, once in their lifetime, have experienced the revelation of Beauty in all its splendor. Faust must return to his quest and move into the world of action.

The hero's soliloquy on awakening in a flowery field was the prelude to the tragedy of Helen; another soliloquy opens the tragedy of action. In the first, Faust was setting off from a " pleasant region " to rise towards Helen; now he is about to descend from the high and rocky mountain where the clouds have set him down, to the shore, the scene of his action. Is this a fall, a return to the real, to utilitarian activity? On returning from his paschal walk, Faust wanted

to translate the Old Testament. Dissatisfied with the traditional rendering: " In the beginning was the Word, " he
had substituted: " In the beginning was action." Hearing
these words, the spaniel-Mephisto barked, as if to show
approval or dissent. Thus Faust had a premonition of his
destiny, which was action on the plane of reality, but which
then presented itself humbly in the features of peasants.
Now that he has known Helen, he can plunge into reality
without danger of losing himself in it. His experience of
Beauty enables him to transfigure the real; his constructive
activity will have the grandeur conferred by the Spirit
and enriched by the vision of Beauty. With Gretchen he
had experienced reality, with Helen he had experienced
Beauty and truth; now he will experience greatness; he
comes into contact with what the Germans call " *das Er-
habene* " (the sublime).

Faust confides to Mephisto that he is attracted by a great
enterprise. He feels ready for " great exploits." He dreams
of power and possession, and proclaims that " action is
everything, fame is nothing." He wishes to subdue the sea
and conquer new territories from her. He succeeds, but
now without destroying the home of Baucis and Philemon,
for the Devil always claims his share; this is his last error.
As he approches his goal his companion is no longer Gretchen or Helen, but *die Sorge*, Care. He is blinded, the
darkness around him grows ever deeper, " but in my soul
a radiant light still shines." He hastens to assemble his
workmen, to whom he explains his grandiose plans. He
imagines millions of men living in an earthly paradise
born of his genius:

> Yes, to his thought I vow myself entire,
> Here is the highest lesson wisdom teaches:
> He only earns both liberty and life
> Who each day new is forced to conquer them,
> And thus, by perils compassed, here shall youth
> And prime of life and age live out their cycle.
> Most gladly would I watch this teeming world,

> Live on free land amid a people free.
> Then to the passing moment I could cry
> "Stop now, O stay! Thou art so beautiful!"
> Then the imprint of these my days on earth
> A hundred centuries could ne'er efface.
> Sensing this future high felicity,
> Instant sublime, your joys I savour now.   (11573-11586).

With his soul full of this vision of the future, he falls dead. Mephisto thinks his prey is within his grasp, but it escapes him, for the problem posed on the human, infernal and divine planes has just found solution for the man, for the Devil and for God.

Faust's lesson to mankind has been much debated, criticized and denigrated. Urged on by his thirst for knowledge, he has cut himself off from life and taken recourse to magic in an effort to force nature's secrets from her. He rejects science and with the Devil's help sets out on the conquest of life. After his three experiences he renounces magic, escapes Mephisto and learns, like Wilhelm Meister, that the goal of human existence is constructive activity in the service of mankind. But was this not exactly the lesson he learned from the peasants on Easter day? Yet it is still necessary to justify this activity, and above all, to integrate the existence of evil into an optimistic conception of life. Perhaps it was precisely the peasants' example which unconsciously led him to accept Mephisto.

Mephisto has baffled more than one admirer, notably Schiller, for he is a complex figure who borrows his many traits from Christianity, from the Faustian legend, from Lucifer and Ahriman (hardly understood by Goethe), from the poet himself, or from his friends Behrisch and Merck, perhaps even from Herder. In the " Forest and Cave " scene, he is an envoy of the " Spirit of the Earth." He, too, is one of those " Demons " who dwell in a sphere between man and God; Faust aspires to rise to this sphere, for he knows that " the spirit world in not closed." The most fruitful way of considering Mephisto is to apply the occult-

ists' formula: " *Diabolus est deus inversus,*" which explains
his negativeness but does not deprive him of his positive
value. He is the absence of faith, of trust, of love and of
enthusiasm; he is ironic and sarcastic criticism; he is para-
lyzing reason; he is delight in destruction, perversions; he is
the imperfection inherent in man and his works; he is
Gretchen's death, the ugliness of the Phorkyade, the destruction of the house where Baucis and Philemon perish.
Yet if he did not exist, man could not fulfil his earthly
mission, as God clearly explains in these lines from the
" Prologue to Heaven ":

> Too easily man's will to action softens,
> Soon with repose complete he is content;
> 'Tis why I gladly give him this companion
> Who stirs him, like the devil that he is. (340-343).

Mephisto is the prime mover of that incessant effort which
is man's fate and greatness.

It was obvious that God would win the wager, but we
must try to justify His attitude towards Faust. From the
beginning of the work to the end, He remains favorably
disposed to him. In the " Prologue to Heaven " He calls
him His servant, even though Faust denies His existence.
God loves those strong enough to seek their trust for themselves, through all their falls and errors: He knows that

> Man errs as long as he both strives and seeks. (317).
>
> A good man, in his half-felt aspirations
> Knows that he follows the appointed path. (328-329).

When Faust's soul is welcomed in heaven, the angels justify
his redemption in these famous lines:

> The noble adept of the the world of spirits
> From durance of the Evil One is freed.
> " He who has always striven with true zeal,
> Him by our intervention we can save."
> And this most easily can be, when Love
> From her high place for him has interceded.
> To meet him now the happy throng advances,
> And celebrates his coming with full heart. (11934-11941).

On June 6, 1831, Goethe told Eckermann that these lines contained the key to *Faust*, the justification of his salvation by "an ever nobler and purer activity" and by the love which brought him help from above, which, he added, "entirely conforms with our religious conceptions, for we feel that we cannot work out our own salvation alone without the help of Divine Grace."

After finishing his *Faust*, Goethe told Eckermann, in August, 1831: "Now I can consider any extension of life purely as a gift; it really matters little whether I do anything further, or what I do." Destiny seems to have taken him at his word, for he had hardly written the final full stop of the work which he had borne within him for sixty years, when, on March 17, 1832, he fell ill. On March 22nd, at half past eleven in the morning, almost at the very hour of his birth, he passed away. Death was the final metamorphosis of the poet who had written:

> To nothingness no creature ever crumbles!
> In all things beats the pulse of the Eternal,
> Therefore with happiness lay hold on life!
> The being is eternal, for the laws
> Preserve and keep the living ornaments
> With which the Universe is richly decked. (*Testament*).

Conclusion
Goethe's importance today

Goethe's importance today

Towards the end of his life, Goethe frequently used the Aristotelian term " entelechy." He explained to Eckermann on March 11, 1828 that, " each entelechy is in fact a fragment of eternity, and the few years during which it remains bound to the earthly body do not age it." In the case of genius, it gives the body an eternal youth, it confers on the old man "a new puberty " (*eine wiederholte Pubertät*) and, he continued,

Man must be brought to nothing again (*ruiniert*). Every outstanding man has a certain mission which he is called upon to fulfil. When he has completed it, he is no longer needed on earth in this form and Providence uses him again for another purpose. But as everything here below happens naturally, the Demons multiply the stumbling-others should haves something

He then cited Napoleon, Mozart, Raphael and Byron:

They had all fulfilled their missions perfectly and it was time for them to go so that in this world, destined to last for a long time, others should have something yet to do.

Goethe could feel satisfied, on surrendering his entelechy to Providence, that he had fulfilled his mission. He had created and earned recognition for German literature. From Carlyle to Gide, thousands of men have expressed their gratitude to him, and his mission had not ended. Yet people have spoken of a " *Goetheentfremdung*," of disaffection from Goethe, as if his message were no longer of value. Maurice Boucher, who brilliantly translated *Iphigenie* and *Torquato Tasso* into French verse paradoxically referred to " an outdated Goethe." It has seemed often as though the world which we had shared with Goethe was about to be buried. Would it be an inverse paradox to speak today of a contemporary Goethe? No doubt Jaspers would answer affirmatively; on receiving the Goethe prize at Frankfurt on August 28, 1947, he delivered a curiously awkward speech in which he alternately eulogized the poet, as expected of him, and endeavored to indicate the limitations of his unique personality, which he called " exemplary but no model." [1] During the course of the year 1949, the second centenary of the poet's birth, Goethe's position in the modern world was heatedly debated. In the limited battlefield of the press, there were two opposed camps: those who claimed that " Goethe has nothing to offer us," and those who sought guidance in his work. He can only retain the greatness so long unquestioningly ascribed to him if he can still serve as a guide to the men of today.

We now know what our fathers and the contemporaries of Goethe and the French Revolution did not know — that we are undergoing, and to some extent making, the history of a planet which has been shaken from its orbit by the convulsions which accompany all birth. A new world will arise, which is bound to oppose the old, to deny it in order to establish its own originality. Then a vital problem will be posed: what are we to save from the past? Is Goethe

---

[1] His speech, published by Artemis-Verlag of Zurich, aroused bitter controversy in the press. Jasper's principal opponent was E. R. Curtius.

a relevant part of our heritage? Either we must put him in a glass case with the dead past, with the civilization which Ernst Jünger called " Museal," or we must admit him among those who point to the future. Though we put the question and offer the alternatives, it is with the conviction that Goethe has a present value for Germany, for modern man, for the citizen of the world. Understanding of the present situation leads us to accept and welcome him as adviser and spiritual guide in three spheres.

Germany may be characterized by its *Zerspaltenheit*, its *Zerslitterung*. Our language contains no expression strong enough to describe the division and spiritual fragmentation which afflicts Germany today. For centuries lacking a single political capital or a preponderant religious center, it long lived within a provincial rather than a national framework, bound by a religion as much territorial as ecumenical. Whereas in France regionalism has always had a somewhat artificial air, it remains a living, if latent, force in Germany. While France has never known the opposition of two religions, it has been a plague to the Germans, and just as at school they have never learned to tolerate, much less to esteem each other, they inevitably feel a religious antagonism which divides them on the religious plane, just as their territorialism divides them on the material plane.

Within these provinces and religious zones and within the German people itself, the divisions are less apparent but no less important. First, as in all countries, there is opposition between parties, which is much more serious there because the Germans had previously been marshaled into a single party, and because they have not yet been politically educated to tolerance and respect for the opinions of others. Next, there is antagonism between former militant Nazis and those who either payed lip-service to National Socialism or rejected it. There is also antagonism between the generations. People age quickly in Germany, and youth, whom propaganda has rendered suspicious of the teaching of its elders, tends to refuse to heed the philosophers. Also, it has so far failed to find new leaders within its own ranks.

Could Goethe, who stands above these antagonisms, play this saving part? Now that the Germans vainly seek a man around whom to regroup themselves, he appears as a common denominator, a spiritual catalyst. As the citizen of a free city, as the minister of a duchy, he can show his compatriots that true greatness does not belong to the material but to a higher spiritual order; that living space is a small thing compared to " the spiritual extent of the nation." And who can be equal to Goethe, the poet, dramatist, novelist, historian, artist, scientist; in short, the universal man?

His death has placed him beyond time. Enshrined in the past and his fame, he offers the advantage of being unequivocal, a necessity the Germans of today demand, obsessed as they are with the fear of being duped. He was not forced to make terms with a régime or even with religion, or to live or think in antagonism to others. It may be objected that he stands at too great a distance from the youth of the present day, but we know that his existence was one of continual rejuvenation through a series of metamorphoses. He may at first appear under a simple aspect, but whoever approaches closer finds him ever ready to reveal a new facet of his complex personality. He is inexhaustible. People have imagined him indifferent to the life of his nation because they forget that he put his intelligence and his heart at the service of his fellow-citizens; that he consented to devote himself to the humblest administrative tasks in order that the little society committed to his charge might live in order and happiness. His idealism never lost contact with reality and his ardour inspired the often quoted cry: " Onwards over the tombs." Would he not be the man who could say to his fellow-countrymen: " Onwards through the ruins "?

Goethe is not dead for the Germans; neither has he lost meaning for us, men of the twentieth century. Although he warned young poets that the Muse can accompany but cannot guide, his confrontation of living reality can still serve as a model and example for us. Those who deny this claim that Goethe's humanity is outmoded in the nuclear age, and that in this century of technology, the poets and the thinkers, once Germany's brightest ornaments, have little relevance. The Weimar humanism was, as we recall, the product of more or less ancient factors, drawn from the civilizations of Greece and Rome, Christianity and rationalism. Lukacs [1] may consider this phase of Goethe's thought a " pause," a " reaction " after the " progress " of the Aufklärung. It nonetheless constituted a magnificent effort to bring Germany into the stream of Western progress, and to enrich this stream with the waters of German spirituality. It did not flourish in a period of calm and relative stagnation as did classical French humanism, but at a time when the French Revolution was disturbing the political and social foundations of all Europe, and which witnessed the birth of the scientific development which was to lead to modern technology. *Hermann und Dorothea*, when forced too soon upon pupils too young for it, inspires the profoundest boredom; yet this bourgeois epic in Homeric form is a humanist's attempt to surmount the Revolution, to use it, as Wilhelm von Humboldt immediately saw, as a means to humanize mankind.

Goethe, who submitted himself to the two great laws of polarity and " potentiation " and who saw everywhere the rhythm of sytole and diastole, reminds us that all evolution is governed by the alternation of periods of expansion and concentration, that from chaos we must seek a cosmos, an organized world. Like the period of the Revolution,

---

[1] In his *Brève histoire de la littérature allemande*. Éditions Nagel, 1949.

the present age is chaotic; its plight is perhaps greater, following in the wake the " decadence " which marked the turn of the century and the scourge of two world wars. Nietzsche's nihilism may appear insipid compared to the outlook which the present world may inspire if we admit with the existentialists that we are cast between existence and nullity, that we are immersed in nullity and may never attain true existence. The major task of the contemporary philosopher is to " surmount," in Nietzsche's sense of the word, this nihilism and to transcend reality, if he does not wish to be reproached with forswearing man and reducing his function to that of surveying the void. Jaspers maintains that " there is no possibility of avoiding nihilism." He seems satisfied to remain poised on the brink of the abyss, for all analyses of existence lead him " *zum schweben in meiner Situation* " (to hover in my situation). He renounces the effort to transcend reality, to give it a value, and logically rejects Goethe when we summon him to our aid.

There is, of course, no possibility of transplanting the humanism of 1800 wholesale into the present, and Goethe would be the first to remind us that life is a process of continual evolution. We must graft Goethe's humanity on to the world of today and adapt it to the age of the machine and technology. In order to form the man of the future, we must first learn from those who, in the course of the centuries, have created superior types of humanity or who have realized them in their own lives. Paul Valéry, who may himself be numbered amongst these exemplars, proposed Goethe as a model in a remarkable speech delivered in 1932: " He represents, *Messieurs les humains*, one of our finest attempts to raise ourselves to the level of the Gods." [1] And ten years later, André Gide concluded his introduction to Goethe's theatrical works with these words:

[1] *Nouvelle Revue Française*, June 1932, Variété IV, p. 99.

" We remain grateful to Goethe, for he gives us the finest example, both smiling and grave, of what man, without the assistance of grace, may by his own efforts attain." [1]

Thomas Mann has described humanism as " a *spirit*, an intellectual disposition, a state of the human soul, which implies justice, liberty, understanding and tolerance, graciousness and serenity." [2] If this definition remains adequate, then Goethe can still point the way. In a romantic trilogy, which has continued to grow in importance during the last century, he first exalted Wilhelm Meister's theatrical vocation in searching for a purely aesthetic ideal. Next, he showed his vocation as a man; recalling the extraordinary *Metamorphose der Pflanzen*, one might call in the blossoming of a human being. Finally, looking deep into the future, he has revealed his social vocation in *Wilhelm Meisters Wanderjahre* in which he has posed and—at least experimentally—solved problems as modern as that of manual labor, and the organization of a social community. Is this not just the lesson we need? Lukacs, in a collection called *Goethe and his Time*,[3] points out the parallel between Hegelian philosophy, which sees history as the realization of the Ideal, and *Faust*, where the successive dramas lead beyond tragedy. Goethe's great work, the summation of his human experience, ends with a hymn to action in the service of society; the thinker agrees to live, renouncing pure speculation to create new lands. The lesson has lost none of its value, particularly if it is given universal application.

Montaigne praised Socrates who, when asked the name of his native city, replied not Athens but the world. Similarly, Goethe did not confine himself to his little capital at Weimar, but became a citizen of the world, incorporating

---

[1] Appears also in *Préfaces*, Editions " Ides et Calendes," Neuchâtel-Paris, 1948, p. 122.

[2] Quoted by A. Gide in his preface to the *Avertissement à l'Europe* Appears in *Préfaces*, p. 67.

[3] Francke Verlag, Berne, 1947.

in his personality the substance of all nations and all centuries to guide the men of the future towards a universal literature which our period may finally achieve.

Goethe never denied his sources; he told Eckermann on December 16, 1828: " I owe much to the Greeks and to the French, I have contracted an infinite debt to Shakespeare, Sterne and Goldsmith. But they are not the last of the sources of my culture; their recital would go on indefinitely, and is in any case unnecessary. The essential thing is to have a soul which loves the truth and collects it wherever it may be found." Indeed Goethe was nourished by contributions of the whole world. Rousseau, who is at the origin of *Werther*; Voltaire, whose *Mahomet* he staged in his own translation; Diderot, whose *Neveu de Rameau* and *Essai sur la peinture* he translated—each in turn offered him examples and armed him against French influence, while Shakespeare suggested models for his plays. In Italy, the Nordic poet discovered the Mediterranean world and evoked the image of ancient Greece, whose beauty he symbolically united with Germanic genius by the marriage of Faust and Helen. Later, Hafiz drew him towards Asia; the *Westöstliche Divan* is a great bridge, erected by the seventy-year-old poet to span time and space from the Rhine to the Euphrates. What endless reading and influences one would still need to enumerate before this subject would be exhausted! Goethe rejected only what could prevent his " becoming what he was." He welcomed all that could enrich him, never doubting that he would remain true to himself; this is the hallmark of the strong.

The heir to a century of cosmopolitans, an avid reader of foreign books and the foreign press, Goethe evolved the idea of a " *Weltliteratur*," whose certificate of birth is recorded in his Journal for January 15, 1827. Fritz Strich [1] speaks of a " literature of liaison between peoples, the spir-

---

[1] Strich, *Goethe und die Weltliteratur*. Francke Verlag, Berne.

itual world in which they meet to exchange their mental wares." The grandeur of the concept speaks for itself in Goethe's declaration to Eckermann of January 31, 1827: " National literature, that is of little account today; the time has come for universal literature, and each must now do what he can to hasten the advent of this new epoch." In his desire to bring writers of all nations and races into contact, he envisaged the creation of a great treasure-house of humanism which, extracted from every literature, should be the leaven of the world; for the translators, who would be called upon to play a vital role, he proposed the high dignity and title of " prophets " of peace.

We have not yet realized this ideal library, dreamed of by Goethe and catalogued by Hermann Hesse. The cosmopolitanism of the eighteenth century has been replaced by nationalization of thought in the twentieth century. Is it too late to alter the course of events? Goethe made Weimar one of those rare places where the spirit can breathe; let the citizens of the world revere it as a shrine!

It was near there, at Erfurt, at half past ten on the morning of October 2, 1808, that Goethe met Napoleon. This interview between emperor and poet may surprise us but in fact, Napoleon was returning the visit Goethe had made in 1792. Paul Valéry recognized the extraordinary nature of this event. It was the meeting of two forces, of two *men*, one of whom had been unable to resist the lure of action, while the other had succeeded in escaping the lure of thought. " We have passed Goethe's limits," writes Jaspers. Is this not the very cause of our sufferings? In his modern version of the great theme of Dr. Faust, Thomas Mann opposes the humanist Serenus Zeitblom, the prototype of the learned German, to the musician Adrien Leverkühn, who represents the Germany of the pre-war years, and who, like his nation, signs a compact with the devil and succumbs to madness and death. This sinister lesson should be a warning to us. In our own struggle against the powers of darkness we have need of this poet who knew the Demonic, yet was able to reject it, or at least to restrict its power, and who, in *Faust*, pressed evil into the service of good and made Mephisto an unconscious auxiliary of God. In 1932, the first centenary of Goethe's death was celebrated anxiously, as if we feared that he might abandon us; in 1949, it is his birth that we honor, and if we have the will it could be for us, as Italy was for Goethe, a " Renaissance."

Index of Names

Stampato
nelle Officine Grafiche Fratelli Stianti
Sancasciano Val di Pesa (Firenze)
— Ottobre 1958 —